TEACH FOR ARABIA

TEACH FOR ARABIA

American Universities, Liberalism,
and Transnational Qatar

NEHA VORA

STANFORD UNIVERSITY PRESS
Stanford, California

Stanford University Press
Stanford, California

Printed in the United States of America on acid-free, archival-quality paper

Library of Congress Cataloging-in-Publication Data

Names: Vora, Neha, 1974– author.
Title: Teach for Arabia : American universities, liberalism, and transnational Qatar / Neha Vora.
Description: Stanford, California : Stanford University Press, 2019. | Includes bibliographical references and index.
Identifiers: LCCN 2018019424 (print) | LCCN 2018022583 (ebook) | ISBN 9781503607514 (electronic) | ISBN 9781503601598 (cloth : alk. paper) | ISBN 9781503607507 (pbk. : alk. paper)
Subjects: LCSH: Education, Higher—Social aspects—Qatar. | Transnational education—Social aspects—Qatar. | Schools, American—Qatar. | Universities and colleges—Qatar. | Liberalism—Qatar.
Classification: LCC LC191.98.Q2 (ebook) | LCC LC191.98.Q2 V67 2019 (print) | DDC 378.5363—dc23
LC record available at https://lccn.loc.gov/2018019424

Typeset by Westchester Publishing Services in 10.5/15 Adobe Garamond
Cover design by Rob Ehle
Cover background: Detail of Doha Tower, Doha, Qatar. "thaslam" | iStock

For Ratna and Susan, who shared this stage of the journey
with me from opposite ends of the globe.

Contents

Acknowledgments

A project like this, which melds academic and field sites, owes many debts. Colleagues in Education City and the Gulf were instrumental in enabling this research. Tanya Kane has been my go-to expert on the ground since I first met her, as well as a fabulous brunch date. She helped me immensely with contacts, as did Hassan Bashir, John Crist, Andrew Gardner, Jocelyn Mitchell, Silvia Pessoa, Mohanalakshmi Rajakumar, and Trinidad Rico. Todd Kent and Troy Bickham at Texas A&M Qatar were integral to securing my classes and contracts there; they were also welcoming and assisted me with my research approvals and networking. Kelly Hammond, Shannon McNulty, Zarmina Nasir, and Hemal Salot made me feel like I had a home base in Doha. The intellectual community fostered by Mehran Kamrava and Zahra Babar at the Center for International and Regional Studies at Georgetown University Qatar was a central part of my Doha experience. I'd like to thank them, as well as Gerd Nonneman and Suzi Mirgani, for inviting me on several occasions to participate in events, including to give a public talk. Alex Caeiro at the Qatar Faculty of Islamic Studies has been a fabulous colleague and ongoing supporter of this project. My students at the Faculty of Islamic Studies, especially Ania, Fedaa, Mehmet, and Ayaz—and our teaching assistant, Rezart—helped me work through some of the arguments I make in the book, as did the students in my three cultural anthropology classes at Texas A&M University Qatar. Of course the students of Education City made this book possible, and it is as much yours as it is mine. I am responsible for all of its errors and omissions.

I also was fortunate in the Gulf to be invited to present early versions of my research at New York University Abu Dhabi (NYUAD) by Nathalie Puetz and Pascal Menoret in their classes. I have benefitted greatly from having them as well as other colleagues at NYUAD, including Justin Stearns and Dale Hudson, as interlocutors. Also in the United Arab Emirates, a workshop at the American University of Sharjah in March 2015 organized by Kevin Gray and Stephen Keck allowed me to present a book chapter. In Kuwait, I participated as a program committee member for the American University of Kuwait's symposium on knowledge economy in 2015, which provided great insight into my project. I thank Farah al-Nakib for including me on that panel and in the conference.

Many other people's labor has gone into this project, including those who were giving of their time to read and comment generously on various chapter and proposal drafts along the way: Attiya Ahmad, Abbie Boggs, Tanya Golash-Boza, Leigh Campoamor, Maura Finkelstein, Rachel Goshgarian, Tanya Kane, Ahmed Kanna, Natalie Koch, Amelie Le Renard, Matt Maclean, Caroline Melly, Pascal Menoret, Jennifer Nish, Kris Olds, Victoria Penziner Hightower, Zainab Saleh, L. Ayu Saraswati, Nada Soudy, and Bob Vitalis (who also gave me the title to this book). I have been lucky to find an academic soulmate in Natalie Koch over the course of travels, conversations, and Skype calls—I look forward to collaborating more with you, my friend.

I also want to thank Scott Morgensen for his fantastic reviewer comments at our 2016 American Anthropological Association panel. Rosie Bsheer invited me to present my work at a phenomenal conference on the Arabian Peninsula at Yale University in April 2016. I also benefitted greatly from feedback I received presenting versions of the book's arguments at Haverford University, where I was invited by Zainab Saleh in 2016; the American University of Beirut, where I was invited by Waleed Hazbun in 2015; Princeton University, where I was invited by Bernie Heykel in 2013; and Wesleyan University, where I was invited by Attiya Ahmad in 2012. My fieldwork was funded in part by a Wenner-Gren Post PhD Grant (#8875), which I received in 2014. I also received a grant from the Program to Enhance Scholarly and Creative Activities at Texas A&M in 2011, and a research grant from Lafayette College's Academic Research Committee in 2014.

Kate Wahl at Stanford University Press has been an extraordinary editor and pushed me to new places with my writing. I thank her for her enthusiasm for this project, and the SUP team for their hard work helping to see it to publication. I would also like to thank my department colleagues for their generous support since my arrival at Lafayette: William Bissell, Rebecca Kissane, Caroline Lee, Monica Salas-Landa, Howard Schneiderman, David Shulman, and Andrea Smith. At Lafayette, Kylie Bailin, Robert Blunt, Erica D'Agostino, Michael Feola, Rachel Goshgarian, Hafsa Kanjwal, Clara Valdano, and Wendy Wilson-Fall have also been invaluable intellectual allies and comrades. There are others in my larger community of friends and mentors whose ongoing support, phone calls, conversations, late-night Facebook chats, recommendation letters, homes, and meals sustained me: Lalaie Ameeriar, Aisha Durham, Maura Finkelstein, Harjant Gill, Inderpal Grewal, Anneeth Kaur Hundle, Alfred Jessel, Karen Leonard, Caroline Osella, Vanita Reddy, Sima Shakhsari, Susan Strickland, and Zulema Valdez. My family—Mom, Dad, Manish, Kathy, Dylan—who I am so glad to have closer to me now—have been a source of joy and strength through the hardest times. Of course I have to mention the cats that give this crazy cat lady life: no one should write without cats. Finally, Ratna, what a journey these years have been—I'm looking forward to the next chapter.

TEACH FOR ARABIA

Introduction

Mythologies of Liberalism

In Summer 2010, I taught Introduction to Cultural Anthropology at Texas A&M Qatar, a course that met daily for five weeks. I had never taught outside of the United States before, and anthropology had never been offered at the branch campus, where liberal arts classes were limited to topics that fulfilled common core requirements for the students' engineering degrees. Although I was uncertain how some topics I taught at the main campus in College Station, Texas, such as patriarchy and intersexuality, would go over in a classroom I presumed would be more conservative, I decided to keep my syllabus basically the same, adding content about the Arabian Peninsula and wider Gulf region to make the class more relatable.[1] I also assigned a popular introductory textbook, hoping that the book's accessibility would mitigate second-language learner difficulties that the denser articles might pose.

Like many anthropology textbooks, ours utilized cross-cultural examples in order to denaturalize assumptions about how societies are organized. Deploying comparative examples to "make the strange familiar and the familiar strange" is a common way to explain cultural relativism to undergraduates. But to make its points, our textbook unquestioningly centered a US reader familiar with American racial categories, American gender norms, and American politics. My students were confused by some of the book's examples, which I clarified in class. This did not pose a great challenge until about midway through the term, when we read the kinship chapter. To highlight how marriage and family were cultural and not universal, the book asked readers to abandon their preconceived notions that cousin marriage is incest, since in some parts of the world, people practice it. As it turned out, we were in one of the parts of the world the textbook used as a primary example.[2] Several of my Qatari students were either already engaged to their cousins or expected to be.

The class—who were about half Qatari citizens and half foreign residents who had grown up in Doha—arrived the morning after reading the chapter uniformly offended; they had clearly had a group conversation prior to our meeting. They told me the reading did not speak to them and also presented them or their classmates as exotic. Overall, they were fed up with the textbook. It seemed that they were also upset at me for assigning it. Just when I felt that I had made an irredeemable error, the class discussion shifted into a sophisticated unpacking of the parochialism of anthropology as a form of knowledge and how it continued to perpetuate American exceptionalism. The students then moved on to tell me how their other classes—STEM classes—contained similar moments of tension, sometimes in the curriculum and sometimes due to their professors' presumptions about what Qataris, Arabs, and/or Muslims were like.

Instead of turning into a failure, our class dynamic grew stronger because of the frank conversation we had that day and in the days following. We continued to discuss not only anthropology but also the American university, the Education City campus where Texas A&M Qatar and other American branch campuses were located, and their role as students within the country's growing knowledge economy. The students amazed me with their willingness to cross rigid social boundaries in order to learn about Doha residents they normally did not have the chance to engage. For their final group ethnographic projects, they researched topics including unauthorized migrant labor camps, shifting gender roles within Qatari marriages, Palestinian diasporic identities, and the experiences of *bidoon* (stateless) people.[3] I heard after I left that some of them went to the dean to request that anthropology be offered again at Texas A&M Qatar; I believe this enabled me to return to teach for the following two summers. Anthropology was eventually added as a full-time line.[4]

Whenever I design a course now, I am reminded of that class in Doha and how much it pushed me outside my comfort zone. It challenged me to question who I center and who I marginalize through my choice of readings and assignments, the language I use in delivering my lectures, how I assign group work, and my overall interactions with students. Today, I am a tenured faculty member at an elite liberal arts institution in the United States that markets itself as invested in critical thinking, undergraduate research experiences, diversity, and global citizenship training. The students at this institution will rarely get to experience these learning outcomes to the extent that I have witnessed students experience them at the American branch campuses in Doha, due to the diversity of students, quality of resources, and number of hands-on learning opportunities available there.

Since I began research for this book project, conversations have been swirling within US academic communities about what the transplant of liberal education into so-called illiberal countries such as Qatar and other Gulf states means for the future of the American academy. Very rarely, however, do we hear about the experiences on the ground of what happens within these transplant institutions, and how different actors engage with liberalism as both a universal and parochial project.[5] My students understood the parochialism of liberal ideologies much better than their professors and the critics of branch campuses. They were quite aware of the branch campus as a space of encounter that rested on longer histories of entanglement that produced East and West, liberal and illiberal, universal and parochial, global and local, anthropologist and native. Their engagement with our anthropology textbook showcased this understanding of how ongoing knowledge transfer co-constituted Arabia and America as mutually exclusive.

There are many unique and spectacular things to write about the multibillion-dollar buildings of Education City, the variety of learners and laborers that inhabited its confines, the uneven transfer of institutional norms, and the local contestations and changes that took place over the seven-plus years that I worked on this project. Pushing beyond these easy targets and thin descriptions, I decided instead to introduce the experience that best animates the stakes of this book. Schools are critical sites for social reproduction, for citizenship training, and for identity formation. They are also spaces where the technologies of governance, surveillance, belonging, and exclusion that exist in the broader social context are rehearsed, negotiated, and contested by various actors. Enabled by an American university in a state where higher education was increasingly seen as a public good, my students embraced certain aspects of liberal education while also challenging the geopolitical and historical inequalities that liberalism relies upon.

Offering an ethnographically grounded account that centers the unique experiences of different actors as they navigated branch campuses in Education City and their relationships to identity formation, citizenship, nation building, and imaginings of the future, this book discusses the role of liberal higher education in the making of transnational Qatar. At the same time, examining the inherent contradictions of American academia from the vantage point of Qatar highlights how ideas about the liberal and the illiberal were constantly emergent, contained within them their own undoing, and revealed investments from both sides of the globe by particular actors in maintaining mythologies of liberalism and its others.

Liberal Deserts

A sprawling fourteen-square-kilometer campus on the edge of Doha, Education City represents the Qatari government's multibillion-dollar investment over the last twenty years in its research and development sector, particularly higher education. Six elite US university branch campuses form the core of the Education City project: Georgetown School of Foreign Service, Virginia Commonwealth University, Texas A&M Qatar, Carnegie Mellon, Northwestern, and Weill Cornell Medical School. They are fully funded by the Qatar Foundation, a nonprofit parastatal that pays for all building construction, office equipment, and annual operating costs and salaries; in addition, it provides generous financial aid and scholarships for students and pays the main campuses

IMAGE 1. Photograph of the entryway to the Texas A&M Qatar branch campus in Education City. Source: Alexey Sergeev, asergeev.com. Reprinted with permission.

in the United States multimillion-dollar annual consulting fees for operating in Qatar. In some cases, Qatar Foundation has also endowed faculty lines in the United States as part of partnership negotiations.

The first branch campus, Virginia Commonwealth University, opened in 1998 as a women's institution offering graphic arts and design degrees. It is now coeducational, as are all the universities in Education City. Most are housed in their own spectacular buildings, designed by world-famous architects. The Texas A&M building, made of red stone, was designed to mimic an Aztec pyramid, with an enormous brass door at the gateway, in which a regular-sized door was discretely placed as the official entrance. (See Image 1.) The Cornell building down the street looks like a spaceship because of its huge oval lecture halls, while the newly opened Georgetown building, built around a beautiful courtyard, has its own private stone driveway with massive decorative pillars. The lawns throughout Education City are manicured and watered daily,[6] and there are ornate open gathering spaces for commencements and other activities. With its many roadways, parking lots, and clear demarcation through fences and gateposts,[7] it truly feels like a distinct space set apart from the rest of Doha—a city within a city.[8]

The focus within branch campuses, as in their metropolitan home locations, is on fostering critical thinking rather than rote learning, on encouraging student citizenship as a form of self-making that goes beyond the classroom through Student Affairs programming, and on maintaining standards of religious and ethnic tolerance, gender equity, and academic freedom. American branch campuses offer almost identical curricula to their home campuses and enforce home country/state and campus-wide regulations. Degrees do not indicate whether a student graduated from the United States or from Qatar. Students are expected to take exams such as the SAT and TOEFL in order to qualify for entry, classes are taught in English, and mission statements, communications, and orientations inculcate home campus identity as transposable to Qatar—thus one regularly hears "howdy" within the hallways and classrooms of Texas A&M Qatar, and admissions pamphlets at Carnegie Mellon Qatar are peppered with Tartan print and Scottie dogs. The rapid growth in American university partnerships with Gulf states over the last two decades has aligned with a larger trend in American higher education over the same period—colleges and universities have increasingly looked outside the territorial borders of the United States for revenue streams, to raise rankings, and to train students to be more competitive for jobs at home and abroad. Not only is the United States the largest host country for international students, bringing in close to thirty-seven billion dollars in annual revenue,[9] it is also the largest exporter of education in the world: as of 2015, fifty-one American institutions operated eighty-one branch campuses around the world, with even more in the planning stages.[10] Like the branch campuses in Education City, many of these campuses are also funded by host countries in the Middle East and Asia and generate large amounts of revenue for their home campuses.

Critics of these internationalization ventures worry that expanding American universities into illiberal societies will undermine liberal education's foundational principles. For example, many have argued against partnering with states that have sexist or homophobic discrimination built into their legal systems, or violate international human rights conventions, claiming that these partnerships would endanger academic freedom and the values of the Western academy.[11] By 2009, the concern over branch campuses in the Arabian Peninsula in particular had become so intense that the president of the Middle East Studies Association, Virginia Aksan, made them the center of her annual keynote, connecting American Empire post 9/11 with the corporate neoliberal aspects of globalized higher education, and expressing concerns that these institutions were complicit in human rights violations. The "vast imitative campuses" of Education City, she argued, were threats to "the very idea of the university and its potential to contribute to the common good."[12]

Similarly, Andrew Ross, one of the most vocal critics of opening a branch campus of his institution, New York University, in the United Arab Emirates (UAE), has argued that moving American universities into the illiberal Gulf "puts at risk some of our bedrock principles."[13] In addition to concerns over migrant labor exploitation, he notes the "problem of hosting liberal lifestyles and open speech" in an "authoritarian" context, asking how "the cultural ethos of Greenwich Village" could possibly thrive on the man-made island in Abu Dhabi where New York University's new campus was to be located.[14] A recent book by a former professor at Georgetown Qatar, who taught there for eight years, laments, despite plenty of examples provided to the contrary, that "higher education's American transplants were not taking root in nurturing, liberal soil."[15] These concerns, which represent the general tenor of US-based faculty attitudes toward Gulf branch campuses and partnerships, both reveal a belief in liberalism as a universal ethos and also recuperate the parochial ground from which liberalism's seeds can grow: fertile soil in Greenwich Village or Washington, DC, but barren desert in the Gulf.

These critiques produce the idea that the world is divided into liberal space and illiberal space, and that moving liberal education into illiberal contexts puts these two supposedly opposing frameworks for understanding and organizing the world into contact for the first time; in the process liberalism, and liberal subjects, are in peril.[16] In these critiques of internationalization, Qatar, the UAE, and other states are classified as illiberal without much incentive to unpack what that means, painting whole territories and the people who reside within them with broad, homogenizing strokes, and in the process also assuming that politics and power work in distinct ways that map onto nation-states (and that nations map onto states).[17]

In addition, most critics present the American university and liberal education as newly entering a homogeneous time-space of the global, instead of considering how liberalism and its supposed universality has been constituted through multiple translocal encounters, including those of scholarly exchange and university transplant.[18] Similarly, the supposedly newly encountered space of the illiberal, often presented in an Orientalist clash-of-civilizations discourse, is itself a product of longer histories of encounter and exchange. It is through these encounters that the ideas have emerged of liberal and illiberal as oppositional spaces, ideologies, and forms of power.

These territorial assumptions and the moralities associated with them occlude how citizenship, subjectivity, and lived experience happen on the ground. They also do not allow us to explore the non-unitary and heterogeneous aspects of how states function or even come to be seen as the state,[19] often through collaboration with foreign agents and corporations, and indeed, with academic knowledge production. Nor are they attentive to the pedagogical work and scholarly partnerships that many academics are already conducting at the non-state scale in so-called illiberal contexts, often based on long-term engagement within communities, linguistic expertise, relationships of trust, and knowledge of local politics.[20]

It is not terribly surprising, then, that so few of the critics of branch campus initiatives are experts in the regions where their universities are expanding. The culture work required to set up these institutions, it seems, does not need the culture experts of the academy. Many who work and teach about the Gulf have also worked and taught and lived in the Gulf, some even growing up there. We have experienced marginalization, self-censorship, surveillance, and discrimination. We have also experienced comfort, intellectual community, teaching pleasure, activism, and collaboration with marginalized communities. These experiences could contribute greatly to discussions about best practices regarding university transfer on the institutional side, and best practices regarding collaboration on the activist side. Yet scholars embedded in these locations are rarely considered to have political or intellectual positions of value, precisely because of these connections—they make us not objective enough, apologists rather than experts.[21]

The categorization of places, ideas, regimes, and cultures into liberal and illiberal is fundamentally a project based in faith rather than fact, one that constantly needs to elide imperial histories, encounters with difference, and discursive and material inconsistencies in order to maintain what I call liberal piety, producing subjects who *believe themselves* to be liberal, cosmopolitan, and inclusive rather than parochial and complicit in ongoing forms of imperialism, Orientalism, exclusion, and American exceptionalism.[22] This is despite US policies representing some of the most egregious human rights violations in the world.[23] A recent controversy over visas that were denied to two New York University professors of Iranian Shiʿi background who were set to teach a semester at the Abu Dhabi branch campus is a clear example of how readily US-based academics, in the midst of Trump's travel bans targeting Shiʿi-majority countries, were willing to write off wholesale the students and faculty at a campus in the Gulf, despite their ongoing activism on the ground, and without providing them any platform to discuss their experiences with academic freedom.[24] Liberalism's universality, therefore, is built on certain exclusions, and those exclusions, both historically and in the contemporary moment of the War on Terror, are particularly Muslim and Middle Eastern.[25]

Academic Crisis

Twenty years ago, Bill Readings identified how globalization was shifting the American university away from its role as an inculcator of a supposedly homogeneous national culture.[26] Instead, the university had become a transnational corporation: the fractured and market-driven effects of globalization and neoliberalism had shifted capitalism away from the national scale, making it seem like the university was somehow newly entangled with capital, when it was just less moored to the national scale. Along with post-structuralist challenges to universal knowledge claims, these changes were causing a sense of crisis among many of his contemporaries. The university had become a "ruined" institution: "What marks the tone of contemporary diatribes, is that the grand narrative of the University, centered on the production of a liberal, reasoning, subject, is no longer readily available to us . . . The liberal *individual* is no longer capable of metonymically embodying the *institution*."[27]

Higher education crisis has over the last two decades burgeoned into a veritable knowledge industry in its own right, with articles appearing nearly daily in the *Chronicle of Higher Education, Inside Higher Education*, and other newspapers, blogs, and dozens of books published every year from a variety of disciplines. Global initiatives and internationalization projects seem to extend claims that higher education is increasingly driven by profit and delinked from the public good.[28] While indeed it is important to study empirically the impacts of specific economic shifts on university management and the everyday lives of institutional actors, it is imperative to dwell in the university as a ruined institution, recognizing that there has never been a pure space of pedagogy or intellectual production outside the constraints of bureaucracy and capital.[29] Rebuilding from ruins, after all, would replicate not reality but nostalgia, thus reinforcing the violent erasures that underpin liberal modernity's epistemologies and institutions. Thus Bill Readings cautioned strongly that "academics must work without alibis, which is what the best of them have tended to do."[30]

Most contemporary critiques of academic neoliberalism do not dwell in the ruins, however. They work from alibis, claiming a space for political and academic life that is outside of economics; and they resort to nostalgia, either eliding the imperial and racial exclusions on which the university, the nation, and liberalism were built, or casting them as exceptions.[31] The turn to nostalgia in crisis narratives evokes a universal public, while in reality the public good that was supposedly lost under neoliberalism has always rested on those who cannot access liberalism's categories of the individual, the human, or the civilized. When applied to more recent international iterations, crisis narratives recuperate civilizational discourses and, in the case of the Gulf, Orientalisms—the very self/other imperial binaries on which liberalism has consistently relied. By diagnosing a state of enduring crisis as a way of defining the present, crisis becomes the marker of its own truth, with no need to provide historical evidence to the contrary.[32]

The American university was foundationally colonial and white supremacist. The earliest universities in North America, which would become the Ivy League, were Christian missionary projects built in the name of manifest destiny and civilizing the inferior Indian.[33] They were funded by profits accrued by white slaving elites, as well as built in part by slave labor.[34] It was through debates about how to manage enslaved and colonized people, and the nature of various races, that the values now considered foundational to liberal education—freedom, secular humanism, and the individual subject—emerged.[35] Slavery—the management of human capital—was one of America's first scientific innovations; the contemporary capitalist crisis of US academia must therefore be connected back to its first instantiation, begging the question then of *who* exactly is in crisis, and who gets to experience nostalgia for a time before it.[36]

The secularism (or presumed secularism) of the contemporary American university is also inseparable from its Christian missionary—and racist—roots. As plantation wealth in the South and the Caribbean funded the rise of Northern cities, the sons of wealthy white landowners and slaveholders no longer needed to travel to Europe to attain their education. With the circulation of European Enlightenment theories, the increase in anti-British nationalist sentiments, and the rise of American industrialism, the university's mission shifted from discovering the totality of God's truth to exploring the truths of Nature and History, thus cementing the secular civilizational telos of liberalism and relegating religion to a separate and marginal sphere of study.[37]

The American university was also originally imperial.[38] The academy was a source of knowledge that, along with military and economic interventions, naturalized a mission to spread principles of rationality and freedom to supposedly inferior races. Older sojourns of the American university connected the domestic technologies of racial management with the growth of higher education in US colonies like Puerto Rico, Hawaii, and the Philippines, and to wider imperial and missionary ventures, such as the establishment of the Syrian Protestant College in the nineteenth century, which would later become the secular American University of Beirut.[39]

The Morrill Land Grant Act of 1862 made higher education a public good accessible to non-elites and expanded the research university model. However, the large state universities created through land grants were also part of a post–Civil War racial project of social engineering intended to create a productive white working class.[40] Land grant universities are living reminders of the settler colonialist legacy of the United States, even as they often provide low-cost public education to first-generation and other underserved populations.[41] These research universities have been key sites for the production of military and other technologies and ideologies that fueled American imperialism, particularly in the Cold War era.[42] Anthropology became of particular importance at this time as a discipline that could help understand the Other in order to promote American agendas abroad, particularly in emerging postcolonial nation-states.[43]

The civil rights and anti-colonial activism of the 1960s and 1970s shook the university's claim to universal knowledge, exposing its exclusionary practices and fracturing unified national identity. Student demands for change focused on increasing inclusion in institutions of higher education and improving representation within the curriculum of excluded histories and cultures. Women and minorities gained greater access to the university, identity-based courses and (inter)disciplines were added to curricula, and more schools implemented affirmative-action policies.[44] In addition, postcolonial and post-structural theories encouraged a decentering of the Enlightenment Western man as the normative subject of liberalism. These oppositional social movements and alternate forms of knowledge have since been incorporated into the university in ways that serve its capitalist entanglements and depoliticize and contain difference.[45] Liberal multiculturalism has made difference an aesthetic, and quantification a measure of success.[46] Exclusion and marginalization are now individualized experiences that are exceptions to liberal education, or bootstraps stories, rather than intrinsic to liberalism itself. Once a marginalized discipline tasked with producing knowledge about the non-Western Other, anthropology's approaches to culture seem to have been mainstreamed as part of this project: civilizational logics, cultural relativism, and the idea of cultural difference as bounded and absolute inform the university's approaches to its domestic Others, who have become markers of liberal humanism's capacity for tolerance. Diversity initiatives therefore imply that diversity is done, that racisms, sexisms, and other forms of discrimination are in the past, or are just a few bad apples of the present.[47]

The actual on-the-ground experiences and activism of students, faculty, and staff indicate the opposite, however. Despite the university's celebration of diversity, it remains in many ways a white heteropatriarchal elite space—the liberal myths of the university cannot contain our marked bodily movements through the spaces of academe, the uneven distribution of academic labor, or the ways that identity work continues to be ghettoized or challenged with extinction within disciplines and institutions.[48] The number of women and people of color denied tenure or unable to advance into the higher ranks of the faculty and administration, pervasive microaggressions and hostile climates on university campuses, the normalization of sexual assault and rape culture, persistent and pervasive homophobia, the demographics of contingent labor, racial profiling of community members by campus police—to name just a few examples—belie the stories of progress and inclusion that appear on almost every university website, recruitment document, and self-assessment.

Academic freedom—perhaps the most pervasive myth of liberal education—is only accessible to the bodies, ideas, and experts who best reflect the university's many entanglements. There is a long history of external surveillance and political repression of academics who do not support US military and imperial interests.[49] Academic freedom dissipates when scholars speak out against national interests or against hostile climates within their own universities, such as post-9/11 criticisms of Islamophobia and the War on Terror, and, perhaps most prominently, in critiques of US military and ideological support of Israel's occupation of Palestine.[50] The violent crackdown on student protestors at the University of California, Davis, and other schools across the country during the Occupy Wall Street movement, along with surveillance of groups like Students for Justice in Palestine and Muslim Students Association, highlight historical and contemporary links between universities, the police state, and wealthy donors and political watchdog groups. This is particularly true of scholarship and teaching on the Middle East and North Africa region, which is intimately tied to US foreign policy interests in the region, thus influencing access to certain areas and the topics that are safe to teach in classrooms.[51] These experiences, however, are not usually folded into narratives of crisis.

Perhaps even more insidious than the institutionalization and depoliticization of difference, many academic crisis narratives, invested as they are in a critique of neoliberalism, incorporate the post-1970s rise of the interdisciplines and inclusion of minority subjects into a narrative of ever-expanding capitalist logics.[52] This has allowed for the dismissal of a very loosely defined postmodernity as anti-truth, which not surprisingly overlapped with right-wing discourses around culture wars in the 1980s.[53] This approach also fetishizes the economy as its own telos, eliding the entanglements between economy, state, and academy that inform everyday lives of scholarly knowledge production.[54] Marxist critique of this kind is thus *deeply normative*, when claiming to be the opposite, even though those most deeply impacted by neoliberal reforms are women of color, first-generation college students, and the working class.[55]

Critique stems most often from a position of authority not powerlessness, as we can see from the demographics and titles of those who are at the forefront of knowledge production about academic crisis; its traction comes precisely from failing to address the (unmarked) position of power from which it is produced.[56] One has to wonder, then, if the nostalgia that crisis narratives express is solely based on corporatization, or if it is also a retrenchment exercise in response to the large shifts in university demographics and curricular offerings also taking place at the same time. It seems that any new regulation, any bureaucratic measure, anything that asks a faculty member at the top of the food chain to change their methods or to adapt to student demands gets painted with the same brush: neoliberalism.[57] This mode of engagement is especially pertinent in understanding how crisis narratives approach the globalized American university, particularly through coupling and collapsing neoliberalism with imperialism, and in the process utilizing unproblematized ideas about illiberal peoples and cultures to claim that internationalization threatens liberalism. Resistance to globalizing the American university by opening branch campuses or partnering with nondemocratic states is not an anti-imperial logic. It revives American exceptionalism and rehearses the very tropes of cultural difference produced through and for the interest of imperial and hegemonic projects, without attending to the ways that scholars who perform critique benefit from their positionality.

If liberalism contains within it excesses and contradictions that need to be exceptionalized or erased in order to perpetuate its mythologies, then illiberalism must be thought of in the same way; both are produced through encounters and collaborations between various actors and institutions. As I made my way out of new faculty orientation at Texas A&M Qatar in 2011, I passed a banner for the incoming freshmen, rendered in maroon and white, outlined with balloons, and hung over a door. It proclaimed, "Welcome to Aggieland, Fighting Texas Aggie Class of 2015!" *Aggie*, short for "agriculturalist," is the name of the Texas A&M

sports team and, by extension, applies to all members of the community, both in Texas and Qatar. I wondered how one becomes a fighting Texas Aggie in Doha. Moving American education to Qatar meant transplanting not only campuses and curricula but also core values and traditions, which are steeped in specific histories.

Texas A&M's flagship campus in College Station is one of the largest public land grant universities in the United States, with an endowment among the country's top ten. The main campus alone enrolls over fifty thousand students and hosts several Division One sports teams. Despite its size, the university's history as an all-male military and agricultural institution is quite visible today in the makeup of the student body, which remains predominantly white, Christian, and conservative, as well as in a number of expressions of school spirit. Students who enroll at Texas A&M are inculcated into a set of traditions that stretch back to the founding of the school and connected to a global alumni network that they can identify with well beyond their college years.[58] Activities that promote a sense of school spirit on campus and among alumni internationally, like monthly Silver Taps and Muster, are often linked to honoring military Aggies killed serving in one of the United States's many foreign wars.[59] Designated a Senior Military College, the university is one of only three nonmilitary campuses in the United States with a full-time active Corps of Cadets. It is not unusual for students to come to class in army fatigues or to conduct military drills with rifles on campus.

Students at the branch campus had a critical consciousness about their relationship to the main campus, school traditions, and the primarily North American faculty. Some felt a strong identification with being Aggie, but they also qualified that identification by telling me that they did not feel as Aggie as the US students at the home campus. Others pushed back against the centering of US experiences in the creation of Aggie identity and traditions. Amna, a Qatari woman who had just graduated from the branch campus, for example, said of Muster, which was also held in Qatar, "Why should we care? Would they care in America if someone died over here? Aggie Muster is not relevant. They wouldn't do the same for us."

Amna's point was especially salient given that Qatar hosts the largest military base and US Central Command in the region, the seat of operations for ongoing attacks under the War on Terror, which had tightened US imperial relationships with its Gulf allies. She challenged the idea of an abstracted and universal form of American liberal education, highlighting instead its inherent inconsistencies and exclusions.

Given the exclusionary and violent histories of the American West that are evoked in so many expressions of Aggie identity, and the imperial ties between the United States and Qatar today, it cannot be an innocent project to produce "fighting Texas Aggies" in Doha. The encounter of a settler colonial land grant university with a modernizing Arabian Peninsula country in the form of the branch campus evokes longer histories of encounter that form the condition of possibility for a project like Education City and for burgeoning academic research on the Gulf region from fields like security studies and political science. Furthermore, the supposed distinction between liberal democracy in the West and illiberal authoritarian regime in the Middle East is a colonial by-product that enables ongoing and uneven oil entanglement between the Persian Gulf and the Gulf of Mexico.[60] In this context, Gulf countries that are US allies are considered by the US government to be safe, stable, and even nationally beneficial spaces to open universities, conduct research, and train students in topics that include petroleum engineering and foreign service.

Manufacturing Illiberalism

American branch campuses in the Gulf are not venues through which the liberal meets the illiberal; rather, they are rehearsals and reconfigurations of a much longer history of encounter. The presumption that Qatar is illiberal forecloses the importance of heterogeneous pasts, hybrid identities, political contestations, and social change in the region. It also elides how two seemingly sovereign and distinct places and identities—Arabia and America—have been coproduced through histories of imperialism, oil extraction, migratory networks, knowledge transfer, and militarism.[61] Scholarly exchange between the West and the East is not a product of globalization or even European colonialism. Rather, many of the ideas that fueled Europe's scientific revolution and the West's ideas about itself were derived from Islamic scholarship and knowledge production—liberalism has Arabian roots.[62] These traces have been lost and replaced by Orientalist constructions of the East as the West's inferior opposite.

More modern entanglements of empire and their forms of knowledge production created the Gulf's illiberalism. The cosmopolitanism of port cities, with their religious and trade networks, were replaced by romanticized images of timeless Bedouins. The pre-oil role of women in many aspects of public life was elided in order to perpetuate "Islamic" traditions of gender segregation and endogamous, patrilineal kinship.[63] The contemporary forms of tribalism and sheikhly rule in the Gulf were not only produced in collaboration with British social science but also modeled on British aristocratic and monarchial formations. Metropolitan knowledge production also produced the idea of Gulf exceptionalism, linked to its oil wealth, political systems, migration/demographics, and supposedly timeless and homogeneous indigenous culture. In this way, a globally connected region with heterogeneous peoples, customs, languages, and networks came to be seen *and to see itself* primarily through Orientalist romanticized tropes of timeless desert peoples relatively untouched by the outside world, even in an era of rapid urbanization and globalization.[64]

The Orientalism that Gulf states recuperate in their own branding projects serves particular domestic and foreign elite interests. Gulf states, like all modern postcolonial states, practice forms of nativism, communalism, and differential governance over their populations.[65] This governance is inherently contradictory, creates insides and outsides to citizenship, and exercises a sovereign right to kill. And, as with any contemporary plural society, ruling power legitimacy is tied to appeasing multiple stakeholders and competing political agendas.[66] It cannot therefore be reduced to terminology like authoritarianism, repression, or fundamentalism. The mythology of Gulf illiberalism and its absolute difference from the West is a holdover from colonial forms of rule that serves Gulf leaders well at particular times as they enact various projects of nation building.[67] However, they also draw from Western aesthetics and international development discourses in crafting visions of modernity, which seem incongruent to many, producing controversy among Qatari residents and internationally, and leading critics to claim that Doha's liberal reforms, including in education, are fake and that its urbanism is lacking in aesthetic value.[68] However, modernization projects in Qatar and the Gulf region are not haphazard or disconnected; they are historically and politically contingent assemblages of globally and locally circulating ideologies, aesthetics, materialities, and imaginaries.[69]

Encounter as an analytic framework can challenge traditional anthropological impulses and help to understand Qatar's complexities, to unpack its nationalist myths, and to de-exceptionalize forms of urbanism and modernity in the region.[70] The American universities that underpin Qatar's modernization agenda are extensions of ongoing and unequal collaborations between Western experts and Gulf ruling elites, collaborations that are imprinted onto the built environments of Gulf cities, their ethno-racial hierarchies and forms of segregation, migration and labor regimes, technologies of governance and surveillance, education systems, citizenship structures, and claims to heritage and tradition. While encounters tend to be asymmetrical, a focus on encounter highlights how multiple actors produce meaning, and how narratives that appear totalizing, like capitalism or imperialism, are instead processes with unpredictable ends.[71] In contrast to academic crisis narratives, which reaffirm Western grand narratives even in their critique of them, an analytic of encounter leaves openings to think about the possibility of decolonized knowledge production and of the branch campus as a site of agency.

American universities have a long history in the Middle East, dating back to the founding of the Syrian Protestant College in 1871, which would become the American University of Beirut.[72] Although it was intended as a missionary and colonial project, the American University of Beirut has been central since its inception to Arab intellectual movements and activism, highlighting how the soft-power goals of imperial institutions result not in hegemonic outcomes but in interesting and unintended localizations.[73] Western schools, both missionary and secular, have been in the Gulf since the late nineteenth century as well, influencing social reproduction of regional elites, and are not newly arrived with American universities or globalization.[74] These entanglements mean that it is nearly impossible to parse a distinction between what is Western and what is Arabian in the production of the modern Gulf. Yet these imaginaries, and their mapping onto ideas of liberalism and illiberalism remain fundamental to how higher education projects in the region are planned, implemented, debated, and contested— by local actors, by educators within tertiary education in the Gulf, and by journalists, academics, and other external critics, primarily in the West.

To understand the ways that liberal and illiberal, as well as Qatar and America, emerge in discussions about branch campuses (and within the branch campuses themselves) as seemingly oppositional spaces and ideas, it is useful to consider these universities as contact zones.[75] Contact zones, rather than assuming a totalizing narrative—in our case, of neoliberalism, imperialism, or transplant—allow us to see the on-the-ground role of the less powerful in the production of cultural meaning and subjectivity.[76] Within the contact zone, as within any space of encounter, difference is not a priori but rather always emergent. It is a space where even the most hegemonic messages are available to be re-signified, allowing the less powerful to "describe themselves in ways that engage with representations others have made of them."[77]

These resignifications do not just imitate the imperial or Western gaze; rather, they pick from its representational archive to construct a new text.[78] These texts have impacts in their local contexts but also circulate in unknown ways in metropolitan centers, changing and adding to understandings of difference in both. They are therefore deeply collaborative, though much of this collaboration is uneven (sometimes violently so). They can appear to be dissonant or chaotic to a reader unfamiliar with the context in which they were produced, as modernization projects in the Gulf often are. Resignified cultural texts are quite ordinary, in that they are heterogeneous and reflect the place and mode of their production; the ways they are received and then reinterpreted continue a process of undetermined heterogenization.

In 2009, Qatar Foundation embarked on an international branding campaign, peppering Education City and Doha with large-scale installations in bright yellow letters that formed words like "think," "innovate," and "learn." These were accompanied by full-page ads with similar one- or two-word messages, in English and Arabic, on billboards and in international print and digital media venues like *Time* magazine, *Al Jazeera*, Twitter, and the BBC.[79] These words are identical to those found in many university recruitment brochures and mission statements in North America and Europe as well as globally. They are foundational to ideas of individual development and the potential for liberal education to cultivate unfettered and unlimited curiosity, reflection, and thought. As such, they mark the universalizing ideas of liberalism and its path toward both individual and social freedom and equality. Qatar Foundation's Director of the Public Relations & Marketing Directorate at the time, Haya Khalifa Al-Nassr, explained that the branding campaign was:

built upon simple, yet powerful, words and phrases that represent Qatar Foundation's unending quest for knowledge and understanding in education, science, research and community development. At the same time, many people will no doubt interpret these words and phrases on a more personal level and find a meaning that is defined by their own individual experiences. The simplicity of this campaign allows it to be interpreted in a variety of ways, all of which are equally valid.[80]

Al-Nassr's invocation of the unending quest for knowledge, a responsibility to community, and the validation of multiple viewpoints echoes the branding campaigns of major American universities, ones who claim the university as exactly that: a universal form of endless knowledge pursuit that can encompass everyone. She continued, however, to explain that the campaign "is a calling from Allah the Almighty to all humans . . . He asks everyone to 'reflect' and has invited people to think about themselves and the creations of the Almighty many times in his Holy Book."

To utilize the language of liberalism and then invoke religion seems like the very incongruous act that gives critics of the Education City project pause. But Qatar Foundation's universal claim to knowledge is not a liberal claim to freedom of thought emanating from an illiberal place; it is a claim to a universal right to knowledge as God-given and inalienable, but linked to Islam rather than to the Christian God of liberalism's secular humanist tradition. The incongruity that Gulf leaders evoke in their liberal development projects for many US-based critics is not a misreading *by them* of the liberal but a reflection of the traces of encounter, of the excesses and contradictions within liberalism *itself* that liberal piety obscures.[81] It is a resignification of liberalism's secular humanist universality and its imperial ethos as underpinned by divine right. The analytic of encounter and approaching Education City and Qatar as a contact zone allow us to better unpack the categories that we have hardened in our anthropological ways of seeing and knowing the world.

Although US critics find flaws in Education City's liberalism, a group of prominent Qatari intellectuals has argued that Qatar's modernization threatens national culture, language, and religion, and contributes to ever-increasing demographic imbalance between citizens and migrants.[82] Many Qatari citizens consider Education City, with its focus on English-language curricula, American campus life, secularism, and especially coeducation, to be exclusionary, and perhaps even dangerous to social values. In 2012, a grassroots campaign, "Reflect Your Respect," led primarily by Qatari women, showcased some of these concerns. Targeting noncitizen residents and tourists in shopping malls and other public areas, the group handed out printed material about how to dress appropriately for Qatar's traditional Muslim values.[83] Showing images of what constitutes inappropriate and/or appropriate clothing, the posters and pamphlets read, "If you are in Qatar you are one of us . . . help us preserve Qatar's culture and values." (See Image 2.)

IF YOU ARE IN QATAR,
YOU ARE **ONE OF US**..

HELP US PRESERVE QATAR'S
CULTURE AND VALUES,
**PLEASE DRESS
MODESTLY* IN
PUBLIC PLACES**

*BY COVERING FROM SHOULDERS TO KNEES

FOLLOW US @ONEOFUS_QA

IMAGE 2. "Reflect Your Respect" clothing modesty leaflet. Source: *Doha News*.

This campaign made international headlines for being discrimina-tory. It showcased Qatar's supposed backwardness, especially in the treat-ment of women, who were most often the targets of this campaign[84]—both nonnational women, whose rights were infringed by being told how to dress, and, implicitly, national women as well, who were already thought to be unfree in their clothing choices because they covered.[85] The contradiction embedded in "you are one of us," but only if you show us your respect, was but one example of Qatar's supposed illiber-alism, and highlighted to many why a liberal ethos cannot thrive within the Gulf. When juxtaposed to campaigns such as this, Qatar Foundation's branding seems rather empty, especially since, from the outside, it appears that both texts are products of the same actors—a homogenized Qatari culture and the elite powers that represent it. How-ever, Qatari state and elite projects of modernization, like Qatar Foun-dation and Education City, are contested by Qataris themselves, and the "Reflect Your Respect" campaign was a response to the ways that changes in the country were including some nationals while marginalizing others. For some in Qatar, Education City signaled a different kind of crisis, and the "Reflect Your Respect" campaign was a reaction to this crisis. This campaign represented a different resignification, one that adopted the very ideas of Gulf exceptionalism and a liberal/illiberal dichotomy in order to assert claims to space that were seen to be under threat by foreign institutions and actors. This included utiliz-ing citizenship-as-belonging and noncitizenship-as-exclusion, which has come to be the a priori framework for scholarship on the region,[86] as part of a narrative of Qatari nationalism and traditional values.

Conversations about the future of higher education and the poten-tial negative impacts of US universities on Gulf societies are rife within Qatar's universities, malls, newspapers, coffee shops, and homes, but from a perspective where the American university signifies a different type of crisis, a different loss—one that destabilizes autochthonous understandings of Gulf history, language, and identity. By centering the branch campus and approaching daily life within its spaces as ordinary iterations of contemporary global processes, the uneven historical and contemporary power relations that underpin mythologies of American liberalism and Gulf illiberalism can come into starker relief.

Encountering Education City

This book provides an entry into studying Qatar and the Gulf region that resists naturalized assumptions about power, place, and belonging by exploring how cultural meanings, subjectivities, politicizations, and materialities are produced through everyday encounters in classrooms, hallways, dorms, and social spaces. Both at the individual university and Education City levels, local manifestations of American academia and its values did not correspond to the top-down deterministic representations in much of the literature on global education. Chapter 1 starts by questioning the concept of knowledge economy itself as a starting point for studying higher education in the Gulf. I highlight how this concept and the narratives associated with it function as forms of received knowledge about Qatar and the Gulf in much academic knowledge production, institutional rhetoric, and everyday conversation, both inside and outside the region. This terminology, like other exceptionalizing vocabulary about the Gulf, forecloses nuanced research and instead invites knowledge production that reproduces statist interests and imperial entanglements. I argue that the rhetorics of knowledge economy and the actual effects of educational reform and nationalist projects in Qatar are quite divergent, and I offer a methodological intervention into the vocabularies of seeing and knowing higher education, national development, and forms of belonging. When we move past received discourses, past knowledge economy as a thing in the world, different stories emerge to help us think about how to access schools as sites of ethnographic encounter and grounded research.

American branch campuses in Qatar understood their pedagogical goals primarily as liberal. However, these institutions were also central to Qatari nation building. University mission, for example, was framed in nativist terms that mirrored state rhetoric: to educate Qatari *citizens*—a group presumed to be indigenous, overly traditional, and homogeneous—to achieve modernity while preserving their supposedly vanishing culture. Despite the heavy focus on educating citizens and preserving culture, non-Qataris comprised more than 50 percent of the student body at most schools. To address this imbalance, branch campuses incorporated Qatarization policies, which were often state mandated, such as preferential selection, extra training, career placement, and financial incentives for reaching quotas of citizen enrollment. These policies resulted in a two-tier structure, where national and nonnational students were treated differently from admission through graduation.

In Chapter 2, I argue that educators acted in many ways as anthropologists, delineating the boundaries of Qatariness through cultural relativism and a salvage approach to culture; in the process, they also constituted the limits of liberalism in ways that made Qatari students unable to fully become the liberal individuals that university missions hoped to cultivate. Qataris learned and negotiated Qatari culture through engaging with these reified ideas—what I call pedagogies of essentialism—as well as by interacting with other compatriots and with nonnationals. Qatarization policies produced effects that might seem paradoxical. Qatari students often felt like they didn't belong, specifically because the privileges afforded to them and the reductive understandings of Qatari culture perpetuated by many faculty made them feel too visible, deindividualized, and/or stereotyped. I explore how their lack of participation in extracurricular activities and supposed self-segregation produced deep anxiety among administrators, which in turn furthered institutional assumptions about conservative Qatari culture and its traditional gender roles.

Qatari women in particular, who attended university in greater numbers than Qatari men, were considered integral to the success of Qatarization and modernity, and were the primary targets of Student Affairs programming. In Chapter 3, I consider how state-sponsored feminism and liberal feminism impacted Qatari women's identity production and social interactions within coeducational space, where they were under constant scrutiny. Qatari state rhetoric portrayed women's education and employment within mixed workplaces as essential to becoming modern, to transitioning to a knowledge-based economy, and to achieving greater Qatarization. Yet gender integration was also considered a threat to women's bodily purity, to their reputation, and to the gender roles and norms attached to Qatar's emergent national identity. The overt and covert ways that coeducational anxiety permeated Education City played out on the bodies and actions of Qatari women, both as a group to be protected from criticism and also as the source of gender threat itself. Young Qatari women were tasked with playing a critical role in Qatar's modernization but were also expected to represent a timeless national culture. I focus on how they negotiated these competing expectations and the parameters of what constituted proper femininity.

In contrast to Qatari students' feelings of marginalization, in Chapter 4 I explore the experiences and narratives of those I call "local expats"—noncitizens who grew up in Qatar. Despite being structurally disadvantaged and precarious in relation to their Qatari peers, they populated most social activities, participated more fully in school spirit, and initiated extracurricular programming, thereby embodying the neo/liberal subjectivities that these campuses professed to cultivate more than the students who they were geared toward. These campuses indeed reproduced privilege for the citizens who were able to access them, but they also increased stratification among citizens while increasing forms of belonging for certain noncitizens. Qatari futures, therefore, were both heterogeneous and hierarchical, and branch campuses reassembled a range of actors, ideologies, and institutions that exceeded the territorial boundaries of the state and the imagined boundaries of the nation to produce a transnational elite that could perform global citizenship as well as reify Qatar's national brand and the illiberal myths on which it relied.

In Chapter 5, I consider my experiences alongside those of my faculty and staff interlocutors, focusing on the illiberal pleasures afforded to Western and white expatriates living and working in compounds, and the forms of labor that these experts were expected to perform. In particular, I explore how expertise in the Gulf mapped on to whiteness, and how whiteness mapped on to Doha's geographic and ethno-racial segregation. American universities in Doha recuperated some aspects of white supremacy that are endemic to US institutions but attributed them to the Gulf and its demographics, thereby absolving institutions and individuals from facilitating change. This enabled racial self-segregation without the white guilt experience of the metropole. The experiences of nonwhite, non-Western, and Muslim faculty and staff were especially insightful in highlighting how the home spaces of academia and the branch campus both required forms of performance and offered different comforts and discomforts. My rights in Qatar and the Gulf were supposedly diminished by its exclusionary citizenship regimes, authoritarian police state, and Islamic gender expectations. However, I have always found modes of belonging, a level of respect from my students, and a sense of physical comfort in my brown body there that I have rarely experienced in the United States. I also experienced new forms of social stratification and had to negotiate different personal and professional expectations and relationships during this project.

The claims I make in this book do not come from a space of critique—a view from nowhere[87]—but instead are highly situated and have been informed by over a decade of researching, living, traveling to, and teaching in the Gulf. In particular, the research conducted for this book included teaching four terms in two very different Education City universities (Texas A&M Qatar and the Qatar Faculty of Islamic Studies), applying for local grants, giving many guest lectures and talks, and sitting in on classes, conferences, academic colloquia, and student events (not only in Qatar but also in the UAE and Kuwait).[88] My pedagogy, my relationship as a non-Muslim to the varied ideas and practices of Islam, and my understanding of how power produces different subjectivities and what I have elsewhere called multiple logics of governance[89] have been shaped by my embodied experiences within academic institutions in the United States and in Qatar, and by daily life as a South Asian middle-class woman in a so-called liberal world, and in a so-called illiberal one. Teaching moments in both the United States and in Qatar revealed incommensurable epistemologies in each place, and I had to rethink the normalizations that go into teaching anthropology, a discipline that has always taken the global as its discursive and material field. Fitting uneasily into either but also feeling at home in both also challenged me to reflect on the norms and centers of each and how they were constituted through encounters—with various actors, with institutions, and with imagined others—and I include these reflections and experiences in the book.

The contradictions and failures I explore in the following chapters do not arise from the migration of Western liberal educational models into new, illiberal spaces; rather, they reflect paradoxes of difference embedded in liberalism itself, which are inextricable from anthropological approaches to culture. The branch campuses in Education City, like all sites of American academia, are spaces of contradiction. This is deeply ordinary, not evidentiary of crisis. Nor are these campuses mere transplants, as they are sometimes framed; rather, they are sites of new agencies and belongings. This kind of exploration, as I return to in the Conclusion, could provide important lessons in decolonizing anthropology and scholarship on the Gulf region. When the branch campus speaks back to the metropolitan university, it further reveals liberal piety for the gatekeeping mechanism that it is. The ruined university's sandy interiors, after all, were always meant to be occupied by the multiple publics that produced and were produced by it.

CHAPTER 1

Unlearning Knowledge Economy

When I began research in the Gulf over a decade ago, the expansion of higher education options in the region, particularly through international branch campuses, had already become a subject of both scholarly interest and lay conversation. Academic conferences and publications, international media, and local newspapers were all discussing investments by Gulf leaders in education, heritage and culture, and technology as part of a larger strategy to shift away from hydrocarbon reliance while also educating citizens to replace foreign workers. "Knowledge economy" quickly became the buzzword for this economic development. The term was circulating in international development discourse as well, which had moved away from "structural adjustment" to postindustrial economic policy suggestions for Global South states.[1] By 2008 the Qatari government had consolidated knowledge economy as the primary goal for the country's modernization with its publication of the *Qatar National Vision 2030*.[2] The standard logic laid out by the *Qatar National Vision* is that Qatar must focus its resources on building human capital in order to become a self-sustaining country, since oil wealth is finite. To accomplish this goal, the state needs to provide its citizens with skills to become entrepreneurs, bolster the private sector, and replace foreign professionals, who now control the workforce. While labor laws have privileged hiring nationals since the 1960s (even before Qatari independence in 1971), state discourses and practices have only recently coalesced around a wholesale strategy called Qatarization, aimed at creating citizen-workers.[3] Qatarization reinforces a narrow ethnic nationalism, since citizenship is patrilineal and not accessible to immigrants.[4]

As a previously untapped citizen labor demographic, women have explicitly become targets of Qatarization policies; however, they are also expected, as in most postcolonial nation-states, to be the bearers and passers on of religious, cultural, and family values.

The Qatar Foundation's mission statement directly references both knowledge economy and the *Qatar National Vision* as central to its mandate, as do other urban development projects, cultural initiatives, and corporate web pages in Doha. Many of the branch campus web pages also make reference to Qatar's development plan as part of their overall goals. The forty-page document has, in essence, become the guide for building Qatar's modernity, national identity, and international brand. Students frequently referred to their own place within branch campuses as being part of knowledge economy as well. Many were proud to be included in the project headed by Sheikha Moza, the chairperson of Qatar Foundation and wife of the former emir. Several of these students, however, qualified their comments about knowledge economy with statements like, "whatever that means." Hawda, a Qatari woman who was finishing up her junior year at Georgetown, said, "More recently I have been questioning just the idea of a knowledge-based economy. Is that even something that's viable, or something that's even true, and can it ever come into existence?" Hawda's question, and the confusion expressed by my student interlocutors—those arguably tasked with bringing the knowledge economy into existence—highlight how this concept and the narratives associated with it function as forms of received knowledge about Qatar and the Gulf in much academic knowledge production, institutional rhetoric, and everyday conversation, both inside and outside of the region.

Like liberalism, knowledge economy is a legitimizing discourse that relies on and reproduces particular categories, narratives, and reductive understandings that are easily undone through grounded empirical research. Yet this terminology, like other exceptionalizing vocabulary about the Gulf, forecloses nuanced research and instead invites knowledge production that reproduces statist interests and the products of previous and ongoing imperial entanglements. The argument I begin to put forward in this chapter, which I reinforce with evidence from my field research through the rest of the book, is that the rhetorics of knowledge economy and the actual effects of national development projects in Qatar are quite divergent. Contrary to what received knowledge presumes, knowledge-economy development is not shifting economic reliance away from petro-wealth, but is rather sustained by it.[5] In addition, Qatarization policies have not been successful in decreasing reliance on Western expertise, nor has the government attempted to reduce the size of the public sector, where most Qataris find ready positions, often without a college degree. And the Qatari government, despite its claims to ethnic nationalism, provides several opportunities for belonging to foreign nationals, thus paving the way for a continued multicultural and transnational future. This leads to questions about what American branch campuses and the knowledge economy they supposedly underpin are actually producing, particularly in the ways they utilize liberalism and liberal citizenship. I present a methodological intervention into the vocabularies of seeing and knowing higher education, national development, and forms of belonging in Qatar and the Gulf. When we move past received discourses, past knowledge economy as a thing in the world, different stories emerge to help us think about how to access schools as sites of ethnographic encounter and grounded research.

Statist Rhetoric and Expert Knowledge

Much like academic critique of university globalization, which reifies certain mythologies of liberalism and its others, scholarship about the Gulf region has produced a mythology of Gulf exceptionalism. This exceptionalism often serves statist interests while also furthering ways of knowing the world that derive from imperial projects and Eurocentric categories. It also assembles multiple, sometimes contradictory, actors into a seemingly unified state. In addition, both governmental and academic discourses elide the entanglements between Western experts and Gulf elites in the making of ruling power and development projects, while also allowing for ongoing erasure of multiculturalism and class diversity in the region.

Gulf exceptionalism pervades scholarship through terminology that is considered regionally specific and therefore implicitly disconnected from global processes.[6] When unpacked, Gulf-specific terms and categories can be traced to broader encounters through which the region became an object of knowledge. The rentier state concept, for example, applied to countries that draw their wealth and legitimacy from the rental of oil prospects, has become an explanatory model for everything from ruling power, governance, migration, labor, culture change, and social relations in the Gulf. This analytic produces an economically reductive narrative of unnatural progress, because it places oil, as an extractive commodity, apart from other forms of extraction, while implying that industrial development in the West was natural and indigenous, even though it was completely dependent on commodity extraction based in imperialism, and on carbon-based extraction.[7] The idea that an economy can be national is in itself problematic, and occludes unequal relations of power involved in producing nation-states, particularly in the Global South, as well as contemporary geopolitics within the framework of development, security, or economic globalization.[8]

Gulf scholarship also tends to presume autochthonous belonging to territorial nation-state, and in so doing naturalizes both nations and states as solely the purview of citizens.[9] This allows scholars to reduce society to state-citizen relationships in many modern histories.[10] Additionally, an economically reductive reading of Gulf societies presumes that migration is solely an economic phenomenon, and that migrants are *homo economicus* actors and not members of society who leave cultural, linguistic, political, and affective imprints, or have religious or ethnic motivations for coming to the Gulf.[11] If mentioned at all, foreign residents, who sometimes outnumber citizens several times over, are considered outsiders whose presence minimally impacts the state-citizen nexus.

The assumption of migrant non-belonging pervades scholarship, punditry, international media, and human rights discourses, which blame the migration sponsorship system in the region, *kafala*, for some of the worst labor exploitation in the contemporary world, along with the ethno-racial inequalities in foreign residents' everyday lives.[12] Approaching kafala as an illiberal extension of Arabian tradition and the rentier state, rather than as a modern form of governance that is connected to transnational processes, elides the encounters through which kafala was systematized and continues to generate profit for multinational corporations, for middlemen brokers, for sending states, and for individual Western expatriates, who not surprisingly benefit the most from the day-to-day impacts of ethno-racial discriminatory structures.[13] It also does not allow us to consider migrant agencies and forms of belonging in robust ways.

Qatari and other Gulf national identities also emerged within British imperial encounter and particularly during labor activism against British (and later American) oil companies, which segregated workers according to nationality and race in order to prevent class solidarity.[14] Gulf leaders, however, many of whom have been educated in Western and American universities,[15] favor narratives of the Arabian Peninsula as an Arab and Islamic space, and deploy ideas about tribalism and cultures untouched until oil development in order to perpetuate ethnic nationalisms. This effectively erases anti-colonial dissent—as well as centuries of maritime hybridity and trade, global religious pilgrimage, and intellectual exchange—from most official national narratives.

While Qatar as an independent country is not even fifty years old, official state rhetoric bases national identity on the idea of a timeless culture that has persevered in the face of rapid change and high rates of migration. It also naturalizes the leadership of the ruling Al-Thani family.[16] Forming nationals was not an easy task at first, however, because the emergence of Gulf countries produced postcolonial land boundaries that split up tribal groups and created resistance from nomadic people who refused statehood. Qatari leaders, like those of other Gulf states, have continuously negotiated policies to create enough citizens, including through the incorporation of manumitted slaves and migrant settlers, while making the category closed enough for citizenship to be a privilege, particularly in the wake of oil wealth. There are many economic privileges associated (though not always experienced) with citizenship: Gulf nationals can claim heavy social welfare benefits, own businesses, and act as sponsors and landlords to migrants, for example. Therefore, who can naturalize, who can have a passport, who can marry whom, and how citizenship benefits are distributed are sources of continuous debate and reformulation.[17] In addition, given the centuries of intermarriage, slavery, cultural exchange, and cosmopolitanism along the Arabian Peninsula's coastal ports, spotting who is and is not local is not easy, for Gulf Arab nationals do not always share phenotypes, accents, or other factors that would easily distinguish them from nonnationals.[18]

Today, elite citizenship privileges are most effectively visualized and rehearsed in daily performances: since Gulf societies have so many foreign residents, the ability to designate citizenship through dress, language, forms of built environment, and access to certain jobs and spaces naturalizes ethnic nationalism, and its technologies of governance and stratification, onto the bodies of Gulf residents and the geographies of Gulf cities.[19] The primary marker of modern Gulf national belonging has become the black abaya for women and the white *thaub* for men. This uniform of sorts is a postcolonial ubiquity that designates national status in Qatar and other Gulf states and influences how people are treated, the spaces they can access, and the privileges they supposedly have vis-à-vis the state.[20]

National identity relies on the large population of nonnationals in order to produce its legitimacy—locals only become one coherent imagined community in the face of so many foreign others.[21] It is through the demographic threat of population imbalance that the need to preserve culture becomes even more imperative. This nativist version of modernity is cultivated inside Qatar but is also projected outward, establishing Qatar's national brand on an international scale.[22] The national brand is a transnational assemblage of cosmopolitanism and heritage, an assemblage that continues a long-standing reliance on foreign expertise and academic knowledge production while obscuring the actually existing historical and contemporary multiculturalism of the country and region.[23]

Abandoning these economically reductionist understandings of Gulf countries, along with the exceptionalizing terminology that has been produced around the region and its connection to oil, allows us to more fully explore longer histories of knowledge transfer that are constantly remade through collaborations between a number of contemporary actors and institutions, which are limited neither to the citizenry nor to the territorial state. Projects that fall under the more recent umbrella of knowledge economy extend these collaborations into new directions, but they ultimately continue to rehearse previous imaginaries of Qatari national culture and Gulf exceptionalism.

Education Reform

Rather than taking the economic for granted as the primary—and supposedly nonideological—reason for development in Qatar and the Gulf, we need to shift our research inquiry to what work economy does as a justification for development projects: how does it mask the interests and actors (both inside and outside the territorial state) involved in producing Qatari modernity, and how does it leverage the idea of future scarcity in order to placate political identifications and mobilizations of differently situated residents in the present? The Qatar Foundation and its American branch campuses utilize knowledge economy as a legitimizing discourse for the centrality of elite liberal universities to national development. The *Qatar National Vision* explicitly states, after all, that education will become a job-producing industry for nationals.[24] As the ethnographic chapters of this book explore, the structure and day-to-day management of American branch campuses, in contrast to their mission statements and even the narratives of administrators and faculty, are not that focused on their existing and anticipated economic impacts on Qatar. They are instead underpinned by ideological assumptions about how liberal education can fulfill a particular civilizing mission: liberalizing the non-liberal Qatari. For local elites, on the other hand, these institutions bring into the domestic context the very kinds of education that they have already been exposed to abroad, helping to build an outwardly focused national brand that reflects global citizenship, modernity, multicultural competency, and geopolitical favor for Qatar.

Qatar was ranked globally in the top thirty-five and highest in the Middle East region in 2016, based primarily on its education and wealth statistics.[25] Qatar's research and development expenditure is extremely high, at over $894 million in 2012, with the largest portion going to higher education.[26] The operating costs of the American branch campuses were estimated at just over $404 million in 2014 alone.[27] This expenditure goes primarily to labor costs and infrastructure, and though slowly shifting to locally sustainable research programs, no aspect of knowledge-economy development in Qatar is currently revenue producing. The setup and operating costs of branch campuses, as well as large management fees to the home institutions, will never be recuperated by tuition. Tuition, while increasing as a revenue stream, is completely subsidized by the state for nationals and heavily reduced through financial aid and interest-free loans for nonnationals. Although other Gulf countries have experienced declining oil prosperity, Qataris today are over-consumers, highly credit oriented (over 75 percent are in debt) and not keen to enter the workforce,[28] especially in the private sector, because the benefits of public sector work are too high—in fact, the benefits of working in the public sector have increased in the same period. Without the revenue from oil and gas that fuels higher education growth in Qatar, branch campuses in particular would probably pick up and leave. The naturalized connection between liberal higher education and economic benefit that pervades narratives about knowledge economy in the Qatar and the Gulf is therefore benefitting certain stakeholders, mostly elites, including many foreigners.

While liberal higher education and education reform more generally are touted as primarily for Qataris and as necessary for Qatarization, they are actually increasing reliance on foreign labor and expertise. The main benefactors of these institutions are nonnationals, who make up almost all of the higher administration and more than half of the student body at almost all of the schools. Expatriate faculty receive high (and practically tax-free) salaries, free schooling for their children, and business class tickets home for the holidays. Meanwhile, foreign resident students are incentivized to remain in Qatar through loan-forgiveness programs, career services, and preexisting connections to the Gulf. The availability of quality global higher education options in the Gulf is therefore increasing noncitizen belonging and transnational futures, despite the insecurities these noncitizens face in residency and job procurement.[29]

Despite special Qatarization privileges in admissions and career placement, as well as access to language and other preparatory training both before entering college and during their first years, as of the 2009/10 academic year, over 65 percent of Qataris attending higher education were still enrolled in the national public Qatar University.[30] While Qatari enrollment in Education City went from a mere 10 percent of the total citizen pool in the 2005/6 academic year to about 50 percent at most schools and rising when I was conducting my research from 2010 to 2014, a combination of inadequate primary and secondary training, lack of English-language skills, and/or family resistance to gender integration and other forms of perceived Westernization was preventing even higher enrollments.[31] The Qatari government also does little to encourage citizens to attend college en masse. National men, for example, have little motivation to go to college because ministry and army jobs pay high salaries right out of high school; huge bumps in pay—up to 120 percent—during the 2011 Arab revolutions added to this, as did the institution of mandatory military service after high school.[32] Those who do go to college still end up working primarily in overpaid public sector jobs, which also increased in salary by 60 percent for nationals in 2011, regardless of whether they graduate from Qatar University or from Education City.[33] And many women, who are targeted as crucial to Qatarization and constitute the bulk of citizens attending college in the country, opt out of the job market after marriage or childbirth.[34]

The private sector, almost twenty years after Virginia Commonwealth University opened in Education City, remains around 99 percent non-Qatari. Even though corporate discourses emphasize a commitment to Qatarization and corporate social responsibility programs target students in Education City, private companies do not seem to be hiring Qataris in greater numbers. Many of my interlocutors believed that because Qataris commanded such high salaries, the private sector could not afford to hire more nationals than the minimum quota imposed by the state. Others felt that the private sector continued to discriminate against nationals, stereotyping them as lazy and only clocking in to get a paycheck. Since the private sector operates primarily in English, some college graduates are not able to work there; this trend will continue as the national Qatar University, which switched many of its programs to Arabic in 2013, graduates more students, unless private sector companies switch to multilingual operations.

Although university growth and other development projects did not increase nationalization of the labor force, it did translate to producing jobs. There were plenty of positions for foreign experts in education, who were tasked with producing a national brand that relied on an essentialized and elite notion of Qatariness while carving space for a variety of foreign forms and subjects to participate in Qatar's modernity. Qatarization, then, was part of the legitimizing project of the state, and of the designation of Qatari nationals as a privileged class, but branch campuses were engaged in an entirely different project when it came to crafting citizen-subjects: reassembling a neoliberal transnational elite.[35]

The role of foreign experts in producing Qatar's development can also be seen in relation to two main publications and their impacts on education reform in the country: the World Bank's *Arab Human Development Report*, and the RAND Corporation's "Education for a New Era." Qatar's greatest period of education reform coincided with the *Arab Human Development Report*, which was published in four volumes between 2002 and 2005. Written by top Arab experts, so thus supposedly an indigenous document, the report rehearsed neoliberal rhetoric of free markets as central to development, democracy, and freedom, and advocated for "knowledge society" as a postindustrial form of development in the Middle East.[36] The report places particular emphasis on education, women's empowerment, and the regulation of religious teaching, all of which will supposedly curb the rise in Islamism in the region.[37] It is not a coincidence that the *Arab Human Development Report* came on the heels of 9/11, and that it advocated top-down depoliticized state-sponsored reform with assistance from the West. It was also written by elites and utilized liberal and neoliberal international discourse, which did not take into account imperial reasons for the economic and social conditions in the Middle East and North Africa region. Though billed as a report produced by Arabs for Arabs, it was initially only published in English, and then translated into Arabic. The report relied on culturalist explanations for Arab countries lagging behind on World Bank development indexes, and thus located the catalyst for development outside of the Arab world.[38]

The discourse of knowledge economy produced by the international development community, especially after 9/11, aligns well with the civilizing mission of main campus administrators in their initial discussions of the benefits of opening branch campuses in the Gulf region: many considered these partnerships as potential soft-power agents.[39] The Gulf region was especially singled out in the report as a source of terrorism, as nondemocratic, and as lagging behind on women's rights, media literacy, and education. After the publication of the first volume, the Qatari government signed a ten-year contract with the RAND Corporation to assist in several education initiatives and began wholesale education reform.[40] The hiring of RAND, and the reforms implemented in Qatar following its report, were seen by experts in the West as positive steps away from Islamic radicalization, reinforcing the idea that global markets and global knowledge were positive counterforces to "Middle East exceptionalism"—particularly Gulf exceptionalism—and its perceived threat to the West, especially post-9/11.[41]

In Qatar, RAND's projects included helping to set up the Qatar National Research Fund guidelines, writing the Qatar National Research Strategy, working with Qatar Foundation on multiple projects, and assessing the national Qatar University.[42] But their main project was focused on how to improve and develop public K-12 education. In 2007, RAND produced a report, *Education for a New Era*, which suggested three options for reforming what it felt was a system that had failed because of Qatari resistance to change and a lack of critical thinking in schools. All three suggested reform options were neoliberal approaches that reduced centralization and focused on parental choice. The first was to make incremental changes; the second, to switch to a charter-school model, which was popular at the time in the United States; and the third, to implement a voucher system that would allow Qataris to attend private schools.[43] The Qatari leadership chose the second option, and in the process revamped the public-school system into what are now referred to as independent schools. With RAND's help, the Supreme Education Council was also set up as distinct from the Ministry of Education and not directly under the state. The Supreme Education Council's job was to assess and regulate schools, primarily through testing.

With this large-scale reform, a whole range of schools offering different combinations of language and subject training proliferated. In interviews, students in Education City related attending K-12 schools that had British, American, Indian, French, Tunisian, and Jordanian curricula, along with some that offered the International Baccalaureate as well as other certifications, to name a few. They were taught in a range of languages, mostly a mix of Arabic and English, but also other European and South Asian languages. And parents were turned into active consumers, constantly moving their children between different schools in order to maximize college admissions success. One of my Iraqi interlocutors, a junior at Texas A&M, had been to six different schools since she moved to Qatar at the age of eight, her parents constantly moving her in order to improve her educational prospects, until she ended up at an International Baccalaureate school that taught in English. My graduate students at the Qatar Faculty of Islamic Studies who were mothers often spoke about the challenges of finding the right school for their children; one student made parental experiences with the K-12 independent school system the subject of her final ethnography for our anthropology class.

K-12 schools were also extremely varied in their gender segregation practices. One student at Virginia Commonwealth told me that she was in classes with boys from grades one through six, then girls were schooled separately from grades seven through eleven, and then in year twelve they were integrated again, without any explanation given. She speculated that "they were preparing us for the workplace and the university. We never really knew the exact reason why." Because policies were always changing, it was also hard for students to know whether these shifts were planned stages of their schooling, or accidental due to implementation of new laws or turnover in leadership.

In 2012, the Qatari government also introduced a voucher system, which allowed Qatari parents to subsidize private schooling (nonnational parents whose children attended independent schools were ineligible). Parents and teachers did not receive the switch to a charter-school system and the introduction of vouchers positively; they felt that schools were competing with each other, creating more division among Qataris because educational quality was no longer uniform, and that the focus on testing and English literacy had overtaken other subjects, especially Arabic and Islam.[44] Many blamed RAND and the Qatari government's choice to partner with RAND for these failures.[45] RAND only used educational reform models developed from challenges facing schools in the United States to produce its suggestions, rather than taking into consideration local cultural, linguistic, and demographic needs; by the time they did present the charter-school model, it was already highly contested by teachers within the United States.[46]

The partnership between RAND and K-12 education in Qatar was one of encounter, where two unequal sides produced reform by creating the idea that Qatari education was in a state of failure.[47] Based on neoliberal development discourse and essentialized ideas about backward Qatari culture, K-12 education reforms only benefitted RAND and Qatari elites, as well as global neo-imperial interests (especially American ones). When I spoke to a RAND employee in 2014 who was involved in the *Education for a New Era* report, she agreed that in hindsight charter schools were "not the best idea" for Qatar. But, rather than acknowledging the cultural bias built into the reforms, her contention was that RAND should have taken into account how the foundations and the capacity "were just not there for this to happen in Qatar: school principals were not trained well enough to run the schools, nor were there enough teachers capable of teaching autonomously. In other words, she saw the failures of the independent-school system as a continuation of the failure of Qatari culture itself to adapt to neoliberal education. She reproduced a narrative of RAND's objectivity and of Qataris' cultural inability to implement a potentially successful model (even though this model had already been thoroughly challenged by educators in the United States). The RAND consultant put a lot of blame on Qataris, saying that they wanted everything to improve too fast and made unilateral changes that teachers could not keep up with, like the Supreme Education Council deciding practically overnight to switch all K-12 math and science to English.[48]

In Qatar, RAND is blamed most of all for the increased focus on English in K-12 schools, as well as for the switch to English at the national Qatar University.[49] However, English curricula in the K-12 system precede RAND's contract in Qatar,[50] and RAND's policy recommendations included no language changeover suggestions. RAND also started a project around 2006 for strategic planning and assessment of Qatar University. They recommended that Qatar University shift from a teaching university, which it had first started as, into a full-fledged regionally and globally competitive research university. Qatar University was an Arabic institution at the time. Since the backlash against these reforms, and not surprisingly corresponding with the Arab uprisings, the university has returned many of its programs to Arabic, even though moves toward becoming a research university also continue.[51] The switch to Arabic immediately impacted many people at Qatar University. Students admitted into an English-language degree program found themselves entering an Arabic one, the university had to scramble to hire new faculty to teach incoming students in Arabic while continuing to offer classes in English to existing cohorts, and many expatriate faculty hired to teach in English found themselves without jobs or with impending termination dates, which would mean they had to leave the country. Today, there are many students, including many Qataris, who feel that the university is not a viable option for them because their Arabic is not good enough and because an Arabic degree is not globally competitive. Meanwhile, others feel more grounded in the national university because it reflects Qatari social norms and religious values much better than the Education City campuses. In addition to language, gender segregation is an important deciding factor for students and their parents when weighing higher education options. Having an Arabic and English option for higher education in Doha in the form of the local Qatar University and the more globally oriented Education City has created new divisions among Qataris, or intensified preexisting ones: as students of the same generation graduate in higher numbers from both places, often from within the same family, they increasingly live in different linguistic and social worlds.[52]

While institutional rhetoric and everyday conversations among residents reproduced the idea that Qatar University and Education City were opposing spaces, both campuses have been impacted by encounters between outside consultants, the Qatari state, and development discourse in the name of knowledge economy. American universities are not the only educational spaces in Qatar that incorporate liberal pedagogy and ideologies: the debates about belonging and exclusion that I explore in this book are rife within the hallways of Qatar University as well. Qatar University is in some ways more international than Education City, especially within its men's college: students I spoke to there felt that nationals and nonnationals integrated well, as did faculty and staff. One recent Indian graduate who I interviewed in a coffee shop frequented by Qataris spoke with Arabic-accented English, for example, and he had a circle of friends that consisted primarily of locals and Arab expatriates. Additionally, portions of Qatar University are also US-accredited or applying for accreditation, including a newly opened medical school, making their standards and curricula not as different from American branch campuses as they might seem.

The constructed tension between Qatar University and Education City reflected increasing stratification among Qataris, and between older (primarily Arabic-speaking) and newer (primarily English-speaking) diasporic communities; and it spoke to different political stances on where the country was headed. Thus, even though there were many research collaborations and intellectual exchanges between Qatar University and

Education City's institutions, maintaining the idea that they were opposing forms (one liberal and global, the other illiberal and local) was productive for interested parties inside and outside of Qatar. It helped to maintain the idea that higher education was (or at least should be) a project primarily for citizens, who were offered choice as part of state social welfare benefits and for the purpose of economic diversification, even though education in Qatar was producing new configurations of social stratification that could not be understood through a state-citizen nexus.

Civic Nationalism

If Qatari nationals are the intended recipients of education reform, it also appears that they are the domestic audience for other forms of national branding as well. Indeed, pictures of happy Qatari families shopping and dining often plaster the fences of construction sites for projects that legitimize themselves through knowledge-economy discourse, cementing the idea that the post-oil future is being built for citizens. However, these projects simultaneously create civic nationalism and transnational futures. The statist and academic literature on the Gulf tends to presume that civic and ethnic nationalism are ontologically different forms that map onto a West/non-West binary, and by extension one could argue a liberal/illiberal binary as well, leaving little room to consider how civic nationalisms might circulate in Qatar.[53]

In reality, these false constructs mix all the time. For example, citizenship regulations and naturalization tests in Europe and North America abound with expectations around language, genealogy, and cultural attitudes that produce a normative ethnic national identity. However, civic nationalism is part of the liberal myth, taken to be true by scholars from the very countries that are supposed to embody it, and therefore this assumption elides the various investments in and by racial, ethnic, linguistic, and religious elites in maintaining the image of inclusivity. It is important, therefore, to separate state and academic rhetoric from the actual ways that nationalism works on the ground to include some and exclude others.

In contrast to Western states, a country like Qatar, with its explicitly ethnically derived regulations around citizenship, and with its stated Islamic identity, is always-already precluded from having forms of civic nationalism because religion, ethnicity, and language supposedly determine who can be part of the nation. But on-the-ground nationalism does not work much differently in its contradictions and fluidity than it does in other parts of the world. Rather, the presumption that abstracted forms are binary and map onto territory, forms of power, and people is what leads to the constant reproduction both of liberal piety and of Gulf exceptionalism.[54] Looking at the *Qatar National Vision*, as well as other statist documents that many noncitizens utilize for development projects and mission statements, as sites of *civic* nationalism highlights two important ways that Qatar's future is not as ethnically bound as one might think. First, the *Qatar National Vision* includes as one of its pillars the maintenance of a "strong expatriate workforce," and the many projects that assemble themselves under knowledge economy and reference the *Qatar National Vision* are heavily invested in nonnational audiences—the buy-in of the majority expatriate population to the idea of a closed nation to which they might not fully belong but have both affection and gratitude.[55] Expatriates, while a source of anxiety in state discourses, are therefore not entirely excluded. The *Qatar National Vision*, as well as the language of the Qatar Foundation, is riddled with slippages between the terms *citizen*, *Qatari*, *population*, and *people* in ways that undermine a purely nativist reading of the nation. Qatar's heritage industry also targets its nonnational residents, who make up the majority of its consumers.[56] Images of white couples and families also peppered the urban imaginaries of construction site fences, for example—projecting Qatar as a Westernized site for tourism, shopping, and business relocation. It seems there was room for a certain noncitizen in most visions of Qatari modernity: the wealthy, cosmopolitan, and Westernized expatriate. This figure, especially when white, was actually central to Qatar's international branding. White Western expatriates brought with them not only expertise but also symbolic capital, in which their whiteness itself became the marker of their expert status, regardless of their skill set in comparison to other nationalities.[57]

Second, expatriates were not only a presence against which ethnic nationalist myth creation occurred; they were also the main laborers in its projects.[58] As newer scholarship has challenged exceptionalist frameworks for understanding the Gulf, it has also revealed how the lived experiences of Gulf residents contain heterogeneous, overlapping, emergent, and messy identities, affects, subjectivities, and politicizations.[59] Many foreign residents feel connection to Qatar in visiting museums and heritage sites and engaging in cultural activities, which are intended to provide them with access to the idea of timeless nation as a generous host for their second home.[60] Qatar's National Day celebrations, Ramadan activities, and other state-run events frequently draw in large foreign resident crowds. The government also provides money to bus in migrant workers, or creates segregated spaces for working-class foreign residents to express their pride in Qatar as simultaneous insiders and outsiders. Civic nationalism as a state project was particularly evident in the official branding of 2014 National Day: two hands of different hues formed a heart, with the tagline "One Love." But civic nationalism is not only a top-down project; when it was announced in 2010 that Qatar had won the right to host the FIFA World Cup 2022, hundreds of people celebrated on the streets of Doha, including many foreign residents. I myself feel a sense of connection to the country after living there many times, and felt a surge of nationalism during the Saudi-led siege in June 2017.[61] Qatar's development and national branding have reconfigured a transnational elite inheriting class, an elite that is English speaking and cosmopolitan, thinks of itself as more liberal, and includes noncitizens. At the same time, some of the Arabic-speaking, parochially educated, and socially/religiously conservative elements of the citizenry feel increasingly unable to access the fruits of the modernization projects undertaken in their name.[62] The pushback from some sectors of Qatari society, especially from citizens, such as the "Reflect Your Respect" campaign, shows how some Qatari citizens feel excluded from the urban space being produced under the rubric of knowledge economy and find that the ethnic nationalist rhetoric is not meant to include all citizens in the country's future.

American branch campuses, as key sites of elite citizenship production, are particularly central to cultivating the type of neoliberal expatriate class that experiences belonging and a sense of patriotism to Qatar, even as they internalize being second-class or temporary citizens, or outside of national identity. Financial aid packages, university marketing at various high schools attended by English-speaking high-achieving expatriates, and career incentives and recruiting, for example, all invite in a middle-class cosmopolitan entrepreneurial subject, cultivate this subjectivity over the course of four years, and then provide opportunities for more permanence in the country. Although civic nationalism produces belonging for foreign residents, it is also masked by ethnic nationalist rhetoric, thus reifying a liberal/illiberal mythology of territory, power, and culture.

Conclusion: Nationalizing the Future

In 2005, Sheikha Moza, chairperson of the Qatar Foundation, gave a speech at the Oxford Centre for Islamic Studies, in which she described the benefit of international branch campuses to Qatar:

> In the past, countries in our region sent students abroad to be educated. Upon their return, such citizens were often isolated from their societies, for they had acquired the education needed to analyze and participate in their societies, but their societies had not developed any mechanisms to accommodate the practice of citizenry. Such people either secluded themselves from others or returned abroad, initiating a process of brain drain in our region. In Qatar, we are bringing institutions to our region, rather than sending our people outside.[63]

On the surface, Her Highness's quote regurgitates the legitimizing discourse of Qatar's knowledge-economy development for international audiences: to educate a future generation to build a post-oil future, maintaining traditional values while participating as global citizens in boosting the country's international profile, and moving away from reliance on noncitizens through decreased "brain drain" and better leadership skills. Indeed, higher education is a key site for the formation of citizenship, and the proliferation of higher education institutions in

Qatar provides more opportunities to keep young people—especially women—in the country, to manage the influence of Westernization on them, and to make them more competent in a range of professional fields. However, to many critics inside and outside Qatar, knowledge-economy projects, particularly Education City's branch campuses, appear to be misdirected (in that they apply liberal education in an illiberal context) or to have failed (in that, in spite of the amount of money spent, Qatari students still lack critical mass, and there has been no tangible Qatarization of the workforce). But as I have argued here, both the seemingly haphazard assemblage of ideas and institutions under knowledge economy and the idea of educational failure require an a priori understanding that nationalism is for nationals only, when in fact it is not.

Sheikha Moza's speech highlights the need to renationalize a leadership class; renationalization includes not only citizens but also noncitizens, and in the process it makes certain expatriates central to Qatari futures, stratifies the national population, legitimizes ruling power, and benefits a range of elite interests, both inside and outside the country. The future that Qatar's modernization is building is therefore one that includes and excludes nationals and nonnationals—categories that are themselves incredibly heterogeneous—in several overlapping as well as contradictory ways, even as it evokes a traditional past in which the imagined nation and the rewards of oil wealth are supposedly for nationals alone. Qatarization is in fact taking place, if we define Qatarization differently, to include the more elite and globally oriented diasporic generation that is essential to Qatar's modernity. Education reform in the Gulf is similarly informed by Western-educated nationals and led by Western or Western-educated experts, like those from the RAND Corporation, or the administrators and faculty at branch campuses.[64] It was these Western experts who were tasked with teaching Qataris how to be better Qataris. In the process, they produced homogeneous and essentialized ideas about culture that then became institutionalized by government agencies, by academic knowledge production and media coverage, and by branch campuses.

CHAPTER 2

Pedagogies of Essentialism

Anna had been teaching at Virginia Commonwealth University's branch campus for several years when I interviewed her in 2010. She spoke several languages and had lived in multiple countries before arriving in Doha. During her time in Qatar, she had married an American professor who worked at another branch campus, and they had two children together. They did not have any immediate plans to relocate and were relatively happy with their lives, although Anna did have concerns about what it would be like to raise her children around so much wealth disparity and labor exploitation when they got older. A self-described feminist, Anna told me she was one of the few people she knew among her colleagues who did not employ a nanny or maid, and she was also active in trying to start an initiative in Education City to teach migrant workers English. She had applied for a Qatar National Research Fund grant to study domestic worker experiences, and she regularly brought migrant rights and other topics that might be deemed controversial into the classroom to encourage her students to engage with issues of concern to the region and to foster debate. Anna was someone who would fit the profile of a progressive and cosmopolitan faculty member on a US university campus. She was heavily invested in social justice and diversity and knowledgeable about many cultural contexts. However, she also reproduced civilizational ideas about her role as an educator. These were not contradictory values but rather embodied a rather typical liberal faculty approach to difference, particularly Qatariness. For example, when I asked her about any changes she had seen in the students over the course of her time in Doha she responded:

The students tell me that they are becoming more liberal, their parents think they are too liberal or too tolerant and they blame it on us and on Education City. And perhaps yes it is a result of where they are studying and the values that we try to instill on them and this critical thinking and questioning and critiquing. But at the same time they still want to maintain their culture and their language and all of that. And you know they could be very articulate and very strong about something but they continue to wear their abaya and they continue to cover themselves. So it is interesting to see how first I thought this could not be possible, but now I am like, this is totally possible. They can still be very Western in some ways and at the same time very much Muslim and still marry their cousins and all of that.

Anna's description of what it meant to be liberal—critical thinking, tolerance—and what it meant to be Qatari—wearing the abaya, marrying cousins—encapsulated how Qatari illiberalism was coproduced with American liberalism within branch campuses by faculty and administrators. In order to promote the liberal forms of critical thinking and multicultural tolerance that supposedly defined American higher education, students were encouraged to interact with each other through their differences from each other—national origin, citizenship status, gender, and religion—thereby hardening these differences. These pedagogies of essentialism, which I explore in this chapter, were central to the functioning of university life and the crafting of student citizenship and identity. They were operationalized by faculty and administrators, as well as by Qatar Foundation planners and consultants—in the classroom, in Student Affairs programming, and in university branding and mission statements. This approach to diversity was not inherently different than that taken by faculty and administrators at home campuses, but the student demographics in Education City, along with nativist understandings of university mission and Qatarization policies, meant that there was an added focus on liberalizing Qatari nationals and preserving and respecting Qatari culture, a culture that often seemed antithetical to the project of liberalism. The resulting climate contributed to segregation between national and nonnational students (as well as other subgroups), further undermining notions of liberal success. In interviews and observations, educators and administrators related a deep anxiety about the problem of what they saw as "self-segregation" initiated by Qatari students within classrooms and social spaces. There were constant conversations and strategic planning about how to get Qatari students more involved in student life and leadership at these schools. I examine how these supposed failures were attributed to cultural difference, particularly the supposed illiberalness and traditional gender expectations of Qataris, rather than the university's structure and climate. Ironically, the misinterpretation of nation building as being for nationals only, along with reductive understandings of Qatariness, naturalized Qatari privilege within campuses, while Qatari students often felt like they didn't belong, specifically because the understandings of Qatari culture that circulated within branch campuses made them feel too visible, deindividualized, and/or stereotyped. Qatariness, then, formed the condition of possibility *and* impossibility for liberal education in Education City.

In contrast, local expats—noncitizens who had grown up in Qatar—more adeptly performed liberal and neoliberal subjectivities, had more confidence and parental encouragement to participate in activities, ran clubs and student leadership, got higher grades, and bonded more with professors, thereby becoming the normative subjects in and out of the classroom, despite being structurally disadvantaged in relation to their Qatari peers by Qatarization policies. Although these effects might seem contrary to the liberal mission of American higher education or by-products of transferring liberal forms into an illiberal context, they actually highlighted ways of understanding difference and culture that are central to liberal education and liberalism.

The Paradox of Diversity

The campuses and classrooms of Education City are perhaps the most diverse in the world, with more religions, nationalities, and languages represented than any US-based campus could possibly achieve. This was emphasized by almost all of my interviewees—students and employees alike—who were surprised by the homogeneity of American home campuses after spending time in Doha. Overwhelmingly, students told me that their experiences in college made them more "open-minded," that "you are exposed to different cultures," and that "you have to be respectful to other cultures." Qataris told me they learned about expatriates; South Asians, about Arabs; Muslims, about Christians; and so forth. Faculty and administrators echoed these sentiments. The classroom discussions I observed and participated in encouraged speaking across difference and voicing different points of view. Like their metropolitan counterparts, the branch campuses celebrated diversity in many ways: through international food days, through icebreaker activities during orientations and other new student events, by touting the number of nationalities they enroll on their web pages, and by teaching students to be respectful of difference in and out of the classroom. Tolerance, diversity, and global citizenship were cornerstones for organizing classroom conduct, activities, field trips, and almost every aspect of college life— one of Georgetown's mission statements is "community in diversity," for example, and Carnegie Mellon's values include "collaboration" and "integrity & inclusion." Unlike their home campuses, these celebrations did not feel inauthentic or forced: what you saw on the website was actually reflected in the makeup of the student body.[1]

At the same time, however, almost every one of my interlocutors related an integration problem between Qataris and non-Qataris across the branch campuses, and I observed this myself in my own classrooms, where Qatari students tended to sit on one side or in the front or back of the class, sometimes also separated by gender. Many non-Qatari students in my interviews referred to how cafeteria tables, lounging spaces, and certain parts of the classroom would usually contain only "abayas" (i.e. Qatari women); Student Affairs officers lamented that Qataris did not come to campus events; and faculty members repeatedly told me that, even after many years in the country, they had "never been inside a Qatari home." In order to address this segregation problem, staff members purposefully integrated students by nationality in orientation activities, even before they officially matriculated, and many faculty members made sure that students could not choose their own groups, splitting up Qataris in particular and forcing them to work with others.[2]

Some faculty members went so far as to rearrange the seating in their classrooms. The message most of us had unquestioningly internalized was that segregation was failure, integration progress.

Diversity and multiculturalism have, since the post–civil rights mainstreaming of cultural difference, become markers of liberalism itself. However, the liberal multicultural university aims to both be universal and account for particular, cultural citizenship.[3] This creates an inherently contradictory situation: difference is desired and considered integral to cultivating the liberal self as a global citizen; it is also precisely that which impedes the supposedly blind universal humanism that underpins the mission of liberal education.[4] Of course, this means that some people and their cultural practices will then be deemed too different to be accepted within liberal humanism's capacity for tolerance and inclusion. For many faculty and administrators, Qataris seemed stuck in this paradox: too mired in particularities like family, religion, gender roles, and national identity to actually realize the liberal individualism of American higher education. This led to culturalist explanations of why Qataris self-segregated or were not able to achieve at high levels.

The paradox of diversity was built into the structure and implementation of the branch campuses. Branch campuses overwhelmingly, like their metropolitan counterparts, presumed universal knowledge as Western or American. They were bound, to varying extents, to the home campus curriculum, and while they had been adding classes to engage the local context steadily over the years, the supposedly universal education students received was marked by American exceptionalism. At Texas A&M Qatar, for example, students were required by state law to complete a semester of Texas history. But this did not account for why one of my Egyptian students, during Egypt's revolution in 2011, told me that he could no longer understand politics outside of "Republican" and "Democrat"—he received this political training not from one required class but through a habitus acquired inside and outside of the classroom over the course of four years. Faculty and staff teach and speak what they know, and what they knew was usually refracted through the

United States. In addition, the texts themselves, written in English, most often published in the United States and reflecting Euro-American disciplinary conventions, were usually geared toward American audiences with unconscious familiarity in American cultural norms. As one student told me, "of course they do bring a lot of current events into the classroom but a lot of the materials in the textbooks are so US-centered."

This was true even of the seemingly objective programs, like engineering and medicine. At Cornell's medical school, for example, American cultural competence was required of students who were attaining a degree that could be used anywhere in the world: not only did lessons contain information unique to the US context (discussion of Vietnam War veterans and Alcoholics Anonymous, for example), they also failed to take into account the context-specific challenges for new doctors in the region: students were not provided with Arabic terminology for conditions they would encounter in a hospital setting, and an imam had to be consulted about the Islamic appropriateness of certain cross-gender training.[5] Similarly, even though Texas A&M's curriculum is accredited with the international benchmark in engineering,[6] faculty at Texas A&M consistently found that students could not relate to the content of distance-learning modules from the main campus's engineering ethics class; therefore, they developed courses that better reflected what new engineers would have to grapple with in the Qatari and wider Gulf context.

Even those faculty who recognized the drawbacks of their texts, assignments, and syllabi—often after students pointed them out, as mine did several times—employed a comparative mode to diversify the classroom experience; class content and discussions usually reverted to a "Qatar versus the United States" framework. In my mode of authority in the classroom, for example, I often used "as an American" to describe situations my students might not be familiar with, even though my Americanness is marked by multiple exclusions at home. In those moments, Qatari students were encouraged to reproduce their difference from Americans and their similarities with other Qataris, and they became the centralized audience of the class. The United States and Qatar were thereby produced as bounded and distinct, and Qatar as a place and an imaginary that was represented by Qatari citizens alone. In the process, non-Qataris were erased from the fabric of Qatari society and marginalized in the classroom. These comparative moments also rehearsed an understanding of Qatariness as standing in contrast not just to an imagined America but also to the liberal university.

Foreigners hired as experts in higher education, who were primarily (white) North Americans, acted—like their counterparts in other industries—as gatekeepers, translating Qatari culture to newcomers, to their subordinates, and even to Qataris themselves.[7] It was through pedagogies of essentialism that expert gatekeepers taught Qatariness to various actors within the university. Faculty and staff utilized both cultural relativism and salvage anthropology to model tolerance through the rhetoric of respect for a simultaneously timeless and vanishing Qatari culture. The discourse of respect allowed gatekeepers to cast themselves as outsiders while masking the ways that they were central to the production of Qatariness. They presented themselves as passive observers or benevolent saviors of culture rather than as active participants in the ways that culture was leveraged to naturalize forms of inequality, belonging, and exclusion.[8] An interview with a faculty member at Northwestern highlights this missionary outsider perspective quite well:

I think we definitely are pushing horizons here, extending boundaries. You know, 'cause the local media isn't really trained properly here . . . So first of all, just educating the local population about what journalism is and, you know, teaching how to do it right. I think that's helping . . . Like 50 percent of our students are Qatari. So they are going to be the ones who are changing the society in the future. So I think we're planting those seeds, you know. I think our students want their society to change, and they're going to have to be the vanguards of that. So, you know, we're trying to help.[9]

The rhetoric of respect is based in cultural relativism, which is premised on the idea of ahistorical and absolute difference. Respect, then, was not actually producing equal treatment of Qataris, but perpetuating civilizational discourses based in imperial histories. It was central to producing Qataris both as privileged recipients of American education and also as incapable of fully attaining the liberal self that American education cultivates. The emphasis on respect reinforced ideas about Qatari conservatism, especially in relation to gender, family, and religion. Faculty told me that orientation, for example, involved learning particular cultural and Islamic dos and don'ts from fellow expatriates, such as restrictions that Qataris supposedly have around heterosocial contact. One faculty member at the Academic Bridge Program said that he was told that he was never to touch a Qatari female student, even in a medical emergency. Others heard they could not teach about certain topics, like Shiʿism or homosexuality, and rumors abounded about books on these and other controversial topics being banned or held up in customs.[10]

I have taught about both Shiʿi and queer Muslims in my Education City classes, including at the Qatar Faculty of Islamic Studies. These topics were indeed sensitive, but they were not the wholesale opinion of Qataris; treating them as sensitive topics reproduced cultural understandings based more on rumor and conjecture than experience. This set up faculty newly arrived to Education City to view Qatari students through a lens of difference rather than similarity. Very rarely did faculty orientation activities at any of the schools I looked into involve sustained interaction with Qataris themselves. They were mostly about learning technicalities of the campus and getting through immigration procedures and other bureaucratic hurdles. Leisure activities actually encouraged the types of self-segregation practices that created so much anxiety for expatriates when they were discussing Qatari student behavior. At most, there would be a visit to the souk or Museum of Islamic Art, or a demonstration of falconry or sword dancing—all reinforcing narrow and Orientalist ideas of Qatari culture rather than introducing new arrivals to Doha's transnational diversity.

My experiences during my recent teaching position at the Faculty of Islamic Studies provide some further examples. Unlike the branch campuses, this institution is Qatari and not secular; it seems to define its identity directly in contrast to the rest of Education City, and it also hosts figures who have created international controversy for Qatar and questions about its investment in liberalism, especially Yusuf al-Qaradawi and Tariq Ramadan. Upon my arrival to start a visiting professor position for the Fall 2014 semester, I was informed by the head of Human Resources, who was Indian and Hindu, that I was obligated to wear hijab as part of the dress code. Apparently, he had arrived at this decision after consulting with some of his Muslimah staff members (both Qatari and non-Qatari Arab). When I questioned my Lebanese supervisor on this, telling him that this rule was not written anywhere in my contract or mentioned in our correspondence when recruiting me, and that it expressly went against Qatar Foundation's own dress code, which allowed for short sleeves and skirts to the knee, he responded, "Well, you know how this place is"—meaning irrational, unpredictable, and overly conservative. It seemed better to Human Resources to make the new non-Muslim and only woman faculty member wear hijab—through the only other non-Muslim South Asian migrant worker manager, who had little actual authority—rather than deal with any potential future problems. There were no Qatari faculty or higher administration at the university at the time, except for the interim dean.

I learned later that my women students, many of whom were converts (and quite dogmatic about their own covering practices), were furious upon learning about this invented hijab rule, and complained about the treatment I received during my visiting term directly to the Qatari interim dean, one of the highest-ranking women scholars in the country. She was entirely unaware of the hijab issue, a rule that was enacted in order to supposedly protect her conservative sensibilities. Her ignorance of such a small issue was unsurprising, given that I was there for only one semester and never saw or met her. It was instead indicative of the role of privileged gatekeepers within Education City, who regularly reinforced the idea that *khaleejis* (Arab Gulf nationals) were backwards or overly conservative, or both, compared to Western and Arab expatriates. Meanwhile, more precarious workers, even those in management positions, like my Indian HR manager, were unable to exercise any authority for fear of their jobs, although they were also participants in perpetuating stereotypes about different national and religious groups. Although stereotyping was pervasive and felt deeply by students, students were not passive receptacles for this kind of culturalist thinking.

Qatarization: Stereotyping and Privilege

Although it appeared to go against principles of meritocracy and egalitarianism, Qatarization was normalized and even promoted by administrators and faculty, who readily defended nativist privilege even as they were missionaries for a multicultural liberalism. Given the historical legacy of how labor and expertise were outsourced by British and American imperial interests in the Gulf, Qatarization could be defended in structural terms that fit into a liberal framework not unlike cultural citizenship models in the United States, which seek to redress past injustices. In this way, perhaps Qatarization could be an allegory to affirmative action; of course, the race and class dynamics are quite different on the ground between Qataris and many migrant groups. However, faculty and administrators placed Qatarization not into this framework but rather into a culturalist one, in which the right to the nation was primordially exclusive to Qataris. This essentialism naturalized Qatari privilege within campuses, while Qataris themselves ended up feeling marginalized. It also created cohesion among students, who may not have thought of themselves as Qatari in the same way before entering college, teaching them to perform national distinction in narrow ways;[11] and it incentivized them to seek out comfort zones through their college career, which were then perceived as self-segregation by university administrators rather than as structural effects of the very system in which citizens were treated as a group and not as individuals.

Qatarization policies created a two-tier education system in which nationals were privileged at almost every juncture—they were admitted into a different pool than nonnationals; they were able to access sponsorships that paid for their education and provided them with jobs; there were opportunities available only to them; and there were remedial classes through the Qatar Foundation and individual campuses to help them with TOEFL and other test scores as well as basic writing and math skills. Some students, for example, were admitted conditionally upon taking a year of coursework at the Academic Bridge Program, which was designed to help high-school graduates gain entry into college, especially those coming from public independent schools. Other students enrolled in the Academic Bridge Program with the hope of gaining admission to Education City or elsewhere after completion.

Branch campuses also had a financial interest in the success of Qatari students, as funding and other resources were often linked to the enrollment and graduation percentages of nationals. Individual campuses, therefore, had started to offer their own foundation courses for Qatari students, and in some cases these were required. At Texas A&M, for example, Qatari freshmen began a semester early—in the spring— to complete these requirements, and they also sometimes had to enroll in summer courses. Qatari perceptions seemed to be that these programs were expected of them, even if they did not need them. Enrolling in these programs added to the feeling among Qatari students that they were singled out and set apart; many also had tighter bonds after attending the Academic Bridge Program together, and the same was true for those who enrolled early at Texas A&M. Early enrollment also kept them from bonding with the rest of their cohort, as they did not experience entering college for the first time together, nor were they expected to participate in orientation programming.

Hind, a junior at Northwestern who had attended the English-language Qatar Academy, a coeducational K-12 school within Education City, explained the marginalization that many Qatari students who went through bridge programs, which she did not have to do, felt:

I feel like they teach more to the non-Qatari students and students like me who are used to this kind of thing. I adapt easier to it for example than people who are coming from independent schools. This is a disadvantage to them and it is kind of sad because they're not valuing what they are learning because of the distance they feel and the anger they feel towards the professor, and that kind of spills into their appreciation of the course and so I feel like lots of people that I know who are really smart from independent schools, they don't do so well in classes because of that reason.

Hind's comments resonated with some of my own classroom observations. In November 2014, I was invited to guest lecture for two sections of a colleague's Engineering Ethics course at Texas A&M Qatar. As a way to introduce my research and connect it to the course topics, the teaching assistant and I decided that I should have the students discuss the impacts of Qatarization policies on their own lives as they moved through engineering degrees and into the workplace. The first class session contained primarily non-Qatari students, including a few Americans from the main campus who were on an exchange semester. A handful of Qatari women sat together in one of the front rows, and two young Qatari men were in the back corner of the room. The discussion slowly started to move along after prodding from the teaching assistant, since Qatarization was such an unspoken yet powerful structuring force within the university. The expatriate students who had grown up in Doha spoke the most, and they overwhelmingly complained about Qatarization and its unfairness. Many also felt it was an ineffective system because it didn't encourage "hard work" from citizens. The Qatari students were silent for most of the class, and I could see that they were taking the comments personally. Finally one of the young men in the back raised his hand to assert that most people deserved to be at Texas A&M, and that the private sector was competitive, even for Qataris. An expatriate student who had been vocal throughout the session immediately countered that some jobs were only for Qataris, which creates the idea of being a "token." After the class, two of the Qatari women who had remained silent stayed behind to talk to me privately. They said the reason they didn't speak in class was because there were a lot of stereotypes about Qataris at the school. If they had spoken, no one would have listened, or it would have just confirmed existing biases. Both women complained about the remedial classes they had to take upon entry to Texas A&M. These classes, they protested, were only for Qataris, which, along with Qatarization policies, led to nationals being perceived as less qualified than their expatriate peers, regardless of their actual performance.

The second section of the class was quite different. There were many more Qatari students, including several men, which was rare compared to other Education City schools.[12] The teaching assistant started the class with the standard Texas A&M "howdy" and then introduced me. I proceeded to ask the students the same question I had asked in the previous class, about their opinions of and experiences with Qatarization. An uncovered woman in jeans and a T-shirt immediately raised her hand. She identified herself as a Qatari and said that she had had several experiences with people assuming she was not as smart as her peers after they found out she was a national; she added, "We are some sort of brand" that universities and companies want. A couple of Qatari men chimed in to back up her point, pointing out that quotas for Qataris in companies were unfair because they limited the number of nationals that would get hired. Some expatriates in the room at that point made patriotic comments about how they preferred living in Qatar over the United States, despite Qatarization, because it was closer to home and a Muslim country, and the community at Texas A&M Qatar was very close-knit. As punctuation to these sentiments, the vocal Qatari men said that Qatar treated everyone well and if it didn't migrants would not keep coming. One man emphasized: "They [Qatar Foundation] could have made Education City just for Qataris but they didn't." Qataris had so many privileges, he explained, because there were so few of them, but there were benefits to all people to stay in the country. To that comment, some of the expatriate students rankled, and mentioned that the kafala system puts undue constraints on them, like the need to get exit visas to leave the country, to which the previous student responded that exit visas were a protection for *kafeels* (sponsors) against migrant workers absconding with money or after committing a crime. Another Qatari man also said, about migrants, "We are developing them."

After class, some of the vocal Qatari men came up to see if I could advocate for them as a faculty member. They complained that they did not get the same courses and privileges that students got in College Station, and they appealed to me to take their grievances, which seemed to

be falling on deaf ears in Doha, to the higher administration. For these
students, my class visit was an opportunity to express their disappointment at not receiving an education commensurate to the main campus, one they felt entitled to. In the first class, the expatriate students
dominated the conversation and highlighted the unfairness of Qatarization, which in turn made the Qatari students feel silenced and stereotyped. Meanwhile, in the second class the Qatari students claimed more
space and turned the conversation into one about Qatari entitlements
to their own country and the benevolence of Qatar toward foreign residents; foreign resident students responded both by rehearsing ethnic and
civic nationalisms and also by challenging some of the claims by Qatari
students about fair treatment, but to a lesser degree. Taken together, these
classroom experiences showcased how Qatari students were expected to
perform in particular ways as a group rather than as individuals in
Education City, and how they negotiated these expectations, which
included privilege as well as marginalization. The scripts that emerged
in my two class sessions circulated regularly within branch campuses,
helping students to navigate their experiences vis-à-vis each other, and
they were reproduced by faculty and administrators, including, when I
reflect back on these and my other classroom experiences, by myself as
an American professor.

   Despite their discourse of respect, many faculty (though by no means
all) harbored preexisting expectations of Qatari failure, which the
Qatari women who stayed back to speak with me after my first class session had internalized. One long-standing faculty member at Carnegie
Mellon told me that when he started at his position, there were many
Qatari women because admissions standards were not as high. The students expected a lot of "pampering" and were always in his office asking for homework help. Since then, because the university's admissions
standards had become stricter, there were fewer Qataris. The non-Qataris
were more "driven." This faculty member's comments were incredibly
ordinary. He highlighted that Qataris did not work as hard, that they
were more entitled, that they participated in groupthink rather than being
individually motivated, and that they were admitted at lower standards

than their non-Qatari counterparts. Attitudes such as these often resulted in treating Qataris differently from non-Qataris. My interviews reflected that Qatari students often felt like they were treated as if they were spoiled by faculty—some even explicitly told them such things, or expressed surprise when a Qatari student got the top mark on a test. Expatriate student interviews related similar complaints: some students told me that faculty members had been accused of using different grading measures for Qatari students, and that the universities had never done anything about it. At Georgetown, a couple students told me that they had even signed a petition against a professor, complaining about biased grading, but that nothing had come of it.

Faculty like Anna, who I quoted at the beginning of this chapter, who were more sensitive to the specific challenges Qatari students faced transitioning from Arabic-medium or gender-segregated schools into Education City, took a more missionary—and sometimes feminist—stance, telling me they were "making a difference" by challenging Qatari conservatism. These professors brought topics like migration into the classroom, but in the process they generally continued to exempt themselves from complicity in the production of systems of inequality. It was through the citizen-noncitizen matrix that assembled student life—in the classroom, in extracurricular activities, through Qatarization policies, and within leadership's understandings of who the target of liberal education should be—that Qatariness was consolidated, both as an object of knowledge and as a cultural form. National students, in turn, were expected to embody and perform Qatariness in ways that highlighted their national distinction, a distinction that was elite but also alienating.

Becoming Qatari

The university was not the first time Qataris encountered each other, ideas of national identity, or expectations of performing national distinction. They, like all residents of the country, were bombarded with state rhetoric and the imagery associated with Qatar's supposedly timeless culture, versions of which circulated through social media, heritage sites, television, and consumer culture. They were also largely visible to each other in public and semipublic spaces like malls, parks, hotels, and souks, primarily through the now ubiquitous national uniform. The Qatari national brand, however, remained rather elusive to them, as it was to non-Qataris as well; and the role that Qataris were meant to play in knowledge economy—and what knowledge economy even meant—was also unclear. Most nationals grew up in multicultural and multilingual home environments, with domestic staff from other parts of the world, or even with mothers and other family members who had immigrated. Their first language was often not Arabic, and they were exposed to cosmopolitan ideas and an array of people from various national backgrounds through media and travel, within their neighborhoods, and within their schools, including public independent schools that were assumed to be solely for nationals. In addition, as Qatar rapidly changed in terms of educational opportunities, and as parents' decisions about where to send their children for schooling shifted, even siblings and cousins from the same family often came away with different notions of Qatari tradition, different ideas about gender norms, and different language skills, including accents. Thus the diverse classroom demographics of Education City were not necessarily new for many students. Social and pedagogical forms tapped into this range of existing cultural competencies. They were, however, assembled differently in the classrooms and hallways of branch campuses, producing somewhat unfamiliar and increasingly rigid understandings of Qatariness and cultural difference.

My interviews with Qatari students revealed that they learned to think of themselves and behave more uniformly as Qataris only after entering university. It was only when students from a diversity of family, class, and educational backgrounds were placed in settings where they witnessed each other more intimately, and where they were expected to behave as Qataris for their professors and peers, that they both realized the fractures within this seemingly homogeneous citizenry and also developed new ways to solidify national identity. Many students expressed unhappiness with the national identity they were expected to naturalize. It made them feel hyper-visible and invisible at the same time. They were sometimes jealous of expatriate students and their ability to fit in within the universities; and they were also ambivalent toward Qatarization policies, which they saw as both their right and the source of stereotypes about them.

I found that while understandings of what Qatari culture and tradition meant circulated within the family, students acquired their norms of behavior primarily from their K-12 schools, which in Qatar were very socially, demographically, and linguistically atomized. Given the range of independent and private school options in Doha, Qataris had very different experiences of pedagogy, friendship, gender mixing, language acquisition, contact with foreign residents, and the development of their identities. Those who attended independent schools usually had not been in gender-integrated classes before, attended the Academic Bridge Program to improve their English skills and gain college admission in higher numbers, and were more likely to have friends who were exclusively Qatari, but this was not always the case. Independent schools varied drastically: some were gender integrated up to a certain age, some taught in English while others taught in Arabic, and there were foreign residents within the independent-school system, usually from other Arab countries. While the perception within Qatar Foundation (especially among Western faculty and staff) tended to be that the independent-school system ill prepared students for American universities, some independent schools were more sought after and had better reputations than many private schools. Private schools varied just as much, if not more. It was difficult, based on so much family and school diversity, to profile attitudes of Qatari students based on their class status, their last names, or where they went to school. The main difference between public and private schooling was that students from private schools, particularly from International Baccalaureate programs, were usually stronger in English than Arabic, had American sounding accents, and did not have as many close Qatari friends as their independent-school counterparts. In addition, they told me they were mostly comfortable with mixed (coeducational) schooling environments. Attending English-language and/

or mixed schools did not necessarily make the transition to university easier, however. Coming to Education City was sometimes made difficult because there were more Qataris there than in high school. Thus students from private schools had to negotiate being under a particular gaze among other nationals and *as nationals* for the first time. Hawda, for example, was surprised to find that shifting from Qatar Academy to Georgetown was so challenging:

Growing up in QA [Qatar Academy], I was surrounded by other locals and stuff. I'd always be like, "Yeah I represent the Qatari culture in all its ways," and as you grow up you realize no, you belong to even a smaller culture than the larger image that is being projected. And that kind of has helped me in understanding other people's perspectives and understanding where they are coming from, not being like this is the only way to do it and just taking the time to figure it out really.

For Hawda, being Qatari came into relief within Georgetown because she left behind the comfortable and small-scale school and the people she had grown up with and entered into a space where she had to perform national identity in a much more conscious way in front of strangers, both national and nonnational, male and female.[13]

Rashid, who went to the American School of Doha for his entire K-12 education, had a similar experience. He told me he had never worn a thaub, except during special occasions, until after he started university at Texas A&M. Because Texas A&M enrolled many Qataris, students felt more pressure there than at other universities to conform to and perform a particular Qatariness under the gaze of their compatriots. Rashid's embracing of his Qatari identity was linked to wearing the thaub. He started slowly, wearing it some days and not others: "I guess I made that decision because I wanted to start getting used to it. Before I wasn't used to it. I was uncomfortable at times. Even if I wear it for two hours, but now I can wear both. And I guess it is about looking more professional, I mean thaub."

When Rashid alternated between different types of dress, his professors wouldn't recognize him on the days he came to class in jeans and a T-shirt. He chuckled when he told me this, but I could see the misrecognition bothered him. Because he had an American accent due to his schooling, and because everyone in Qatar was so accustomed to identifying nationals primarily through their modes of dress, his professors did not see him—and therefore did not treat him—the way he wanted them to when he wore jeans. By his junior year, he was wearing thaub daily. When we met, he had just graduated and was working at a large oil and gas company. From his ease of comportment, I would not have guessed that national dress was such a recent part of his life; the only days he didn't wear thaub now, he told me, was when he was on site for his job. Rashid said he had always felt more like the expatriates than like a Qatari because of his school friends but that this had slowly changed as he had moved through university:

Before, when I was at ASD [American School of Doha], I used to see Qataris and feel that I was separate from them. I noticed as well that a lot of the expats that come from abroad, when they first get off the plane, they see the Qataris as aliens, a bunch of aliens walking around among them. They are very, very afraid. And I guess I was like that, about Qataris, 'cause I was from an American culture. Right now I feel as though we are all brothers and sisters, and if I see a guy on the street I can just go say hi.

Wearing thaub was a key way for Rashid to perform and embody his national identity, gain recognition from others for his national distinction, and fit in with his new university peers; it was therefore central to his *becoming* Qatari. Like Rashid and Hawda, other Qatari students related a constant sense of having to perform national identity, and of being surveilled by others.[14] On the one hand, they benefitted structurally from being Qatari within Education City, and many claimed its spaces as "for Qataris" in our interviews and in classroom discussions, even as they often told me they felt left out of the culture of the university or marginalized by professors and other students. On the other hand, they were highly critical of their compatriots, felt that other Qataris (but not them) were too materialistic, too entitled, too lazy, too snobby, and so forth. They disavowed the stereotypes that impacted their daily lives in the university even as they applied those stereotypes to others. There was a simultaneous sense of constant policing, hierarchies, cliques, and gossip by other Qataris, a feeling of being singled out as a group through positive and negative stereotypes by non-Qataris, as well as a strengthening of identity around elite status.

Performing national identity also meant that many Qatari students began to identify with the nation, have nationalist pride, and internalize state and university rhetoric about post-oil citizenship. Bahar, who was also obtaining an engineering degree, felt strongly compelled to participate in Qatar's development in some capacity after she graduated, and said that she eventually would love to be involved with the 2022 FIFA World Cup: "I am so proud of Qatar. I think our Emir is doing this for our own good. I love the way he talks, I love his ideas, I support him. I think this happening [the tensions in 2014 with other Gulf countries] is more jealousy. But I support everything, and I want to be a part of it." And Maryam and Rania, two sisters I interviewed together, defended Qatar's choices against detractors and felt pride as Qatari women in getting degrees and eventually getting jobs—employment for them was something they associated not with economic need but rather with citizenship expectations, like most Qatari students I interviewed.

Having pride in Education City or in Qatar did not mean that Qatari students were on board with all of the changes that were happening around them or all of the decisions taken by the government. My students in 2011, for example, were openly divided about whether the World Cup would bring positive changes to the country, and they had several debates in class about the topic. One group even conducted an ethnographic research project on older Qataris' feelings about the World Cup and mega developments in the city. Over the course of that and other summer sessions, we debated migration policies, gender roles, social media, and even Qatarization. In interviews, however, Qatari students related that they felt pressure (or perceived pressure) from other Qataris around certain topics to "save face" for the country. So while they were quite outspoken about their views on a range of topics, they also felt that they could not directly criticize social structures or say negative things about the country or the ruling family. They were especially defensive about Qatarization privileges, and they consistently rehearsed a nativist narrative of Qatari belonging when discussions turned to inequalities between citizens and expatriates. Rifat, a student at Northwestern, told me she felt pressure in her classes from compatriots to avoid certain opinions, especially around structural inequalities in Qatar:

RIFAT: I take a lot of politics classes, and I cannot talk, because if I am it is usually saying negative stuff, and if I am I know I won't get away with saying these kinds of things.

NV: Because you are Qatari you can't say that?

R: The thing is that when non-Qataris say it, the Qataris get *very* angry. And then when I say it, they are like, "You are from here, *you* can't say that." Because I've done it once or twice in class, but then when I go home and tell my parents about it they say, "Just don't talk about that."

Clearly, Rifat felt comfortable criticizing state policies with her family and her friends (and even to some extent with me), but part of becoming Qatari meant internalizing the idea that one was representing the nation at all times, and then self-policing behavior and speech accordingly. National performance thus provided elite status to Qataris over nonnationals but also produced dissonances that students had to carefully manage in the multicultural spaces of Education City, leading to practices of segregation.

Segregation and Failure

In all of my conversations, students, faculty, and staff mentioned student segregation as a problem that was evident from the minute they entered college. Rashid, for example, called coming to Texas A&M a "reverse culture shock" after his experiences at the American School of Doha, where students were much more integrated:

There people [Qataris] didn't really have many differences [from other students] in terms of culture, political views, whatever. Of course we were Muslim and we were in an American school, but it was no problem at all. ASD gave the culture of accepting the person, celebrating the person. But at Texas, even though it was an American school, most of the students were from Qatar and the Middle East, and parts of South Asia. So it was a culture shock because, you know, the Qataris work together, the Omanis work together, the Saudis work together, the Indians work together, the Egyptians work together. I didn't really like that.

Danny, who had worked at Carnegie Mellon for several years, discussed various Qatari student complaints he had heard about faculty insensitivity, and even overt racism, around the topic of segregation. Referring to Qataris as "thaubs" and "abayas" was relatively common, as was shaming them for self-segregating in cafeterias and other social spaces, even though *desi* (South Asian) and Arab students did the same thing. Expatriate students regularly told me they also found comfort zones with those of similar national, regional, or linguistic backgrounds, something that they were familiar with from their childhoods growing up in Qatar in relatively segregated communities and schools, and understanding their identities as tied primarily to national "homelands" elsewhere. Although their parents worked with Qataris, expatriate students rarely encountered Qataris of their age group until they came to university, unless they attended elite international schools. In Education City, they found that Qatarization, as an abstract and material reality, shaped their life experiences and produced anxieties about their futures. They were also aware of their second-class position within the university and within the country, and of the fact that knowledge-economy development was not centered around them, but rather a privilege extended to them by a supposedly benevolent state. This understanding—that Education City was a space intended for Qataris—extended beyond structural policies and the classroom into all aspects of student life, creating a rift between citizen and noncitizen students. Despite this, noncitizen students actively participated in the life of the institution, effectively embodying the liberal subjectivity promoted by the branch campuses.

While faculty and staff tended to attribute segregation to Qatari students almost wholesale, students took ownership of a "two-way" problem that was embedded within and enabled by the structures and practices of the branch campuses.[15] Almost all of my student interviewees had cross-national friendships that they valued very much, and those friendships sometimes extended beyond the boundaries of campus (e.g. going out for dinner or being invited to a wedding). None of the students I spoke to liked the way they were segregated, and many told me they felt more comfortable in diverse groups. Several Qatari women, for example, said they found studying and hanging out with non-Qataris easier because they did not feel as scrutinized in their behavior and speech in a mixed-gender group with expatriate men as they did with other Qataris. But these women also emphasized that expatriate friendships were mostly contained within the boundaries of Education City. They also felt that, given family expectations, high levels of homework, and the types of programming in the evenings, they were not interested in attending student events, especially ones like dances, which encouraged heterosocial mingling.

For noncitizen students, on the other hand, the campus became the main place for socialization, usually with friends from their national and linguistic backgrounds. They lingered late into the night, sometimes even crashing with international students that lived in the dorms. These expat-international friend groupings were fairly common: expatriate students often had cars and lived with their families, so international students were able to get a ride to the grocery store or go to a friend's house on the weekend for a meal. For expatriate students, Education City felt like a real American college experience, many told me, despite certain restrictions on mixed-gender interaction and heavy crackdowns on drugs and drinking. They organized and attended social functions and clubs and even religious meetings, like Bible study, and they used the library and the student center at all hours to get studying done, hang out, and flirt. Many understood that Qataris as well as others were unable to stay late on campus due to family expectations. For some noncitizens who came from less privileged backgrounds, social interactions with Qataris were made difficult by the fact that Qataris often insisted on paying for the whole group when they went out somewhere. Since this was a common practice among South Asians and Arabs (fighting over who got to pay), not being able to return the favor due to either lack of funds or a sense of unequal status led some to give up on those kinds of social activities.

Student understandings of the nuanced ways that segregation happened but also was not complete were not reflected in most faculty and staff narratives, which, while cognizant of Qatarization as an inevitable structural divider, regularly turned to culturalist explanations for what they saw as Qatari self-segregation, basing potential solutions to segregation off of these presumptions. Qatari failures to integrate and embody liberal subjectivities became a source of deep anxiety about the future of American branch campuses as integrated and sustainable educational forms in Qatari society. These anxieties were particularly acute among Student Affairs staff, who seemed to be tasked with alleviating this problem. I found a contradiction within most Student Affairs programming between being charged with creating student life experiences that were inclusive of all students, which almost all of the staff members I spoke to articulated, and a desire to cater primarily to Qataris in order to solve the problem of segregation. Attempts to work around perceived Qatari cultural sensitivities, particularly around gender, reinforced essentialized ideas about difference, furthering instead of alleviating Qatari feelings of being set apart and deviduated, thus perpetuating the very problem they were trying to fix.

Danny, from Carnegie Mellon, described some of the ways his office had attempted to integrate more Qataris into student activities. Orientation, which was student led, for example, had historically chosen icebreakers and bonding exercises from a standard American repertoire. In order to make Qataris comfortable, orientation leaders had recently discussed how to make those activities more "conservative," especially since the university was expecting the freshmen class to grow to about 60 percent Qatari by 2016. The presumption that Qataris, and Qatari women in particular, were more conservative than other students and needed protection echoed the discourses of the state as well as colonialist representations of covered Muslim women as repressed.[16]

Many staff members and faculty were of course aware that supposedly neutral programming replicated from the home campuses was laden with cultural assumptions. Primarily, however, they addressed this problem through initiatives that reproduced pedagogies of essentialism and furthered segregation, even when they were sympathetic to the forms of discrimination Qataris experienced. Carnegie Mellon's new conservative approach to orientation, for example, made all the activities opt-in, leading to the reproduction of previous problems: Qataris still participated in low numbers, even though the changes made to the programming were geared toward them. Even worse, some of the incoming non-Qatari freshmen at another institution told me that Student Affairs staff and orientation leaders actively encouraged them to go up to Qatari students during orientation to introduce themselves and mingle. This highlighted a familiarity and insider status afforded to expatriate students that Qatari students did not get. Qataris were more alien to many staff and faculty, and the discomfort interacting with them was evident; thus it was not surprising that segregation remained a problem despite deliberate attempts to make Qatari students interact outside of their comfort zones. These types of changes made Qataris continue to feel as if they were treated as a homogeneous group, separate from the rest of the students, and targeted as a problem to be solved. Expatriate subjectivities were inadvertently reinforced and cultivated within universities, but foreign resident successes were not as highly celebrated. The primary indicator of liberal success or failure remained *Qatari*.

There were examples I found where Student Affairs took approaches that did not fall into reductive attempts at liberal multiculturalism. One was at Virginia Commonwealth, where the Student Affairs officers better understood the heterogeneity of Qatari backgrounds. A staff member told me that she had spoken to many Qataris over the years; some entered university with what could be considered very liberal values, while others were quite conservative. Interactions among Qatari students, more than between Qataris and non-Qataris, caused rifts that were particular to Virginia Commonwealth being an art and design school. For example, some students placed sticky notes over nudes in library books, while others viewed their exposure to the use of nudes in art and sculpture as part of their own exploratory and creative process. She discussed an artist in residence who had caused a lot of controversy the previous year by painting a mural of a woman with exposed breasts on one of the school's walls. Some of the women students were worried that if their parents came into the building, they would pull them out of school. Student Affairs staff members told me that the students constantly struggled with faculty insensitivity to their opinions about these kinds of topics, and that faculty had been resistant to training to be better equipped to communicate with the diversity of their students.

Virginia Commonwealth's Student Affairs office had made significant efforts to implement programs on intercultural communication at their campus and across Education City, but they felt that other campuses had not recognized these efforts. The staff shared a presentation with me that they had put together for freshmen, "Working Together," which differed greatly from the descriptions students and staff at other branch campuses provided of orientation and other activities. They had pursued certification in intercultural communication, and when I spoke with them in 2014, they were in the planning stages of bringing the certification program they had attended in the United States to Qatar for a three-day workshop. Getting other campuses on board for this program was proving difficult, however. Some staff members had heard that faculty at Cornell had called them "intellectual lightweights" and scoffed at their efforts. They also told me that they had been accused by other campuses of not participating enough in leadership activities—they were considered unwilling to be part of Education City, when really it was, according to them, the Eurocentric structure of leadership and community building that marginalized their students. Other campuses did not consult Qataris, Qatari women especially, in the planning of programming, but rather expected them to be conservative in particular ways; then, when the predominantly Qatari Virginia Commonwealth students did not show up at Education City-wide events, the school was accused of being less engaged. In contrast to events at other campuses, Virginia Commonwealth had a weekly informal drop-in gathering called "*karak* (tea) and conversation" every Wednesday around noon.[17] This timing worked well for students, particularly those with family obligations such as small children. And the Student Affairs staff members, instead of shying away from concerns and tensions around segregation and Qatarization, which other schools seemed to want kept hidden, immediately welcomed me to speak about my research there openly with any community members that showed up. Virginia Commonwealth was also the only American branch campus where I met a Qatari Student Affairs staff member.

Another example that diverged from other Student Affairs programs was the recently opened Hamad bin Khalifa University (HBKU) student center. This space and its activities were meant to transcend those of individual campuses and serve all of Education City. They provided coeducational trips during spring break, as well as other trips that were either women only or open only to Qataris. Student Affairs staff at HBKU, who included several Qatari members, were clear that their primary goal was to integrate nationals into Education City, rather than with nonnationals. Thus, although they admitted that some of their tactics were exclusionary, they also noted how these programs were works in progress and were already successful by the standards that they had set—a recent trip to Oman, for example, only open to Qataris, filled up quickly, and included ten women. Fully funded by Mersk Oil as part of their corporate social responsibility initiatives, the trip showcased how HBKU Student Affairs centered principles of Qatarization in ways that did not claim to also embrace the liberal values of inclusion and multiculturalism that the branch campuses did.

Conclusion

Diversity initiatives in higher education often have the opposite effect. They depoliticize difference by appropriating the vocabularies of resistance into administrative celebrations of flattened multiculturalism, thereby preventing institutions from becoming truly inclusive. By enacting diversity mission statements and initiatives, liberal universities imply that their diversity work is already done, thus making it harder for discussions about existing inequality and the structural changes required to address it to take place.[18] When liberal education moves overseas, diversity gets linked to civilizational progress as well. According to the metrics of US universities, diversity has actually been achieved in

Qatar—the sheer number of students of color, languages spoken, national backgrounds, religions, and women in STEM would be an end goal on any home campus. However, the numbers at Education City's branch campuses did not stand up to liberal notions of success. Instead, faculty and staff were obsessed with segregation, groupthink, and of course the literal and figurative Muslim woman as the limits of liberal multiculturalism and diversity. They applied a different metric in Qatar, one that was about civilizational training of certain students more than it was about the prevailing standards at home campuses, which were based solely in a numbers game. In the process, branch campuses were able to open space for discussions about inequality, but in ways that reconfirmed certain existing social hierarchies while also producing new ones. And segregation, in the end, was a problem that went unresolved—not unlike diversity. Both highlight a fundamental problem with the liberal university's approach to culture and difference, an inability to frame change around the experiences of those most marginalized by existing institutional norms. Students therefore learned tolerance and multiculturalism as discourses that were part of being good citizens of the university space, but those discourses also allowed them to interact with each other in ways that avoided discussing the deep power differentials built into the university system.

Ironically, given that Education City was viewed as a Western and foreign entity by most residents in Qatar, as opposed to the public Qatar University, the faculty and staff within branch campuses seemed more invested—through their deployment of nativist understandings of school mission and justifications for Qatarization—in being *national* than the national university itself. Branch campuses were producing Qataris who identified primarily as citizens in relation to their peers and their educational experiences, rather than forming political and other subjectivities built around the heterogeneity of Qatari backgrounds and family expectations. And it was within Education City that Qatariness was most at stake.

CHAPTER 3

Mixed Meanings

In August 2014, Vodafone sponsored a student charity trip as one of its corporate social responsibility initiatives. Seven high-school and college-aged Qataris, named the Qatar Firsts Adventurers, were selected to rebuild a school that had been destroyed by fire in an Amazonian village. A dedicated Vodafone website was set up to chronicle the excursion and provide profiles of each team member. As the group left for Brazil, other social media venues also began sharing tweets and photos of them trekking through the rainforest.[1] However, when a short video clip of the team started to go viral, there was an unexpected backlash on Arabic and English Twitter, mostly from other Qatari citizens.[2] The clip showed the team members hiking in loose T-shirts and pants, the women with their hair in ponytails. The backlash was aimed at the women not wearing hijab and the casual gender mixing within the group. According to social media critics, these practices were un-Islamic, went against Qatari culture, and were a misrepresentation of national values. A slew of rather vicious personal attacks on the young women team members called into question their virtue and reputation.

This was not the first time social media had erupted around what some considered problematic representations of Qatariness: speaking out against migrant labor abuses, claiming a gay identity, or championing more tolerance for multiculturalism have caused backlash from elements of the citizenry who define Qatar's national identity through orthodox Islam and tightly bound understandings of tradition and belonging.[3] Often, these public contestations over national identity involve policing women's bodies and actions, as women have become a symbolic site for debates around how to preserve supposedly vanishing traditions within the context of rapid modernization. In response to the criticism of the Qatar Firsts Adventurers, there was also a groundswell of support for the team. These posts called out critics for their cyberbullying, saying they were sexist, old-fashioned, and antithetical to the spirit of Islam. Many highlighted that a hijab was a Muslim woman's choice, and that mixed—or gender-integrated—environments were increasingly common in Qatar, particularly in workplaces and universities.[4]

The controversy was a regular topic of discussion in Education City when classes resumed a couple weeks later, just as I was arriving in Doha to complete fieldwork for this project. That semester, I perceived a heightened sensitivity among administrators and students to how events, activities, and even everyday social interactions, particularly those highlighting the coeducational nature of Education City, might appear to those outside campus. By 2014, a small but vocal subset of the Qatari citizenry had established itself as critical of the modernization projects being implemented by Qatari leadership. They felt that rapid urbanization privileged a secular Western version of the nation that pandered to international standards of legitimacy and the interests of certain elite nationals and expatriates. In the process, they claimed, many citizens were being disenfranchised.[5] For its detractors, Education City had come to stand in for many of the ills that modernization brought. It had earned the nickname "Sin City" around Doha, primarily due to rumors about impropriety around gender mixing at the branch campuses. Some Qatari families were worried about their daughters' reputations if they attended a branch campus, while others wondered which citizens, if any, knowledge-economy development benefitted.

The focus on women's education in the Gulf region, particularly in the expanding higher education sector, has created what some scholars call a reverse gender gap, where national women are now overeducated in comparison to national men.[6] Among Qataris, this education gap correlated with changes in heteronormative family structures and gender roles: women married later, birth rates were lower, domestic violence was increasing, and divorce was more common. Some women told me they felt they had educated themselves out of marriageability altogether, since there were so few men who had university and postgraduate degrees. Meanwhile, American branch campuses saw coeducation as integral to the liberal project in Doha. Branch campuses perpetuated the idea that students could not attain liberal academic progress without being in mixed classrooms, and that they could not attain full citizenship without heterosocial participation in activities outside the classroom.[7] These understandings stemmed from the mainstreaming of liberal feminism into the US academy, and from the yoking of gender and sexuality to civilizational metrics for branch campus success.

In this chapter, I explore how Qatari women produced, negotiated, and contested the "Qatari woman" and the parameters of proper national femininity amidst competing expectations within Education City's coeducational spaces. Although coeducation was considered a fundamental aspect of the American higher education experience, certain segments of Qatari society saw mixing as a threat to women's bodily purity and reputation, and more generally to national culture and traditional gender roles. Not surprisingly then, the covert and overt ways that coeducational anxiety permeated Education City played out on the bodies and actions of Qatari women, both as the vanguard group for liberal success that needed to be protected from patriarchal criticism, and as the source of gender threat itself. Qatari women experienced mixing, therefore, as both imperative and impossible. Tasked with playing a critical role in Qatar's modernization, but also expected to represent a timeless national identity, young Qatari women constantly negotiated the parameters of possibility as gendered citizens, sexual subjects, future wives and mothers, and working professionals. Despite a range of challenges they faced entering and staying in college, they also overwhelmingly experienced the branch campus as a space of freedom and empowerment. Their challenges to patriarchal gender norms might resemble those of liberal feminism, but the complexities and contradictions of their experiences do not readily fit into Western civilizational narratives of success.

Feminist Parentis

Images of women in abayas going about their daily lives within the class-rooms, labs, and recreational spaces of the university have now become synonymous with branch campuses in the Gulf.[8] The various Educa-tion City websites, the marketing material for its institutions, and the media coverage that it received, both from domestic and international venues, were peppered with Qatari women studying chemistry, playing basketball, or interacting with men in classroom discussions. These im-ages utilized the optics of gender mixing among supposedly conserva-tive nationals to index Qatar's modernity, as well as the liberal and civilizational success of the branch campuses. For detractors, they marked the incongruity of moving liberal institutions into illiberal space, or the threat to traditional values that Western education brought.

Within branch campuses, Qatari women were considered the pri-mary group that needed to benefit from liberal education. Coeducation was part of a missionary approach that highlighted the mainstreaming of liberal feminist values into the American university.[9] These values also included striving for professional careers, expecting equal access to the public sphere, and speaking out against sexist behavior and language. For the most part, the liberal feminist values of the American university, especially when they focused on neoliberal forms of career preparation, aligned well with the state-sponsored feminism promoted in Qatar's *Vision 2030* and other official rhetoric, although there were points of friction when it came to questions of women's role in the family and the decisions they faced upon graduation. For faculty and administrators, co-education was integral to their pedagogical mission. Within classrooms and through extracurricular events, they promoted coeducation as an es-sential component of liberal citizenship formation and part of the process of improving what was seen as a conservative or even backward Qatari culture. All of the students I spoke to—both citizens and expatriates—told me that gender integration was built into how groups were assigned, and that educators were open about this tactic.[10] Missionary approaches to heterosociality were particularly prevalent among self-identified feminists.

In conversation over drinks one evening, a young white American professor who had been at Georgetown for three years emphasized how much she loved teaching, and especially teaching Qatari women, because she "makes more of a difference" than she would in the United States. Her language during our conversation emphasized a belief in universal patriarchy, but also in Qatar as a place where women were more oppressed than in the United States. This attitude was common among faculty in Education City, and reproduced the idea that Muslim women needed saving by Westerners, particularly by Western feminists.[11]

The mainstreaming of heterosociality into liberal and civilizational notions of progress elided the centrality of women's homosocial spaces to white liberal feminism, especially in the academy—it was at elite women's campuses like Smith, Barnard, and Wellesley, after all, where white middle-class women began much of their consciousness raising around work equality and sexual desire. Women-only safe spaces are still common today on many college campuses in order to discuss topics such as sexual assault and body image. And, despite the gains of transgender theory, feminist politics and scholarship are still anchored to notions of identity that have trouble delinking from biological difference.[12]

The civilizing mission of heterosociality built into the branch campuses was easy to naturalize, however. I also assigned mixed-gender groups the first two summers I taught at Texas A&M Qatar, tried to get Qataris and non-Qataris into conversation in the classroom, and felt discouraged by what looked like self-segregation by nationality and gender catalyzed by Qataris. I was essentializing gender as well as Qatariness in my pedagogy. It was only through my fieldwork experiences and interactions with various students, including at the Faculty of Islamic Studies, that I started to rethink how certain pedagogical techniques that seemed like a given needed unpacking. In particular, I came to see how coeducation and other measures of liberal feminist success in Education City presumed a baseline voiceless Qatari female subject on which to inscribe liberation, not a woman who entered the university with her own forms of personal power and agency.

The liberal feminism promoted by branch campuses was one that was marked by Qatari difference and an in loco parentis approach to Qatari women[13]—they were meant to reap the benefits of mainstream feminist ideologies, but they were treated as if they were not agents in their own right. Education City recruitment efforts, for example, presumed that Qatari women were first and foremost daughters. Parents chose coeducational universities either because they were Western educated themselves, or because they respected the quality of schooling offered but still harbored concerns about mixed environments. That women chose their own education or advocated for themselves did not factor into the way branch campus admissions offices approached the Qatari family. Nor was it imaginable to many of my colleagues that women would choose Qatar University, gender segregation, or even what appeared to be anti-feminist stances on gender roles. Therefore, branch campuses attempted to solve what they saw as a social crisis around mixing by actively inviting Qatari parents and other family members to campus through open houses and recruitment activities. These meetings were meant to show parents that there were academic reasons for their daughters to stay late on campus, participate in group work with men, or attend mixed extracurricular events.

Liberal feminism often focuses on gender equality in the public sphere, and grudgingly accepts gender complementarity in Islam through discourses of cultural relativism, if at all. Forms of Islamic feminism, which are less concerned about gender difference and gender segregation but focus on equality in domestic relationships through a revisiting of the Quran, are not readily visible or even imaginable through a liberal way of seeing. Often, Islamic feminists have also pointed out that the kinds of rights that liberal feminists advocate for, which come from the state or through recognition by other secular authorities, also create new forms of surveillance.[14]

Liberal ways of seeing were evident in the way branch campus actors hailed Sheikha Moza as a symbol of modernity, a proponent of women's rights, and a legitimizer of liberal education. High enrollments of women within branch campuses and the support from Qatar

Foundation for coeducation were often held up as proof of Sheikha Moza's feminism and as what distinguished her and Qatar Foundation from other less liberal spaces and people in Qatar, most importantly the gender-segregated, national Qatar University, and the families who would rather send their children there.[15]

There had been citizen criticism against Sheikha Moza since the start of the Qatar Foundation initiative, particularly against her style of dress, which included Western designer clothes, a turban instead of a hijab, and close-cut long dresses instead of an abaya when she traveled abroad. She also allowed herself to be photographed, and these photographs circulated regularly in the national and international press.[16] Sheikha Moza's rhetoric and performances, however, resisted appropriation into the liberal feminist framework through which both her champions and detractors seemed to read her. She was a strong proponent for women's education as well as civil society in the Arab world, making a clear distinction between culture/tradition and Islam: according to her, limiting women's education had been claimed as Islamic by various states and religious authorities in the Middle East, when this was actually due to patriarchal understandings of tradition or misinterpretations of religious texts.[17] Some of her rhetoric resonated with Islamic feminist traditions—looking to the Quran for women's ultimate equality with men, for example—and she called for democracy and political participation rooted in an Islamic state, but she also reproduced more secular and state-sponsored feminisms, by constantly invoking her husband, the former emir, and since succession, her son Tamim, the current emir, as the source of Qatar's vision, and herself as just an outlet for that vision.[18] She also rehearsed a Qatari femininity that was family focused, maternal, and based on the complementarity of male and female roles rather than in their sameness or even equality.[19]

The internal conflicts between the citizenry that played out on Sheikha Moza's body and representation—for some, she was the quintessential Qatari woman and a role model, while for others, her feminine and feminist performances and speech acts threatened the idea of Qatari nationhood—were not very different from the multiple expectations and divergent messages my Qatari women interlocutors grappled with daily. Public contestations over what defined national identity and the social roles associated with it were embodied by them, shaping how they negotiated their visibility and mobility in public (and semipublic) spaces. Increasingly, Qatari women seemed to find themselves in a space where they were both expected to excel and criticized for their gains. Although there was much that Qatari women gained from higher education, and much they were unable to gain despite it, their returns went well beyond the gendered metrics of success set by development, state, and branch campus discourses.

Almost ʿayb

One afternoon in October 2014, Maha, a junior at Virginia Commonwealth University, visited my office. She had heard about my project from her professor and contacted me for an interview. Like almost all of my Qatari women interlocutors, Maha wore an abaya and *shayla*, but she was dressed very modestly: all of her hair was covered, her abaya was not open like the ones that were on trend that year, and she was not wearing any makeup. This was atypical of Qatari women in Education City, who usually sported designer heels, handbags, makeup, and jewelry, or challenged this norm with their Converse, ripped jeans, rocker tees, and more masculine accessories. Maha came from an elite cosmopolitan family; her father held a high-ranking ministry position that had taken the family to several overseas postings while Maha was growing up. As a result, she spoke Japanese and had traveled extensively, but she said those experiences made her feel even more rooted in Qatar now.

As part of our interview, I asked Maha whether there were any particularly memorable intercultural exchanges or misunderstandings that had happened in her college classes, either between students or between students and professors. Before I had even finished this question, she chuckled and answered with an emphatic *yes*, "especially when we are talking about culture and the professors are asking about Qatari culture." When I probed further, I realized that her biggest cultural learning moments had not been when she had encountered students and professors from different national backgrounds—she had interacted with non-Qataris her entire life—but when she engaged with other Qataris, and especially other Qatari women. This was one of many turning points in my research project; it helped me recognize how much I presumed Qatari gendered sameness as a starting point for my research instead of exploring how norms of femininity were produced within the university setting itself. It also highlighted Qatari cosmopolitanism and not insularity—of course, most Qataris of Maha's generation, whose families employ domestic workers, who probably have traveled outside the country, and who grew up in a consumer culture staffed entirely by foreign workers, had extensive experiences interacting with non-Qataris. Some of those experiences might be quite intimate, such as learning a housemaid's native language before learning Arabic because she was your primary caretaker.[20]

Maha described the class assignment that had stirred up discomfort and debate the previous year: "We had this project last year it was called *almost 'ayb*. Do you know what *'ayb* means?"

NV: Like *haram*?

MAHA: No, it's not *haram*. *Haram* is like forbidden in Islam, but *'ayb* is cultural.[21] It means like something that is socially unacceptable or shameful. So we had this project . . . we had this collaboration between two studios. And basically we would choose an *'ayb* and we would represent it through stop-motion. When the professors first introduced the project there was a lot of tension in the class. The students didn't feel that comfortable because they felt they were taking it a little too far by talking about *'ayb*, like *'ayb* is something we don't talk about . . . and there was a lot of conversation that came up that kind of stirred things, like, because even though we in Doha have the same culture, it really varies depending on the family.

NV: Like your family is more cosmopolitan?

M: Actually, even though we went to international schools, my father's family is very strict, very old-fashioned. But my mother's family on the other side, my grandfather was very educated. He studied in the UK in the 60s . . . so I come from two different faces. And my mother, even though she is very open-minded, she still enforces cultural values on us. Like in my father's family, my grandpa doesn't allow us to drive. And he's very serious about it. But my cousins on my mother's side they all drive, and I want to drive. And my mother drives. But because I carry my grand-father's name, she's not that keen on it because it might stir up conflict in the family. So in the class, one girl would say it's not 'ayb to do this, and another would say no it's 'ayb to do this, and sometimes it's 'ayb to dance at a wedding but other families it's not a wedding if you don't dance. That kind of thing. This was between the Qataris.

The debate over 'ayb showcased how Qatari women had not defined or internalized a cultural norm for femininity. Rather, their understand-ings of what was culturally acceptable were based primarily on what they learned and negotiated within their immediate and extended families; sometimes those families came from two different faces, like Maha's, and thus women received contradictory messages. Their gen-eration was also far removed from the memories of Qatar's pre-oil past—the poverty and hardship that many families faced, the built envi-ronment of the *fareej* (neighborhood) and the mobility it enabled among women, and the fluidity and syncretism of Arabian and Islamic norms.[22] Without those touchstones, the production of national femininity was all the more abstract and emergent.

Maha's father chose coeducational English-medium private schools for his daughters. Maha told me that he pushed his children hard to get a good education and wanted his daughters not only to attain bache-lor's degrees but also to pursue postgraduate training and careers. When Maha chose Virginia Commonwealth over Qatar University, some mem-bers of her extended family were unhappy that she would be on a mixed campus. But her parents were enthusiastic about the quality of educa-tion she would receive; her mother highlighted that people would talk regardless, and that Maha should not worry about gossip as long as she was behaving properly.

When women from different families and different backgrounds met at university, they realized that they were interpellated as one group— Qatari women—and that they really had no clear consensus of what proper Qatari femininity and behavior meant. The university context and engagement with a wider range of people, news events, and social media meant that they began to form their identities in relation not only to each other but also to larger frameworks, such as the state and segments of the citizenry they had been unaware of before. For example, Hawda, a junior at Georgetown, was working on a paper about the relationship between the Qatari leadership and various strands of political Islam when we sat down for our interview. Hawda and I talked a great deal about gender roles and the way that external societal forces that opposed what they saw as improper mixing between men and women in Education City informed her behavior, other female students' behavior, and the attitudes of family members. She had always felt she had to perform a particular identity based in gender segregation, one that was loosely enforced if at all in her family. She told me that in her mother's time, weddings used to be mixed gender, and that her mother went abroad for university education, but all of this was taught to her as having been *jāhilīya* or ignorant of Islam.[23] Her parents were completely supportive of her attending a mixed K-12 school; in university, however coeducation became more sensitive to navigate because of the amount of unknown people there and the external criticisms of American universities from other Qataris that she and her family heard regularly, either directly or through the media.

Hawda and other Qatari women I spoke to were well aware of the way they were represented in discourses of state-sponsored feminism, both inside and outside of Education City, which encouraged their entry into the gender-integrated private sector. But they increasingly felt the contradictory pull of knowing that branch campuses were under a microscope by certain detractors in Qatari society, some of whom were also extended family members. Their understandings of their role in national development were shaped by these larger forces, as well as by the liberal university model of citizenship, which focused on critical thinking and expected a cultivation of the self among students through both academic and nonacademic activities. These women's narratives highlighted the overlapping and contradictory expectations that pulled at them as college students, including those of the state, the family, consumer and beauty standards, and the stereotypes that circulated in Education City. As they navigated the constant tension between patriarchal expectations of preserving reputation and their educational and work aspirations, they internalized a sense of surveillance and also began to police each other, leading to a state of being almost-always *'ayb*.

Negotiations, Performances, and Debates

Although branch campuses enabled the emergence of Qatari femininity, they did not produce uniform Qatari women; rather, women developed their identities and sense of citizenship against and through the Qatari woman as an evolving object of national desires and contestations. Qatari women's crafting of their personal parameters—around proper behavior, negotiations with authority figures to gain more mobility and power, criticisms of others' behavior, and responses to boundaries they felt were unfairly imposed on them—drew on a range of feminist and other discourses about the role of women in society. In the first instance, these negotiations began with family members, although for most of my interlocutors, they were not as challenging or as top down as universities seemed to think they were. Most women I spoke to said their parents, especially their fathers, were supportive of them attending Education City schools, drawing from Islamic principles of women's right to education, as well as trust of their daughters to make decisions for themselves. Mothers were almost equally involved in these conversations. Families were not as patriarchal as most admissions officers presumed.

Branch campuses had acquired a reputation for excellence and were considered by many Qataris to be status symbols, especially since the national university had a reputation of being in decline. In addition, for many young women, Sheikha Moza gave Education City an added level of legitimacy and pride. Many families, seeing the opportunities Education City provided, were willing to consider potential social risks of sending daughters there, but others did need more convincing. Several women used the exact language of state feminism and their role as future workers to speak to family members about going to Education City and choosing certain majors. Rifat explained that she had to work to convince her father that she should go to Northwestern:

My dad had a bit of an issue, because I was in a mixed school until year seven, then it was the same school and they just separated us, so he didn't really accept the idea of me being in classes with guys, but then I said, what, I am going to work, I am going to be working with men, it's gonna be the same thing. The more you separate me, the more when I work with them, then it's gonna be oh my God now she's working with a guy.

Bahar had no issues with choosing to attend Texas A&M but was negotiating with her family as a petroleum engineering major, which required training on rigs and going out to field sites, although she seemed confident that she would get her way in the end:

I'm prepared; my family are not. My family are totally against it. Actually, my parents are. From early on they would compare me to my sister, and like, "No, you can't go. We didn't allow your older sister. You're not ready," or, "You know, you are a girl. You can't do it, but your brother can." But you know, from here until I graduate they are going to have that. But this is my major. I study four years of doing this—they can't actually not allow me to do it.

Negotiations with family also included balancing obligations that extended beyond academic work. Some women were married, for example, and universities were only now beginning to understand that nontraditional students had different needs. At the time of my research there was no day care available on campus for either students or staff, although I heard several women mention that they had complained to administration about this need. Family members, faculty, and others often didn't understand the amount of responsibility women had to juggle, along with the constant sense of having to protect their reputation in terms of how late they stayed on campus, who they were seen with, and the activities they engaged in. My joint interview with Maryam and Rania, two sisters attending Texas A&M, highlighted many of the contradictory expectations they had to negotiate around time:

M: Junior year, my school starts at 8 and always I finish at 8. From 8 till 8, and I want to stay more but I don't have time, I am very tired. My friends whose parents agreed to let them stay on campus, in the dorms, they stay. They still work and study and are doing homework until 3 A.M., all together. But my parents, they don't let us, so we leave.

NV: Your parents don't let you stay later?

R: Maximum until 10.

M: C'mon, our mother, she told me you can finish before 10. She don't know that my labs finish at 7 or 8. It's very difficult.

NV: So it is difficult for Qatari women because parents don't understand the hours, and the universities don't understand the restrictions?

M: Yesterday I had an exam, it starts at 7. I finished the exam at 10. In the middle of the exam my mother called me. I told the prof I have to answer. My mom, she called me, and I told her, "I'm in exam, Mom. I'm solving the exam." She said, "What, till now you are doing the exam?!" Only in Texas I think they start exams after 5.

NV: But what if people have parents who won't let them stay that late?

M: You can't say this is for the purpose of my parents.

R: Any parents who have decided to put their children in Qatar Foundation, they should be open-minded and they should let them.

The script that most women normalized was that academic hetero-social engagement was acceptable because it socialized women and men into working together. As Rifat said, "I think it is becoming more normal for girls and guys to talk, be friends, communicate, whatever. But then when you go out of the university, people see that as a sin. Like I'm not allowed to have male friends, but there are a lot of guys at university who have my number on WhatsApp because it is work related or whatever, but not just like talking. But that's ok, work related."

Women did find academic work with men difficult, however, because they often got blamed for the restrictions on their communication and on expectations that they be home by certain times. They were then perceived by their peers and/or by professors as the problem members of the group or as lazy. So even though most professors actively utilized mixed-gender group work as part of their understandings of pedagogy, and women normalized work-related heterosociality, they also told me about how they were disadvantaged in groups. Sara, for example, who was a former student of mine at Texas A&M, liked the idea of group work—it enabled her to get outside of her comfort zone—but also found that "some guys make it easier, others don't work and it is hard to get them to. It sucks to send emails, [but] you can't call them, [so] what do you do? They can also do the work at the last minute, late at night. A lot of the girls can't do this."

While men and women, and citizens and noncitizens, worked to-gether in academic groups, there was deep segregation in the branch campuses when it came to social time and space. Women had to navi-gate ambivalent feelings about this segregation and how it impacted their university success and sense of belonging. I asked Amina, a journalism student at Northwestern, for example, "As a Qatari woman, having these restrictions on time, giving out your phone number for group projects, meeting outside, all of those kinds of things, do you feel like it has im-peded in any way on your education?" She replied by telling me that some of her projects required her to go off campus to report. She would just go to the site and come back, whereas her non-Qatari female friends would be able to stay back and hang out in a mixed group, go out to a restaurant or go for a hookah. She felt left out in situations like these, so even though restrictions did not impact her formal education, they did affect her overall college experience.

Although Qatari women used work to delineate appropriate and in-appropriate forms of communication with men, they also transgressed these boundaries on a daily basis: in cafeterias, study areas, and class-rooms, on mobile phones, and in the student center, you could regularly observe men and women, Qatari and non-Qatari, flirting, chatting, sharing contact information, and socializing over coffee—all loosely revolving around group work meetings. Some students also had mixed-gender parties with alcohol in rented hotel rooms and villas off campus, dated, and socialized openly on school-sponsored trips.

Women would actively push for suspension of curfews and the legitimacy of the time they spend on campus, and some restrictions were suspended or more easily transgressed within the bubble of Education City or the liminal space of being a college student. But women also felt a sense of constant surveillance by other Qataris, and a fear that some students would misrecognize their behaviors. On the other hand, women themselves judged each other on certain behaviors that they felt took gender mixing or being in an American university too far. For Daria, smoking went past the limits of acceptable behavior. For Maryam and Rania, it was low class to go to parties on campus. As Rania said, "At all the parties they are wearing dresses and playing music and dancing. Can you imagine a Qatari wearing abaya and dancing? So why would she come and sit and look at the others?" Policing mixing was not only about staying away from contexts that women deemed *'ayb*, but the construction of *'ayb* also rested on their sense of being a designated class set apart from the foreign residents (of both genders), who populated most social events on campus. The repercussions for women's tarnished reputation may have been much more imagined than real, but they did occur, and thus served to maintain the constant self-surveillance and surveillance of others embedded in negotiating the boundaries of proper national femininity, in relation to Qatari men as well as non-Qataris.

When Rifat, who I introduced in Chapter 2, told me she had struggled to adjust to university at first, having come from a segregated independent high school, I asked, "So it was a culture shock? Or a gender shock?" She had trouble parsing the question because gender meant something different with Qatari men, even though there were parameters to how much one could interact with non-Qataris or adopt behaviors that were seen as foreign. Her hesitation highlighted for me how gender could never be a culture-neutral term within Qatar, as in any university setting; therefore my question needed unpacking and rephrasing. Pausing for a while, Rifat finally answered, "It wasn't a gender shock because I was ok with the non-Qatari men; it was just the Qatari guys in a sense. If I talked to them, then they would think something of me. So it's not ok for you to just have a random conversation with a [Qatari] guy in your class. If you have a random conversation with a guy who's not Qatari, no one says anything." Rifat had felt direct repercussions from her compatriots speaking critically about Qatar in front of non-Qataris, so her self-policing behavior had to do with gender integration but also with being in a multicultural American university. This was key to why the branch campuses were singled out by some Qataris as threatening, usually through the language of mixing.

Repercussions could happen at any time both within the university and outside, which heightened anxiety for young women. Within campuses, women feared the judgment of Qatari men most of all, who could sometimes be quite rude and end up silencing them. Bahar, for example, recounted:

I remember one experience. One day I walked into class late and I sat in the back. He wasn't even sitting next to me. I don't even know him. Between him and me there was a chair. I sat there, and then he just walked out of class. I never noticed this, but the other day some girl was talking to me and said, pay attention he's the type of person, he doesn't really accept that you are talking with guys when he is there. There was a free chair, and I sat there. I never wanted to talk to him in the first place! I think some guys, they didn't change. Even when they got accepted into this type of university, their mentality didn't change.

Bahar highlighted a tacit understanding among most women to maintain a safe bubble, while they also criticized each other for inappropriate behavior, too much materialism, not being stylish enough, being from less cosmopolitan backgrounds, being too shy with men, being too flirtatious with men, sticking only with Qataris, not having enough Qatari friends, going to events, not going to events, and so forth. Several women, for example, would remove their shayla on campus, but put it back on when they left. Or they would put on makeup after coming to school, only to remove it at the end of the day. They justified these practices on the grounds that they were cultural rather than religious transgressions, and also relatively minor in a contained space like Education City. Daria, for example, did not wear shayla on campus, and also resisted norms of consumer femininity among her Qatari peers, preferring to keep her hair natural, not wear makeup, and throw on an older style abaya over her jeans and Converse sneakers. She emphasized that you could see how shayla and abaya were about culture and thus malleable norms, telling me that she didn't wear abaya when traveling, nor did her mother, although her mother would wear hijab. She was upset at what she saw as the "blanket of religion" through which many Qataris judged women's behavior as well as Education City and gender integration. She was quite angry about the social media backlash against the Vodaphone-sponsored trip to the Amazon: "A few of the women weren't wearing shayla and a picture was posted on social media, and it spurred lots of criticism, people calling them profanities, because they bring in religion and culture [together]." She finished by saying that "people tend to forget that hijab and modesty exceeds just the way you dress. It's the way you behave and the way you act, and by people calling those women profanity, they are not acting peaceful and modest. So they are kind of going against what they are saying."

The branch campuses were sites of anxiety because of the threat of mixing, but in their day-to-day lives Qatari women experienced them as spaces that were primarily female, since Qatari men were mostly missing or formed a very small percentage of the student body, except at Texas A&M, where they attended in larger numbers. Nonnational men were not considered part of mixing anxieties, though there was a discourse of threat attached to the Western or foreign influence that so many noncitizens might bring. Thus the symbolic presence of coeducation, much more than actual interactions between Qatari men and women (though these did take place and were important), catalyzed women to begin to put together a rubric for proper national femininity. Their constant performances, negotiations, and debates around femininity were for other women much more than they were for men, and they produced a hybrid form of femininity that came out of being together as national women, but in a space populated by, and in many ways, geared toward, nonnationals.

Empowerment

I got to know some Qatari women over multiple interviews; others, I met briefly over one session. I conversed with some women in the context of guest visits to colleagues' classes; several others, I interacted with more regularly as my own students. Regardless of the depth of our relationship, these women overwhelmingly described their choice to come to Education City as one they were ultimately happy with, and they also told me, without prompting, that they felt the type of education they received had empowered them by opening up career options or by encouraging them to take a more active role in determining the course of their marriage and family life. Of course, many women had criticisms to share about particular classes or college policies or professors, which came out more in my in-depth conversations; several also had broader commentaries on the Education City project.

These women reflected attitudes that could be considered feminist by US university standards, and some openly identified as feminist. They overwhelmingly described themselves as more open-minded, both in terms of gender roles and in terms of their attitudes toward other nationalities, for having attended coeducational, diverse universities. Sara, who was entering her senior year at Texas A&M when I met her in 2011, said that she would raise her daughters differently than her parents had raised her because of her university experience. She told me she found it hard to "keep your identity but in ways that you still can interact with others," and that she would encourage her daughter to talk to her about these struggles, and "not to judge people and treat them how they are." She also said she expected her daughter to go to university and have a career—gender integration would not be an issue at all: "I'd expect her to do things for herself, things that come from her heart, be passionate, to be passionate about the things she is doing, and not just to do things because, you know, to have the name and the culture that you're an engineer, or that you're a doctor." For Sara, empowerment was about having the freedom to choose one's path. This was the kind of rhetoric espoused by the liberal university, but it also overlapped with much of the entrepreneurial language of the state and its corporate partners. Similarly, Bahar credited her heterosocial college experiences with empowering her for the workplace and marriage:

I am *so* glad I am in a mixed university. My mentality is more open to all kinds of stuff. I respect. I don't judge. I don't just take everything in an inappropriate way, you know? It made me look at stuff in a more different point of view, and it makes me think more rationally. And yes, I should interact with men, 'cause life is all men and women. We are not gonna [be] spending my whole life interacting with women. I wanna know different people, I wanna have friends from different sexes, that's how life should be. For example, I'm going to get married, I can know what type of person he is. I mean, if I'm never interacting with men, all of them I would judge in the same way. I know what kind of man he is, I know if he's good or bad.

Although most women were not pressured by family members to marry while in college, and most felt that the coeducational experience gave them access to better marriages, they also saw women around them struggling to find spouses or to stay with them. Women felt empowered, but they also felt expectations of family and motherhood that created anxiety about their futures. Amina felt that coeducation was very positive, but she also highlighted that "with the whole society there is always a negative look on females who graduate from these kinds of unis. A lot of people who don't want to come here is because of marriage. Because a lot of girls who come to these universities are looked at as loose."

Women felt similarly empowered yet ambivalent about higher education's impact on their ability to have successful careers. While many had naturalized the idea that they would work after graduation, and some had even begun to do so through internships, they were learning that the workforce was unequal and discriminatory. Maryam and Rania—particularly Maryam, a petroleum engineering major—faced gendered discrimination in their academic lives, which they knew would extend into their careers. I asked them if the branch campuses were empowering Qatari women:

R: If the job takes women, then yeah you are giving power to the woman. Everybody studies in the university, and then if the job they say no I don't take women because they don't go to the field, then it is not good.

NV: So even though you are getting a really good education, there is discrimination in the workplace for women?

M: Yeah. Even you know when I went for the internship, I went two days for Dukhan,[24] there I went home, *khalās*, I want to die. Very hot, two hours in the car, then you are with all workers, no females. I have to stay and see the rig and it's very difficult for the girl, and wearing abaya, and half of the offshore and onshore you have to wear their clothes. It's difficult every day for the girl to go there.

NV: Do you think if the girl wanted to go, she could go?

MARYAM: At the beginning they give you a paper that you can go to the offshore two days a week, *ya'nī*.[25]

NV: Like a permission slip? Who has to give the permission?

M: The girl herself and her parents. Parents or, if she's married, husband.

NV: So you can't go on the rig unless you have permission? (Yeah). So this means that you are not treated the same at work.

M: For other departments, yes, but for petroleum, no. Because half of our work is in the field.

R: It should be different. You can't put a woman in the field and then tell her, *yalla*,[26] go work in between the workers. A man, go. Or if he has today, tomorrow he can sleep there, in Dukhan. They have rooms, but we can't do that.

My conversation with the sisters reflected many of the issues that Qatari women faced: they were expected to enter the workforce and wanted to, but certain work environments were men's spaces and not appropriate for women to occupy. In addition, they did not have full autonomy to make choices about their careers. What Rania and Maryam were suggesting was that the workplace itself (along with larger societal structures), rather than women, needed to change to accommodate their needs: instead of just putting on coveralls for a day, they should have been able to get the training they needed, travel to field sites that had made certain concessions for them, and then get equal employment opportunities and treatment at work. Thus workplaces needed to cater to the forms of femininity espoused and permitted by state feminism.[27]

Instead of finding themselves in accommodating and challenging workplaces, many Qatari women were instead treated like princesses who did not want to work, or who were not as capable as men. Daria felt that while women were empowered to work, they faced a "glass ceiling" in many workplaces. She recounted an experience she had when she accepted a summer internship in a bank. She "didn't get responsibility" and on top of that:

I was getting special treatment from non-Qataris for no reason; they were praising me, saying I know your dad. It was easy for me to apply because they know my dad. I didn't even have an interview. When I was there I had requirements to write a paper [for school], so I asked for substantial work to do but wasn't given anything. At one point I was given a task to hand out gifts to everyone on the floor.

Daria's experience at her internship was not just about a glass ceiling in relation to men, but also, as she herself told me, about the problems of *wasta*[28] and Qatarization—noncitizens in particular did not challenge her to do her job, because her father was prominent in the company. They also resisted providing any constructive criticism when asked, probably because of their precariousness in relation to Qatari employees. Others told me that while women were encouraged to be entrepreneurial, they mostly were expected to create small businesses they could run from home, like baking. Thus the phrase "abayas and cupcakes" was common in the country to reference the small businesses that Qatari women started, but in a derogatory way.

The Qatari women I interviewed were aware of the backlash against women's education and employment, even though it did not change their take on coeducation. Bahar said, for example, "Some people are living in old tradition and culture of girls not speaking up for themselves." She framed her empowerment through language that sounded like liberal feminism, challenging the old tradition of patriarchal gender roles within the family, specifically by speaking about her power in terms of identity and voice. Other women, however, challenged patriarchy through religion, by pointing out that ideas about women's inequality were cultural, or a misrepresentation by men of the Quran.[29] Daria's explanation for why she didn't wear shayla, and the language she used to clap back at social media outrage over uncovered women, was an example of Islamic feminist discourse.

In many cases, however, women drew from a range of existing discourses. One example comes from my own classroom experiences. In my Summer 2011 Introduction to Sociocultural Anthropology class at Texas A&M Qatar, on a day when we were discussing gender roles, the young Qatari women were extremely vocal about gender inequality in Qatar, directly criticizing what they felt were sexist claims made by some (primarily Qatari) male students. We had just finished reading two texts that challenged naturalized ideas about women's biological inferiority. The men defended the idea that women are biologically weaker, commenting that they would never let their sisters go work on an oil rig, for example, because women were not suited for such jobs. The women argued back that nowhere does it say in Islam that women and men are suited for different jobs. The men countered that women don't want to do such physical work. Would the men be willing to stay home with the baby and take care of it while the women did those jobs, some of the women asked? Well, a couple of the men chuckled, thinking they had won the argument: "We wouldn't have to; the maid would be doing it!" At that point in the conversation, the Qatari women started to discuss their anxieties about procuring stable jobs. They worried that they had to compete for jobs with expatriate men, and suggested that there should be better policies to ensure women's access to the workplace. When I described this conversation, which was one of the first contentious debates between men and women I had experienced teaching in Doha, to two of my colleagues the following day, they were very excited. They said they would not have expected so much mixed interaction between Qataris even two years ago at Texas A&M, especially so many opinions from the Qatari girls (it was common for faculty and staff to refer to students as boys and girls). They regarded my class as a moment of success toward gender equality and coeducation. They did not comment on the latter part of the debate, however, which rested on scapegoating expatriates and asserting elite national distinction. My classroom conversation, although my colleagues readily accepted it as so, could not easily be co-opted into the language of mainstream US feminism, because the Qatari women had not defined gender equality in terms of liberal democratic access to rights and civil society but first through Islamic notions of equity and then through calls for differential treatment by the state as privileged national subjects. This privilege relied directly on excluding the large noncitizen majority to support the benefits provided to the citizen minority.

Many Qatari women had expressed to me over the course of my fieldwork that expatriate men were preferred for jobs over them (though this claim was not necessarily backed up by fact). They also had expressed unease about moving around in spaces that were occupied by South Asian foreign resident males. And they were angry about their mothers having to leave their younger siblings with housemaids because their fathers did not do an equal share of domestic work. Equality, liberation, and freedom, applied from a liberal feminist perspective, failed to account for the particularities through which Qatari women deployed these terms—claiming their grievances against the state and their male compatriots as moments of feminist liberation also meant being complicit in alienating noncitizen groups and the power and labor hierarchies within which they lived their daily lives. It also meant, however, not recognizing that Qatari women's feminist positions were sometimes more radically presented than those of their liberal faculty and peers, since Islamic feminism included the domestic and intimate within its conception of equality instead of locating gender liberation within a primarily rights-driven conversation about the state and civil society.

Conclusion

Although education was an acceptable and even expected venue through which Qatari women could gain social status, the coeducational and Western environment of the branch campus brought out anxieties about changing social norms and values that pulled students in multiple, conflicting directions. Qatari women formed their sense of femininity, identity, and citizenship through self-surveillance and the policing of other women's actions, but they also created a collective identity within the spaces of Education City and shared a tacit understanding that the university should be preserved as a site where they could experiment with gender norms and different forms of sociality. Qatari women's increasing public presence and everyday transgressions amounted to a "quiet encroachment" on patriarchal power, one that did not fit neatly into the branch campuses' liberal feminist scripts of liberation or state-sponsored versions of modern Qatari womanhood.[30]

CHAPTER 4

Local Expats

About a decade ago, during fieldwork for my first book, I came across a UAE-based blogger who went by the handle "localexpat."[1] I thought this was a clever way to index diasporic hybridity in the Gulf: he was technically an expat, as he was a second-generation foreign resident who did not have access to citizenship, but he was also identifying as a "local," the colloquial term for Gulf nationals, since Dubai was the only home he had ever known. His handle highlighted how second-generation diasporic youth in the Gulf, like their counterparts in other parts of the world, were a blend of home and host societies, with affective, material, and even political ties to both.[2] I found this name could readily apply to the identities and experiences of South Asian young people I was interviewing at the time, many of whom were attending newly opened American-style universities not unlike those in Education City.[3]

In 2006, for a noncitizen in Dubai to name himself local was intentionally provocative; not only did it directly challenge the UAE's restrictive citizenship policies, but it instigated growing anti-migrant sentiment, which was a response to media attention around labor exploitation, Westernization, and the fast pace of urban development.[4] Not surprisingly, localexpat's attempts to discuss belonging among longstanding diasporic communities, and his choice of handle itself, were met with some vitriolic backlash in the UAE English-language blogosphere, from self-described nationals as well as from some foreign residents. Similar online and offline policings of citizen/noncitizen boundaries and behaviors played out in Doha almost a decade later within the context of its rapid urbanization. Qatar's shifting geographies and demographics mirrored those of Dubai's boom period in several ways. And like Dubai, Doha faced international media scrutiny, especially around migrant labor abuses. I found it surprising, then, that I heard university students in Education City use the term *local* more frequently over the years to refer to their second-generation diasporic peers. Our interviews would often include explanations about students' social lives and friend circles in which they would say things like, "I [Qatari] hang out with a few Arabs and Indians, but they are locals," or, "Qataris understand that we [Arabs] are local so it is easy to make friends with them," or *"Desis*[5] tend to hang out together, the international students and the locals; the locals usually have cars and will give us [international students] rides."

I wondered what this resignification of a term usually reserved for citizens alone meant, if Education City was providing pathways for foreign residents to lay claim to official forms of belonging to Qatar—if they were indeed becoming more local. In this chapter, I explore how the liberal and neoliberal ideologies embedded within American branch campuses enabled new forms of identity and belonging for noncitizen students, particularly local expats—those who had spent all or most of their lives in Qatar. This belonging took place simultaneously with having to navigate the structural disadvantages of a two-tier system produced by Qatarization policies, which impacted almost every aspect of their college lives and career prospects. These challenges were amplified by the knowledge that their educators, while interested in their individual success, were more concerned with how the project of liberal education impacted Qatari students. I explore how the seeming incommensurability between global citizenship, on the one hand—a philosophy that is open and inclusive—and Qatarization on the other—one that is specifically closed and exclusive—led to rather shallow neoliberal investments by the institutions themselves in learning to work together across presumably distinct cultural norms. However, in both the praise and critique that foreign resident students had for Education City, we can see that their belongings were more drastically reconfigured. They were

becoming local, more firmly rooted in Qatar and its transnational
future, yet always marked by the specter of foreignness.

I pay particular attention to the material investments by Qatar Foundation and the Qatari government in these reconfigurations, which
were not well incorporated into branch campus rhetoric or pedagogy. I
also consider the affective ways that student citizenship activities on
campus created civic nationalism, and how politicized critique of inequality in Qatar was itself grounds for new claims to belonging that
grew out of the middle-class liberal and neoliberal values of diversity
and global citizenship that circulated in branch campuses, values that
were brought into starker relief because they existed alongside Qatarization as a structural and ideological practice. Higher education as a public
good, despite Qatarization, increasingly included local expatriates; in
turn, they increasingly took ownership of higher education. The experiences of local expats and the structural ways that they were included
showcased the transnational future that Qatar Foundation and modernization projects more generally were producing.

Understanding the contradictions built into their branch campus
experiences also prompted students to criticize the metropolitan American academy, which, in their view, failed to live up to its egalitarian
promise. Thus students understood that global citizenship, meritocracy,
and egalitarianism, as constituted in the United States, were inherently
unequal and did not become less equal or more flawed when they moved
to a supposedly illiberal space like Qatar. In many ways, then, the narratives of the students I introduce here, while relatively unnoticed by
administrators anxious about Qatari integration and other citizen-
centered metrics of success, reflected the critical liberal and global citizenship that American higher education claims to be premised upon.

Working Together

Universities in the United States have long touted the value of global
citizenship as a cosmopolitan ethos of tolerance and cultured intellec-
tualism. Increasingly, global citizenship training has also become a value

add to career-oriented degree programs in an arena where universities are competing for resources and students. Global initiatives take a number of forms, including the recruitment of international students to home campuses; the implementation of global studies, international affairs, and other interdisciplinary programs; the availability of study-abroad opportunities; and, of course, expansion through partnerships or branch campuses into areas outside the United States, particularly those with growing economies like the Gulf Arab states.[6] Global citizenship's meaning is not entirely clear, however, when American campuses are tasked with serving national populations while adhering to host country exclusionary laws, whether they be in the United States or elsewhere. Understanding how branch campuses teach global and national citizenship in Qatar, especially when nonnationals make up over half of the student body, can provide important information about higher education's role in producing citizenship and exclusion. This information can also reflect on how metropolitan campuses, which are presumed to be more inclusive spaces, are similarly stratified.

The mission statements of Qatar Foundation and many of the branch campuses highlighted global citizenship as a main student outcome goal. Orientation activities, culture fairs, and student discussions were all designed to undo stereotypes based on nationality, religion, gender, and other forms of difference. I found that structural inequalities also mitigated the ways that students learned about each other across difference. Students were indeed taught to be global citizens, in that diversity and tolerance were emphasized before they even reached campus. This teaching, however, translated almost entirely to pragmatic skills of learning to work together within a plural society, where ideas about essentialized cultural difference were not broken down but rather recalibrated into forms of multicultural celebration.

In August 2011, I was winding down a summer of research and teaching. It was the middle of Ramadan, and though most of the fasting population of the city was resting, I found my last few days in Doha packed with interviews and meetings. Word of mouth about my project had spread rather quickly, and I was scrambling to interview all of the students who were interested in speaking with me. Although this was indeed a windfall for a researcher still in the early stages of her project, I came to realize that the eagerness to participate in research and share narratives was also a product of Education City itself. These students embodied a particular kind of citizenship—learned in university but also for many in their K-12 education—that made participation in ethnographic research projects like mine a natural extension of their civic modes of engagement with campus life, and with faculty and administrators. One especially enthusiastic interlocutor, Aman, had just graduated from Texas A&M and was about to start a master's degree program in California. Like most foreign resident students in Education City, Aman was born and raised in Doha. However, despite growing up in such a diverse city, he had attended an Indian K-12 school that was gender segregated, and he had little contact with Qataris or other Arabs growing up. Texas A&M was initially quite challenging for him because he had to learn to interact regularly both with women and with students from other national backgrounds. In addition, he was unable to access lucrative sponsorships that could pay his way through college and guarantee him employment after graduation.

Aman's Qatari peers had all entered university with sponsorship from major petroleum companies, from Qatar Foundation, or from the Supreme Education Council. These sponsorships paid full tuition, provided summer internships, and came with generous stipends. In return, students were required to work for the sponsor company or for a company that fell under the umbrella of their sponsor organization for the number of years they were in school. The Qatari students who had just graduated with Aman were all either subsequently employed, getting ready to start jobs, or beginning postgraduate degree programs, usually also under a sponsorship arrangement. The sponsorship system keeps Qataris tied to the domestic economy by providing them with free education and guaranteed employment. Often their undergraduate (and graduate) stipends added up to thousands of dollars per month, making college life profitable for them and their families, especially at Texas A&M, which tended to recruit students from less elite

backgrounds, who might choose engineering because of its earning potential. Unlike their Qatari peers, foreign resident students struggled to
find internships and jobs during college, and they had to compete for
limited scholarships or pay tuition out of pocket. They were, however,
able to apply for generous financial aid through Qatar Foundation in
the form of interest-free loans to be paid back after graduation, which
was how Aman financed most of the cost of his education. These loans
were also available to international students. They could be paid back
as a flat percentage taken out of one's monthly paycheck, or they were
completely forgiven after a number of years working in Qatar, which
also encouraged noncitizens to remain in the domestic economy. Noncitizens were not guaranteed employment after graduation, while nationals enjoyed preferential hiring. Therefore noncitizens often faced tough
competition for open positions, even those below their skill level.

This two-tier system spilled over into other aspects of college socialization. It was evident in the way students interacted with each other or
avoided each other in hallways and social spaces, within student clubs,
or in other extracurricular venues. However, despite these structural inequalities and their effects, Education City also gave rise to new ways of
thinking about similarity and difference among students. These exceeded
and challenged existing social divisions, increasing belonging and
enabling new friendships for local expats, who despite their structural
disadvantages were able to embody liberal and neoliberal citizenship expectations of American college life. Aman told me that he did not regret
his decision to attend Texas A&M "one bit," despite the financial challenges and his awareness that he was a "second-class" person in the place
he called home. He felt that he had received a better education than he
would have on the main campus in College Station. He was astounded,
for example, at the equipment and laboratory space the school
provided—including his first personal laptop—and at the opportunities
to travel at no cost to conferences and trips to the main campus, which
he took full advantage of. All of my local expat and international student interlocutors, even when they came up against the difficulties of

Qatarization policies and financial aid structures, had extremely positive things to say about the resources and personal attention offered by the branch campuses, which effectively made them more similar to liberal arts colleges than large universities, but with the opportunities of the latter. This started with the admissions process, when admitted students were invited to lavish events on campus, including fly-outs for international students (with an accompanying parent or guardian), in order to get a sense of the institution, Education City, and residential life.

Once students enrolled, they were placed into small orientation groups with upperclassmen leaders, who created Facebook or other online networking opportunities, introduced them to campus resources, and helped them enroll in classes and set up their Net IDs. Class sizes were small, and student-faculty ratios low, enabling professors to be regularly available to discuss course material with students or just to have a conversation with them, which students much appreciated. In addition, the funding available for applied learning, student clubs, and community outreach—along with Doha's geographic accessibility to many parts of the world—meant that students were able to take international trips for classes, spring breaks, conferences, and humanitarian projects in conflict zones and disaster areas—all opportunities that American universities and liberal arts colleges advertise as central to the increasingly global orientation of their citizenship training.

While he enjoyed all of these resources and opportunities, Aman insisted that what made his Doha education so much better than attending a university based in India or the United States was its incredible diversity:

This whole opportunity has pushed me to get out of my comfort zone, to, you know, make friends, to just learn to talk to people from different backgrounds. You know they teach you what to say, the social dos and don'ts when you are in a multicultural or multinational environment. I guess there has been a lot of learning experience subconsciously . . . The next generation of people that comes out is gonna be way different than the one that exists right now. And I can see and I can tell you that. People who have that mindset, that I appreciate and respect you regardless of where you are from.

All of the students I spoke to during the years I worked on this project similarly expressed that the Education City experience positively challenged their stereotypes about other nationalities. Although South Asians in particular told me that they were surprised to learn that Qataris were not snobby, lazy, or rude, Qataris expressed a greater respect for their non-Gulf (and particularly non-Arab) counterparts, who they otherwise only interacted with primarily as service workers. Amna, for example, related an incident during her freshman year at Carnegie Mellon that changed her outlook on being Qatari and also showcased how identities in Education City developed relationally in classrooms and other spaces:

Some Qataris treat the Indians like they are servants. This is not right. One time there was a fight in class. They were in a group, an Indian and a Qatari. The Qatari was telling the Indian what to do, do this, do that. And the Indian said, "I am not your servant, you should talk to me properly."

Witnessing that encounter made Amna more cognizant of how she interacted with her non-Qatari peers, and it led her to go out of her way to diversify her group of friends. She went from seeing Indians as either invisible or as servants to seeing them as colleagues and potential friends. Many Indians, on the other hand, went from thinking that Qataris were entitled and pushy to recognizing them as hardworking group members, and this led them to be more open to the idea that they could have egalitarian interactions with Qataris in the future. Non-Qataris, especially non-Muslims, also found their presumptions of Qatari conservativeness challenged in classroom encounters as well as through everyday conversations on campus. It was particularly eye-opening for many foreign nationals to realize that just because a Qatari woman wore an abaya and a shayla did not mean she was unwilling to discuss women's rights, or work on a film project in the city, or question government policies. This was so particularly because foreign nationals received these normative messages from within their university spaces.

The multicultural experiences students had in their universities also ended up at times reaffirming and reassembling the very forms of difference that they had begun to dismantle. This was Maya's takeaway from her freshman year at Texas A&M, which she had just finished when we met for coffee in the student center. Maya's parents were from Tamil Nadu, India, but she had been raised in Doha since the age of two. She explained how meeting people from different nationalities changed her outlook on working together, challenged her stereotypes, and taught her how to interact with difference more successfully:

Working in any sort of a multicultural environment, everyone faces some sort of challenge. More often than not it is because a certain set of people think differently, are taught to think differently than you. For example, if you look from afar you would think that Arabs are lazy; they like to take their work at their own pace. But that is their style, and if you are in a place where there are more Arabs, then you have to adapt yourself to that style, to get the best out of it. You can't say, "OK, work only according to my style." There was a project last semester where a lot of people had trouble working; they had a lot of conflicts. But if you just try to see the other person's perspective, people could get along.

Maya's exposure to global citizenship training did not teach her that she should *not* treat people differently based on nationality; in fact, she learned quite the opposite. She continued, "Now if I am working with an Egyptian, this is how I deal with them, and if I am working with a Lebanese, this is how I deal with them, and if I'm working with a Qatari, this is how I deal with them, because it's different. You work with different people differently." In the narratives and passing comments of students, faculty, and administrators, the tendency to reify national difference after noting how it got disassembled was quite common. The multinational environment of Education City therefore provided new experiences that challenged stereotypes through organized activities or through everyday social interaction, or even emerging out of conflicts and tensions between students, which were fairly common. However, the branch campus emphasis on a neoliberal global citizenship aimed at working together also reconfigured understandings of people that were still in many ways based on nationality; through finding modes of engagement across ethno-national difference, students began to recuperate and reassemble ethno-national stereotypes and parochialisms. Students were, to varying degrees, aware of these drawbacks and of ways that Qatarization policies made working together not enough to overcome structural differences from nationals. This was especially the case during career fairs, when potential employers would only consider Qatari students for certain internships or jobs. Administrators, faculty, and foreign resident students all acknowledged the structural disadvantages to noncitizens of Qatarization, but they simultaneously professed a belief in the possibilities of meritocracy within their education system. Despite these contradictions and the ways that noncitizens were ultimately excluded from the social reproduction project of knowledge economy as understood by the branch campuses, there were ways that the students themselves *as well as* Qatar Foundation and Qatari state actors perceived higher education as a public good that included them.

Education as a Public Good

The evolution of financial aid practices during the course of my research demonstrated that Qatar Foundation defined its public as one that included foreign resident diasporic youth and, to some extent, international students as well. Branch campuses, on the other hand, did not recognize local expat belongings or saw them as tangential to their narrowly defined nationalist missions, even though they recruited internationally and within Qatar for enrollment numbers and diversity metrics. How a transnational institution both impedes certain transnational connections while reinscribing others can shed light on how global citizenship is always a localized concept, and how the parochialisms built into understandings of what constitutes the global are reproduced as institutions and experts migrate. These parochial underpinnings influence how the state, as a supposedly unified actor, is understood by institutions, and how institutions in turn act as ideological state apparatuses—those that are meant to socially reproduce or hail a citizenry.[7] Most academics and foreign consultants involved in implementing branch campuses understood the Education City project as a nativist endeavor, as did US-based academics and journalists. If the demographic majority of noncitizen students even registered in most external coverage of the project, it was as a source of anxiety or an indicator of failure. Qatar's leadership, however, had never espoused a fully nativist future but rather one where, as formal citizenship was reengineered, so too was diasporic belonging. This future was heralded by a vision of higher education as a true public good, one that was not limited to the legally defined group called citizens.[8]

Gulf branch campuses are some of the most accessible elite institutions of higher learning in the world for those students who are able to learn about them through their high schools or other networks. The Qatar Foundation and the admissions offices of branch campuses recruited students from high schools in the Middle East, South Asia, Africa, and other parts of the world, as well as from high schools in Qatar and the Gulf that serve expatriate populations. This recruitment strategy diverged from the ideological focus of school mission and from the prevailing discourses within classrooms and Student Affairs programming, which pinned success first and foremost to the production of Qatari citizens as liberal subjects. These recruitment efforts, particularly for international students, often included substantial financial aid packages in the form of interest-free loans from Qatar Foundation starting from freshman year, with additional merit-based scholarship opportunities available from individual branch campuses from sophomore through senior year. For several students I interviewed, receiving aid made Education City the only financially viable high-quality option available to them. It was more affordable than comparable campuses in the West, and often even more affordable than elite colleges in their home country, whether they were coming as international students to Doha for the first time, or as local expats who may have never even set foot in the country where they held citizenship.

Interest-free loans, scholarships, and other resources were an investment by Qatar Foundation in the education of noncitizens. Despite Qatarization policies, then, the public good of the university also extended to local expat populations and international students, albeit in different ways. Students availed themselves of all sorts of opportunities offered by branch campuses, Hamad bin Khalifa University, and Qatar Foundation, including residency programs at media companies offered through Northwestern, study abroad to home campuses, access to top-of-the-line lab equipment, trips all over the world for conferences or community engagement, and free books and gear. Jobs were not guaranteed for foreign residents or international students after graduation, but the payment structures for their loans actually encouraged them to stay within Qatar, highlighting how Qatar Foundation was invested in growing a transnational workforce even as it focused on professionalizing Qatari citizens for the private sector. Many noncitizen students I spoke to planned to take advantage of Qatar Foundation's loan-forgiveness policy by working in Doha after graduation if they could secure a position, not only because it made sense fiscally, but also because they felt a sense of patriotism or connection to Qatar, and particularly to the Qatar Foundation, for investing in their education. Many also saw larger benefits of staying in Qatar for the long term—it was a Muslim and/or Arab country, family oriented, stable, and safe within the region, and a place where it was possible to earn high salaries and save money with a relatively low cost of living (many jobs provided accommodations, and expatriate students would be able to continue living at home with parents). These forms of nonnational belonging, however, were not uniform, and became more inclusive of local expats over the course of my research, while international students felt increasingly insecure about their financial viability and career prospects after graduation.

One of my final interviews for this project was with Jimmy, a senior at Georgetown whose journey to college had been especially challenging. From a Pakistani family of modest means, Jimmy had attended a British-curriculum high school in Lahore on scholarship and had graduated at the top of his class. During his senior year of high school, his mother fell very ill, and her medical bills quickly left his family destitute. This pretty much killed his hopes for attending college. He had started to apply to Ivy League and other top US universities during high school but quickly realized that his family would never be able to pay for room and board, as well as international flights, even if he received a full scholarship. So he resigned himself to working multiple jobs in order to save money. After about a year, a friend told him about Qatar Foundation and the aid they offered and encouraged him to apply. At that point, Jimmy's SAT scores had been frozen by the College Board because he owed them money—about ten dollars—which he couldn't afford to pay; so he sent in a photocopy. He explained in our interview how generous Georgetown had been in accommodating his financial situation:

I sent them an emotional email telling them I didn't have the money to send them the files; if you can make a decision based on this well and good, otherwise I am sorry for wasting your time. The next day my dad got a call on the phone, and they scheduled an interview. Not only did they make an admissions decision, they also gave me a scholarship that is only offered to four students in the incoming batch based on the strength of your application. This waived 50 percent of the tuition. The other was a loan from QF [Qatar Foundation], which is very flexible. They even offered me a ticket to get here. It was like a breath of fresh air for me, like when someone is suffocating.

Over the three and a half years he had been at Georgetown, Jimmy took advantage of every possible opportunity he could. He procured full scholarships for the remaining three years of college; he visited nine countries on sponsored trips; he won several competitive fellowships and grants; and he worked as a resident advisor, which provided a stipend, but more importantly, waived his housing fees. He also studied abroad at the main campus. While he appreciated the opportunities Georgetown had opened up for him and enjoyed meeting people from all over the world, Jimmy also had felt what he referred to as "culture shock" when encountering the lavish wealth in Education City and the income disparities between himself and other students, especially Qataris and elite local expats. He vividly remembered his arrival to Doha and how much it had troubled him:

I was the first to check in to my dorm. Turns out, that air conditioner had been working for the last two months. I come from a place where most people don't have it, and if they do they only turn it on in one room when they need it. And even then it is interjected by periods of load shedding where you don't have any electricity. I was just astonished to see the amount of affluence that is enjoyed by the people here. And the orientation activities: they took us to the desert with twenty Land Cruisers sand duning; I found the difference too stark and I took that as motivation to work hard.

Though maybe not as financially challenged as Jimmy and his family, several international students I met would not have been able to attend college without Qatar Foundation's relatively need-blind approach and the individual campus recruitment policies; the Foundation even had a program to provide full scholarships for a small number of state-less Palestinian students every year. Several students referred to this financial aid as "need blind," but this was not a transparent policy. Students had to apply annually, and packages varied from year to year, leaving families insecure about what the next year would bring, and with bills they sometimes struggled to pay. Additionally, international students, unlike their domestic peers, were required to live in residence halls, which, even though subsidized, still cost a significant amount of money. Therefore, many applied for resident advisor positions and other on-campus jobs to make ends meet. Pakistani international students, in particular, relied on a combination of loans and merit-based scholarships to fund their education. In addition, they took as many jobs as possible to pay for room and board. There were some international students who were quite affluent, whose parents were diplomats or well-paid executives; these students lived in their home countries or other parts of the world and often attended expensive private secondary schools, including boarding schools, sometimes in the United States. But they were a small subset of international students. Class differences were not as stark among local expat students, whose parents had to be earning a minimum salary in order to sponsor families in Qatar.[9] Thus foreign residents ranged from middle-class to very affluent.

When I started my research in Education City in 2010, international students did not seem to distinguish themselves as a group set apart from their diasporic peers—everyone would identify primarily with their passport nationality or with broader ethnolinguistic group-ings, such as Arab, *desi*, Levant, *khaleeji*, Western, and so forth. These identities shifted as international students became a critical mass and as their place within Education City became less certain. Although inter-national student numbers increased as Education City's reputation im-proved and as recruiting efforts extended to high schools outside of the

2016 Applicants, Accepted, and Enrolled Students

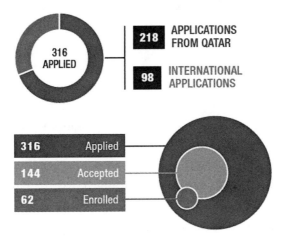

IMAGE 3. 2016 Applicants, Accepted, and Enrolled Students. Source: Georgetown University Qatar 2015/16 Annual Report.

Gulf, there was also a simultaneous push to privilege more local and regional populations of noncitizens, often through financial aid incentives that resembled Qatarization privileges. Thus, while admissions officers worked to diversify the student body, through direct visits to high schools and recruitment fairs abroad (particularly in other Arab countries), and e-marketing aimed at prospective international students, such as email blasts, social media campaigns, and live-stream open house events, they were also pressured to conduct more outreach within Qatar itself.

Admissions reporting did not always distinguish between local expats and international students, perhaps due to rising concerns about whom Education City was serving. For example, when reporting on the incoming class of 2020, Georgetown Qatar's annual report mentioned the number of international student applications but not the percentage of students accepted or enrolled from that pool. (See Image 3.) Georgetown Admissions then reported that the sixty-two students in the class of 2020 represented thirty-nine nationalities, and that twenty-six of them spoke three or more languages, while thirty-four were bilingual. These were amazing diversity statistics, but they could easily have been true of domestic or international students, and there was no way to distinguish within the report.

As recruitment efforts and reporting, shifting financial aid structures, and my interviews highlighted, budget cuts and citizen pushback against Education City did not lead away from investing in noncitizens altogether. Rather, there was a move to distinguish between noncitizens who constituted part of the local imaginary and those who were understood as foreign. Investment in expatriate belonging and civic nationalism came at the expense of international students and their ability to feel financially secure through the four-year college experience. Nabeel's story highlighted the difficulties that international students faced as Qatar Foundation restructured its financial aid and scholarship mechanisms. When we met in 2014, Nabeel had just started his sophomore year at Northwestern. He was an extremely high-achieving student from Pakistan with a 4.0 GPA. In addition to holding two on-campus jobs, he worked as a journalist for the student newspaper and was a member of student government. However, he was not sure if he would be able to afford to come back after his sophomore year. Not only were loan amounts becoming smaller across the board, but merit scholarship structures had changed, in order to privilege those noncitizens who provided the most "benefit to Qatar"—this included expatriates who had been born and raised in the country, students whose parents worked for Qatar Foundation, and others who had made a significant contribution to the country, although this latter category was never clearly defined. While the previous structure of this competitive scholarship was based solely on GPA, the new structure only allowed 50 percent of the points a student could earn toward the scholarship to come from their GPA; the other 50 percent came from the benefit-to-Qatar metric. This new rubric made it practically impossible for international students to receive the scholarships they heavily relied on. In addition, students were only notified of the change after they were already on campus and had submitted their applications, which meant that they could be left with large

bills they would be unable to pay and might have to consider withdraw-
ing altogether as early as the middle of the school year.

Nabeel considered this new policy discriminatory to international
students, and he was not alone. A group of students petitioned Northwestern about it and wanted to take their concerns to Qatar Foundation. But the university administration refused. Nabeel found this stance
from the administration very frustrating; he felt that "they didn't want
to rock the boat." He told me that across Education City, he had already
heard of three students who had dropped out due to funding changes.
In addition to the changes in financial aid, student job openings had
also shrunk due to Qatar Foundation budget cuts. South Asian students
were having an especially difficult time procuring resident advisor positions due to a new push for diversity hiring in dormitories. Nabeel felt
that he had not received a resident advisor position that year because of
his nationality:

They told me, "We ranked everyone by their applications and interviews, but
then we also brought in the element of diversity. Last year we had too many
Pakistani CDAs and this year we are trying to like make it more diverse."[10]
There was only one new Pakistani CDA selected this year. And I really needed
it. Their demand for diversity is discrimination and it affects the students and
this is why I want to go away from here as soon as I can.

When Nabeel tried to cover student employment and housing issues
in the Northwestern student newspaper, he didn't receive support from
his *desi* peers or the administration, highlighting for him growing cleav-
ages between local expat and international students, and an increasing
lack of investment by his institution and Qatar Foundation in international student inclusion and success.

A high-level administrator at Georgetown, who had been with the
university since its first year in Doha, confirmed that there had been a
turn away from international students in favor of investing in local expats. He told me that while there originally was no uniform attempt by
Qatar Foundation or the branch campuses to link to official state rhetoric
and development plans, they were now actively making those links, especially since the founding of Hamad bin Khalifa University. One major

change was the increased investment by Qatar Foundation in non-citizen locals (he also used the term "local"). Since Qatar Foundation couldn't reconcile how international students helped them with Vision 2030 and other national development goals, they were tightening loans and other benefits. For the branch campuses, however, who were beholden to home campuses, international students were of a very high academic caliber, and they brought diversity, but they were very hard to recruit without financial incentives. So there was tension between Qatar Foundation's imagining of the public that it served and the needs of the branch campuses, which continued to recruit international students but were unable to guarantee support for them and unwilling to advocate for their needs, since they were beholden to Qatar Foundation for their operating budgets. Looking closely at financial aid structures and how they changed over time highlights how the public hailed by Education City was not merely Qatari, and in some ways excluded certain Qataris—those who could not access its English-only mixed-gender spaces—while making room for local expats, who were increasingly incorporated through technologies that looked similar to Qatarization, such as the points system for benefits to Qatar in the new scholarship policy.

Affect, Performance, and Politics

Local expat belongings were marked by class status and a particular habitus that was often cultivated through childhoods spent within Westernized private K-12 schooling systems and cosmopolitan life in Doha. The most elite secondary schools resembled the international partnership models of higher education, such as branch campuses. DeBakey High School in Doha, for example, was a branch of an elite Houston high school. The Varkey group, a multinational firm that had a stronghold in the Middle East and was owned by a wealthy Indian businessman, managed several prominent schools.[11] These schools provided the preparatory liberal citizenship training required to successfully maneuver within Western universities. Many wealthier cosmopolitan Qatari families, especially after voucher programs were introduced, opted for these types of schools, as did upper-class expatriate families. Given the predominantly privatized K-12 educational landscape, most local expat students, along with many of their Qatari peers, came into Education City equipped with the basic vocabulary and cultural capital required to succeed within American university spaces. This elite generation was decidedly transnational. Belonging on campus for noncitizens, however, meant modeling liberal student citizenship, exhibiting civic nationalism, *and* accepting that being local did not mean being any closer to becoming Qatari, except in rare circumstances. The experiences of local expats suggested a shared sense of home, however tenuous and uneven, that branch campuses enabled between Qatari and non-Qatari residents. Local expats overwhelmingly occupied the center of campus life and were exemplary student citizens. They participated in multiple extracurricular pursuits, frequently organizing activities, applying for research grants, and running student government and clubs. In our interviews, they enthusiastically recalled the relationships they had built with faculty and staff, and especially the pride they had in their friendships with Qatari students, although the ability to form those friendships was impacted by linguistic, class, ethnic, and religious backgrounds.

Several of my Arab interlocutors, especially those from diasporic communities that had been in Qatar for multiple generations, such as Libyans, Palestinians, and Yemenis, or those from mixed backgrounds (usually with Qatari fathers), had many Qatari friends. Some had grown up in Qatari neighborhoods and attended Qatari schools. Many spoke with *khaleeji*-accented Arabic, and a handful even wore thaub or abaya. A few were also naturalized or in the process of naturalizing. These intimacies highlighted how the official boundaries of citizenship were constantly shifting. At the time of my research, exceptions to citizenship regulations were also linked to Qatari national vision and branding goals, such as sports team membership and medical training.[12] As areas in the Middle East became less accessible due to war and political repression, some of my interlocutors looked at educational achievement as a path to relative permanence, if not formal citizenship. Degrees from Education City could lead to enough income to sponsor family members to live in Qatar or purchase freehold property (which came with a visa), to better marriage prospects, or to the ability to migrate and obtain citizenship elsewhere, and then possibly return to the Gulf.

In addition to the cultural capital with which they entered college and the cross-national intimacies the university space fostered, South Asian and Middle Eastern local expats also told me that they felt comfortable in Qatar in ways they could not imagine in Europe or North America, and often in the countries where they held passports as well. Few of them experienced racial and/or religious minority status in the Gulf, and they also enjoyed middle-class stability, all of which they would have to sacrifice attending university in the United States or Europe. This concern was legitimized when they experienced discrimination upon visiting home campuses, where they had to fend for themselves away from parents and domestic workers. The ability to stay within the comforts of home and access such high-quality education, with the likelihood of attaining a lucrative job eventually, even though it meant enduring a period of insecurity that their Qatari peers did not have to face, increased their patriotism toward Qatar. Unlike international students, local expats were not as critical of Qatarization, perhaps due to their class status and stable homes in Doha, and perhaps because they had been raised in a space where politicization was not encouraged.

Generally, the sentiment seemed to be that jobs were hard to find, but that there were connections in Qatar one could leverage in ways that one would not be able to in larger, unfamiliar countries. A graduating senior told me, "Everyone eventually gets placed but it takes the *desis* longer." Residency and sponsorship rules were also more flexible in practice for middle-class expatriates than they might appear: while sons technically could not stay on their parents' visas after graduating college, many still managed to stay sponsored as dependents for several years as they looked for employment.[13] Daughters, meanwhile, did not face as many career-related anxieties, because they could stay on their parents' visas until and even after marriage, and some preferred to do so because jobs were more readily available if they did not require sponsorship. In addition to the sense that "everyone eventually got placed," students acknowledged that Qatar Foundation and the private sector were investing directly in high-achieving local expats. A Qatari company had sponsored Aman's master's degree in the United States, for example, which further deferred his undergraduate loan payback time and guaranteed him employment upon return. Other programs, like the Qatar Science Leadership Program, were designed to encourage Qatari and foreign resident scholars to pursue postgraduate education abroad and then return to Qatar and work in the growing research sector.[14] These scholarships similarly guaranteed jobs, waived loans, and even included generous stipends for living expenses during graduate study.

In my previous research, I found that South Asian diasporic youth who grew up with the knowledge that they might not be able to settle in the UAE normalized uncertain futures and created globally dispersed networks of friends as they moved into college life, marriage, and the workforce.[15] Like my interlocutors in the UAE, seeming less concerned might have become a script for local expat students in Education City. Their seemingly lax attitudes did not mean that local expat students were complacent about the structural inequalities built into higher education, migration, and residency in Qatar, however. Some of my Arab student interlocutors during uprisings in their home countries, and especially Syrian students as my research project progressed, were clearly quite desperate to find jobs in places where they could procure citizenship for themselves, their parents, and their siblings. Many expatriate students acknowledged that the system was unfair and expressed frustration about it. Some also grew politicized by drawing parallels between the structural inequalities and racism that shaped their lives and the lives of migrant laborers, including *chaiwallahs*,[16] groundskeepers, and janitorial staff on campus, who they often identified with as co-ethnics. Their narratives diverged from those of international students and some Qataris, who more directly challenged state policies and educational structures. Instead, local expat students used the civic participation skills they learned in university as a platform for initiating forms of change, producing a greater sense of belonging to Doha and Qatar, but without advocating for rights for themselves in terms of a liberal sense of citizenship and equality before the state.

During my time in Doha, I met a diverse group of Georgetown students and alumni who had used the skills they had learned running clubs on campus to start an NGO (registered outside Qatar) that focused on migrant labor support. Donating volunteer hours and tapping into contacts around the world, they conducted casework, raised community awareness, applied for funding, and consulted with international human rights groups. Other students had taught migrant workers English, used their language skills to make sure that Qatar Foundation maintained the best practices it had adopted under its migrant welfare initiative, used the journalism skills they were learning at Northwestern to report on labor abuses and other social justice issues around Doha, and participated in mental health and other community outreach campaigns.[17] Their class papers and projects did not shy away from controversial topics, such as Islamism, women's rights, or internet censorship.

They also maintained a belief in Education City as primarily an egalitarian space, however, and often described Qatari inequalities as milder than those in the United States, where international students had almost no chance of procuring jobs after graduating from university. These seemingly contradictory observations of the university as a space of hierarchy and egalitarianism did not seem to create much conflict for students, whose narratives would contain, sometimes even in the same sentence, acknowledgment of how both were structuring forces in their everyday lives. For example, while Aman praised Texas A&M Qatar and Education City for challenging students' preconceived notions of other nationalities, he was aware that jobs and sponsorships were preferentially given to Qataris, and that expatriates like himself would have a harder time procuring employment and would never be able to officially belong. Global citizenship, while an ideal that he and his counterparts believed in, was therefore inextricable from the bifurcated system that Qatarization produced. To illustrate, Aman described two classmates, one a Qatari woman, one a Bangladeshi man. They both were hired at the same time at the national gas company: "He was better in grades but couldn't get hired as an engineer because of their policy. He is a tech and she is his boss now. I put myself in his place and I wonder how I would feel. I would feel bad . . . but also be grateful for the opportunity."

Aman and his peers mostly navigated their criticisms of Qatar through their positions as guests in a host society, and through forms of activism that could be framed as leadership, philanthropy, or part of Islamic duty. Local expats stressed that the preferential treatment Qataris received in admissions, sponsorships, and placement was necessary because Qataris lacked the competitive advantage that other expatriates had from their international K-12 schooling, and because it was "their country" after all. They overwhelmingly espoused neoliberal understandings of their own successes in the Gulf, attributing their ability to succeed vis-à-vis both their compatriots and expatriates from other nationalities to self-entrepreneurship.[18] Aman's neoliberal understandings of work ethic and success therefore coexisted quite seamlessly with his acceptance of the illiberal policies of Qatarization, with systems of white/ Western privilege that were built into the American university system, and with a discourse of respect for Qatari customs and laws. These multiple logics of belonging permeated the spaces of Education City and of Qatar in general, but they were not unique to the Gulf context.[19] The comparisons my interlocutors made with American academic spaces and the United States revealed an understanding of similar multiple and contradictory logics at work there as well. Understanding these contradictions in Qatar prompted students to criticize the American academy, which, in their view, failed to live up to its egalitarian promise. Criticism of liberal education and home campuses by all students, but especially by local expats, was itself a site of citizenship production, one that highlighted the inherent contradictions of liberalism but also the branch campuses' unintended success in increasing belonging to Qatar among a population that they were not directly targeting, and in producing a located global citizenship that adopted liberal and neoliberal skill sets to frame postcolonial challenges to Western hegemony.

Aman told me that he understood Education City was primarily for Qataris, and he was mostly fine with that, but because he had lived in Doha all his life and his father had done well there, his family members should have some kind of security. At this point in the interview, I asked him whether the branch campuses could ever be commensurable with the home campuses, since they provide built-in advantages to citizens. Aman disagreed quite strongly with my assessment of the difference between American home campuses and branch campuses: "But they have a bias there [US] based on your visa status, you know, if you are an international student. Good luck getting a job, good luck getting an internship. Here you see what you are getting into." Aman's sentiment was echoed in many of my interviews across Education City and within my classrooms as well—the United States was inherently discriminatory of certain groups, particularly international students (especially those who were read as Arab or Muslim), who paid higher tuitions, had trouble procuring visas, and were less likely to find employment after graduation than they would be in Qatar, since the one-on-one opportunities to network and meet people in a small place like Doha were much higher. Thus, for local expats, American universities in the United States were more unequal in their treatment of noncitizens than American universities in Qatar.

In addition to the inequality that international students felt they would face in the United States, many who had visited the home campuses of their institutions came back disillusioned, particularly due to the coldness and racism they experienced. Aman had learned so many of the Texas A&M traditions while in Doha, but after seeing them up close, they did not feel as special as he thought they would. He had trouble navigating the large scale of the institution. And he felt out of place in a white rural Southern town where he felt that people were unwilling to make the effort to understand his accent. Most of all, his classroom experiences were disappointing and made him realize how much personal attention he got from faculty at the branch campus and how many more resources he had access to there. In addition, he was able to stay at home with his family while in college instead of having to adjust to living alone in a new location, where he had to learn to buy groceries, do laundry, cook, take public transportation, and had no friends who spoke Urdu or were Muslim. I heard from almost all Muslim students that they felt disrespected and out of place in the drinking and dating culture of home campuses: South Asian and Arab students noted discrimination at the airport, in college towns, and even in classrooms; and all students struggled to make friends, navigate the larger scale of the main campuses, and get face time with faculty members. One Egyptian student at Georgetown told me, "Qatar is very warm, especially the university—one guy goes to the vending machine and he brings back seven Pepsi cans because there are seven of us. That kind of environment, it's so warm. That's not an American mentality." Several of my interlocutors had even started university abroad and then transferred to Education City. Nisreen, a Bangladeshi woman with Canadian citizenship, attended a university in California for one year and was so unhappy with the treatment she received in the college town there that she transferred to Northwestern Qatar, even though she was not interested in pursuing any of the majors offered in Education City. As a *hijabi*, she was tired of the constant stares and fear of harassment, as well as the effort of trying to find halal food everywhere she went. After weighing her options, she decided, "I prefer my freedom so I would rather come and study here." In doing so, she sacrificed the public health career that she originally wanted to pursue. Other students were surprised by the homogeneity of US universities, which tout diversity in all of their recruitment brochures.

Lara, a graduate of Georgetown Qatar whose family was originally from Lebanon, had started her studies at the main campus before transferring to Doha. After growing up in international schools, she found the whiteness of Washington, DC, jarring, proclaiming, "Thirty white kids and two Latinos in a class, how is that diversity?" Coupled with feeling homesick and not fitting in among the Muslim Students Association on campus, which she felt was overly dogmatic and expected a singular performance of Muslim identity, Lara decided to try the branch campus, where she enjoyed smaller class sizes and closer relationships with her professors, and made a close group of friends from many backgrounds, mainly Qatari and diasporic Arab. After graduating from Georgetown Qatar in 2013, Lara had been working in Doha, still under her mother's sponsorship. When we met, she was contemplating going to graduate school in the social sciences to study the Gulf region. Her social position and life experiences had driven her critical engagement with the topics she studied in college as a politics major, and now she wanted to take those interests even further, a sign to me and to her mentors, who had referred her to me with great pride, that she was a successful student who not only excelled at course material but also embodied the subjectivity that liberal education purports to cultivate.

The local expat students I met articulated a global citizenship that distinctly pushed against an American or Western form of being global, in favor of localized understandings of both their opportunities and their limitations as situated actors in Qatar and in a globalized economy. This was not a view from nowhere or a non-grounded global citizenship at all, nor was it simply the product of increased neoliberal creep into higher education (the product of a project to work together). Instead, it was very much a view from somewhere that was also cosmopolitan at the same time, as all cosmopolitanisms are.[20] Students, understanding quite well the contradictions of being educated in an American university, were pushing back against the social engineering that was implied by this educational form. In this way, they were quite similar to their postcolonial predecessors educated in the West. As one South Asian faculty member—a mentor of Lara's—told me, reflecting on this comparison based on her experiences of attending an undergraduate college in the United States:

We are not brainwashed. We continue to think critically about US foreign policy. We continue to think critically about Orientalist approaches . . . we continue to think critically about hegemony, right? It's not just the sort of . . . I'm wearing jeans, I'm drinking Coke, and you know, you suddenly think America is wonderful. That is what I think is really strange, is that people assume, you know, if you're going to eat McDonalds, you're going to an American school, you're going to love America. I think that's not true.

Conclusion

The forms of global citizenship that branch campuses in the Gulf produced were not disconnected from forms of postcolonial citizenship or from prior forms of colonial education in the Global South.[21] The contemporary process of institutional transplant creates a binary in which the academic metropole seems to produce scholars (those who can be cosmopolitan), while branch campuses seem solely focused on civilizational uplift and neoliberal outcomes of self-making and economic success after graduation. Education City's multiversity model, for example, where each branch campus granted degrees in their specific areas of international expertise—Northwestern for communications and journalism, Texas A&M for engineering, Virginia Commonwealth for arts, and so forth—could be read solely in neoliberal and neocolonial terms. Although we should rightfully be suspicious of both of these aspects of the transnational American university, Eng-Ben Lim argues that we should also allow "room for speculations of an ethical plurality and mimetic infidelity at the satellite campuses" rather than writing them off under these grand critiques.[22]

The small class sizes, availability of resources, and access to faculty made the branch campus experience feel more like a liberal arts college for many students, especially local expats, than the supposedly more authentic home campus. Branch campuses for these students inspired forms of citizenship, cosmopolitanism, engagement, and critique that looked more liberal than outcomes in the United States. Student criticisms of metropolitan American higher education, and the comparisons they made between the United States and Qatar, challenged the normalizations through which home and branch, center and periphery, local and global, and university transplant in general were discussed and debated. Even though most of these students could not become legal citizens of Qatar, they were indeed part of its emerging transnational elite, and as such their experiences might gesture to similar class-based divides that were taking place elsewhere. But at the same time, many of the noncitizen graduates of Education City were not wealthy at all, and although some were pulled into the Qatari workforce, others did not stay in Doha or even the region. The experiences of this student population provide an excellent site for exploring the unanticipated effects, or mimetic infidelities, of university transplant, operating within two seemingly incommensurate frameworks—Qatarization and global citizenship.

CHAPTER 5

Expat/Expert Camps

In my first days conducting research for this project, I met Margaret, a human resources staff member at one of the branch campuses. We immediately became friends.[1] One Thursday afternoon, after a late lunch in the upscale Landmark Mall, we decided to start our weekend early and not return to our offices (Thursday was the last day of the work week in Doha). Margaret invited me to hang out at her place, in a newly constructed gated community near the mall. About a ten-minute drive from Education City, Margaret lived alone in a three-bedroom villa, provided to her as part of the benefits package that came with her employment. I was a bit surprised to see its state of disarray, since most expatriate housing I had been in before was sparsely furnished and cleaned regularly by paid workers. The front hall was lined with goods that Margaret stocked up on during weekend errands: flats of diet cola and water bottles, beer and wine cases, and plastic shopping bags. The living room was packed with furniture and other objects Margaret had collected over the five years she had lived in Qatar, ranging from modern pieces to antique styles reminiscent of Indian or Persian designs.[2] Her most recent purchase, a baby grand piano, took up most of the center of the room, and everything else had been pushed to the edges in order to accommodate this new arrival. Between work, her boyfriend (who lived in a compound nearby), music lessons, socializing, and a charity she was involved in, she hadn't had time to pick up around the house lately, she apologetically explained. I understood the feeling quite well. Since I had arrived in Doha ten days earlier, I had been rushing around as well. Between finishing my syllabi and familiarizing myself with a new institution, learning my way around the city, and dealing with the bureaucracy of establishing residency, my hotel apartment in Doha's swanky West Bay neighborhood—also provided by my employer— looked like a tornado had come through. The housekeeping staff cleaned around my mess, not wanting to disturb what might be my own form of organized chaos.

Margaret's busy Doha life took place, like mine, in three or four key sites: work in Education City, where she arrived every morning at eight and left around four;[3] upscale shopping malls and hotels, where she ate her meals, did her shopping, and spent leisure time; and villas or apartments in gated compounds and high rises, where her friends and associates lived.[4] In those spaces, she encountered a multinational group of people, including a large number of (mostly white) Americans, Canadians, and Europeans who, like her, had come to Doha on renewable contracts to work in managerial or upper-level administrative positions. In Education City, for example, the majority of Margaret's coworkers and friends were American or Canadian. Her interactions with Qataris, Arabs, and South Asians were mostly limited to students and clerical or service staff, although through her philanthropic work she was acquainted with a small group of wealthy Qatari and Arab expatriate women who occasionally invited her to their homes for tea.[5]

This final ethnographic chapter focuses on Education City's faculty and staff, who were central to the ways that ideas about culture, difference, progress, and liberal education manifested within branch campuses. Like Margaret, these actors were primarily recruited from North America and Europe as experts in education and earned more than they would for comparable jobs in their home countries. Their seemingly cosmopolitan ethos, their English-language skills and, for many, their whiteness, translated to a value-add within Qatar's job market. They were often able to leverage their identities and networks to advance quickly through the ranks of the branch campus, when similar positions on main campuses would have required further years of training or experience. On top of receiving higher salaries than their Arab or Asian counterparts, these Western expatriates also had their housing, children's schooling, and travel back to their home countries subsidized by their employers. And they had access to top services and consumer products from around the world that were brought into the country for their consumer desires and national tastes.

The 2008 global economic recession made it harder to procure and maintain employment in Europe and North America for young people with college degrees, making the Gulf region even more appealing as a site for labor migration. Thus Margaret and those like her were embedded in the same economic systems that drove South Asian, Filipino, and African migrants to places like Qatar. Once in the Gulf, Western expatriates, like their Global South counterparts, also established forms of belonging, affective ties, and community formations that exceeded the economic narratives through which they expressed their reasons for coming and deciding to stay. Margaret, for example, told me she felt at home in Doha more than she had anywhere else in the world. The people were friendlier, more family oriented, and more cosmopolitan. However, when she referred to people in Doha, Margaret mostly meant other expatriates like herself. She rarely mentioned lower-wage foreign residents, except to express pity or complain about their poor work; nor did she share many positive views on Qataris beyond the few she personally knew. I introduce the term "expat/expert camp" to highlight how Education City's faculty and staff were both laborers segregated into compounds and a privileged elite who could enjoy the pleasures of racial and class segregation. They largely disavowed their complicity in the structural inequalities that produced white/Western elite status and geographies of segregation in the city; and they felt they had little ability to enact change in a system that they attributed to an illiberal, repressive state. Margaret and those like her were both enabled by our social and geopolitical locations as well as circumscribed by them. I include myself in this category since I benefitted from my Western expertise while in the Gulf, although white privilege was not available to me.

Embodied Expertise

Despite their intended goals of achieving Qatarization, knowledge-economy projects have created many job opportunities for foreign professionals, particularly North Americans and those educated in Western university settings, who moved to Qatar in large numbers over the last two decades to work as faculty, administrators, consultants, and service providers in educational venues, culture and media industries, and health care.[6] Both Qatar Foundation and individual branch campuses employed headhunting agencies to recruit foreigners who embodied the expertise required to achieve global competitiveness and modernity. These hiring practices built on an established legacy of reliance on Western consultants for nation building in the Gulf. The branch campuses placed a high value on American degrees for faculty hiring, as well as for most mid- to high-level administrative staff. But this preference did not explain why faculty and administrators were recruited so heavily from the United States and other Western countries, when elites from around the world, including the Gulf, held degrees from top American universities. Given Qatarization goals, it was also surprising that there was only one Qatari faculty member across all of the branch campuses during the span of my research, who left a couple years after I started the project for a local institution within Hamad bin Khalifa University (HBKU). When branch campuses employed Qatari staff, of which there were few, they were usually tasked with human resources liaison work in order to capitalize on their Arabic skills and *wasta* (connections), or they served as receptionists. Higher-level Qatari administrators worked either for Qatar Foundation, or were hired later, as part of HBKU staff or for the newer local institutions opening within Education City. They were therefore part of Qatar Foundation's direct restructuring toward a more publicly oriented university that focused on local heritage and community outreach.

While branch campuses marketed themselves as bastions of diversity, they often sold their expertise through whiteness, featuring white faculty on their websites and marketing materials, a common marketing technique overseas for Western as well as non-Western goods and services, including education.[7] Branch campuses were not very diverse as one moved higher up the ranks of faculty and administration. This contrasted sharply with the diversity of the student body, and with staff in other departments, such as IT or human resources. Different jobs were allocated for those hired internationally and those hired locally. The preference for Western, mostly white, faculty and higher administration was compounded by pay and benefits structures that divided along national, racial, and gendered lines. The resulting hierarchy was often blamed on Qatar's ethnocratic migration and residency regime, when it was actually set rather autonomously by the branch campuses themselves.[8] I heard numerous complaints of discrimination from nonwhite and non-Western educators and staff during our interviews, which fed into Gulf social hierarchies as well as American academic ones, some of which I myself experienced as a woman of color faculty member among primarily white colleagues.

I sat down one afternoon in December 2014 with Bill, an administrator at Georgetown who had been with the institution from the beginning. He explained how pay scales had changed over time. At first, top executives like him were recruited from the corporate world, not from academia, using corporate pricing benchmarks, and utilizing private search firms. For this reason, pay scales within Education City were not that much different than in other business sectors. Individual branch campuses paid exorbitant salaries and gave generous incentive packages to US-based academics and administrators in order to encourage them to relocate. This included a moving allowance (often over ten thousand dollars), business class tickets for the entire family twice a year, free housing or a housing allowance, free schooling for children, a car allowance, and sometimes even a furnishing allowance, cell phone allowance, and other perks. In some cases, Canadians, Brits, and other Europeans also received these top packages. This meant that faculty and middle administration from the United States became significantly overpaid in comparison to their counterparts in the United States, as well as their counterparts from other countries at the branch campus. Salaries were usually at least 25–30 percent above what a tenured faculty member could make at the home campus. None of these benefits were available to those staff members hired from less privileged national backgrounds into lower status positions, such as South Asians working in IT; nor were they available to non-Western faculty members.

Many administrators I met when I first arrived would have been underqualified were we to compare their credentials to similarly situated deans and heads of staff in the United States. Some were even recruited into high-level positions with almost no qualifications when the branch campuses were in the start-up phase. One of my interlocutors, now back in the United States, told me she was hired as an assistant dean at the age of twenty-five, when she was working in an entry-level administrative position at the main campus; she did not have a completed PhD at the time. She simply attended a recruiting meeting for the branch campus and got the job on the spot. She added that if she were a man, she might have been able to get the job with just a bachelor's degree, since she had seen less qualified men come in with higher salaries than hers during her time in Qatar.

Due to several complaints of discrimination, Bill told me Georgetown changed their hiring policy around 2008 and designated every non-Qatari as an expatriate. Pay was then set based on letter grades. All faculty would be at grade A, for example. This way, there would be no discrimination based on country of origin or residency status. However, according to staff members I spoke to in 2014, not much had changed, for jobs that tapped into local talent (i.e. people already residing in the country) were usually ranked at a lower grade, and therefore paid less and came with fewer benefits; these jobs were filled primarily by Arab and South Asian foreign residents. Often, these were women on their husbands' sponsorships, working in administrative positions and not eligible for the lucrative housing, schooling, and travel allowances that their North American peers received. These women often felt they could not ask for employer sponsorship without risking being turned down for jobs, or risking losing the job after they were hired. Nor did they feel they could bargain for higher salaries, because they were not getting this incentive. Thus the gendered inequalities in pay among staff were readily perpetuated by branch campuses, which saw benefits not as money but as perks that should not matter to some subjects in (Islamic) heteropatriarchal society.[9]

The stratified recruitment and pay scales in the branch campuses, as well as the lack of diversity at the top levels, reflected the ways that, even in spaces where there was no white majority, academia and liberal imaginaries of higher education remained inflected by whiteness.[10] Since I started my research in 2010, Qatar Foundation has attempted to make Education City more accessible to the public, and HBKU's growth made the branch campuses a much smaller part of the campus as a whole. Doha's rapid urban growth also meant that the campus was no longer remote but within the borders of the city. However, these changes did not impact the perception by Doha's residents (on social media or in personal conversations) that Education City was a distinct, inaccessible compound and a Western and white space, similar to the city's hotels and luxury residential areas, despite the variety of people one encountered when inside.

White Liberal Enclaves

It is commonplace to name certain multinational and multiethnic spaces in the Gulf as Indian or Filipino or Lebanese, while also acknowledging that this naming does not encapsulate the diversity of people that inhabits these spaces. There seems to be a reluctance, however, on the part of many scholars to similarly address the whiteness of certain spaces—spaces they themselves often occupy—when the on-the-ground experiences of most field researchers include racial segregation, boundary policing, and a naturalized sense of where one does and doesn't belong in urban space based on skin color, nationality, gender, and/or class status. Whiteness operated in conjunction with other markers to produce exclusionary spaces and communities in Doha.[11] Education City's expat/expert faculty and staff were inculcated into a system of race that was not disconnected from the one they experienced in their home countries. Their discourses and everyday practices, in turn, reified the imperial underpinnings of ethno-national labor market segmentation in Qatar, and the ways that white supremacy structured multiple forms of value, both inside and outside the university space.[12]

Margaret preferred her cosmopolitan life in an international city like Doha to living in the United States because she was able to participate in and benefit from practices of cultural and racial segregation, preferring to be with like-minded individuals without having to explicitly acknowledge her complicity in the discriminatory structures that gave her access to elite white, Western spaces. The sense that whiteness was in peril at home due to multiculturalism, immigration, and post-9/11 fears of terrorism ironically intensified the sense of comfort that many Western expatriates felt in these exclusive communities.[13] Taking pleasure from structures of racism and segregation—a practice that by definition was the opposite of the liberal values that expatriates promoted in their academic lives—was readily passed off as a product of illiberal Gulf authoritarianism or backward Qatari culture, rather than attributed to legacies of white supremacy. In the process, white liberal belief in liberalism became even more solidly entrenched. My everyday interactions with colleagues in Education City and with other Western expatriates I met in Doha highlighted how quickly these beliefs became normalized.

Lizbeth and her husband Mark had been living in Doha for three years when I first met them. In a post-recession economy, Mark was thrilled to get a lucrative management position at an oil company, and the couple relocated from the United States with their two small children while Lizbeth was writing her dissertation. She had procured a permanent teaching position in Education City soon after obtaining her PhD and was quite happy there. The family lived on the Pearl, the most exclusive luxury development in Doha, which was on an artificial island near the West Bay neighborhood where I stayed when I was employed for short-term teaching. Their large four-bedroom apartment was provided by Mark's employer, and they employed a live-in nanny to help with childcare. The couple also had a driver who seemed to be on call most of the time, although they both drove their own cars, rather expensive SUVs. I remember noting their incredible generosity when I visited their home: they ordered delivery of a sushi dinner, poured several bottles of expensive wine over the course of the evening, insisted I stay in one of their empty guest rooms the next time I was in town (why should I pay for a hotel when they had so much space?), and even sent me home with their driver so I would not worry about paying for a cab.

Arriving as a faculty member from the United States to Doha, I found the lifestyle of Lizbeth and her colleagues jarring, since faculty in the United States did not get paid nearly as much as their counterparts in the Gulf, nor did they tend to spend their money in the same ways. Lizbeth was always decked out in designer clothes, as were her children; the family went to Europe or Asia at least once a month on short holidays; weekends were spent dining at expensive hotels or luxuriating at spas; and no one seemed very concerned about money and spending at all. Lizbeth's friends, mostly other women faculty and staff in Education City, would, like me and my colleagues in the United States, go out regularly for drinks to gripe about college bureaucracy and departmental politics, but that was where our similarities ended. When I tagged along on their girls' nights, they would also talk about their nannies, either complaining about them and their quality of work, or asking for recommendations for new ones, or bragging about how they had done something nice for them, like paying for a flight home to the Philippines when a relative there passed away. They also spent a lot of time telling me or other newcomers about Qatari cultural norms and taboos, often lowering voices to discuss the latest human rights violation or labor abuse scandal to hit the news. It would be impossible to get through an evening without hearing generalized statements about practically every nationality that had a presence in Doha. As a South Asian American woman, this was particularly challenging, because most generalizations would be about Indians, Nepalis, or Pakistanis—the term "Indian" was a stand-in for almost anything negative that was being discussed about South Asian migrants, such as sexism, poor quality of work, lack of hygiene, and bad driving.[14] I found myself leaving such gatherings either blowing up at someone or quietly fuming and vowing to never go out with white expatriates again. But, as social options were limited among colleagues, I regularly found myself back out for drinks with white faculty. As I spoke to other faculty of color over the course of my research, I realized that I was not alone in my experiences and frustrations.

While the above paints my Doha-based colleagues in a disturbing contrast to academics in the United States, I want to suspend this criticism, for my description is meant as a way to explore first, how we all participate in contradictory practices and discourses wherever we live;[15] and second, to point out that while the content of conversations with predominantly white faculty in Doha might have been different, faculty of color's sense of exclusion from the social spaces of academic life was not. What the above sketch highlights is how certain pleasures of explicit racial segregation and elite status were a normalized part of everyday life for white expatriates in Doha in ways they were not—or rather were implicit or had to be hidden—in the United States due to the same structures of white supremacy, structures that produced ideas of liberal/illiberal and civilized/barbaric through which expatriates understood and explained their migratory decisions, social status, and everyday lives in Doha and Education City. Almost all of my interlocutors expressed a sense of shock and guilt about the racial hierarchy and labor conditions they encountered on arrival. This white liberal guilt manifested in awkward attempts to engage custodial staff and *chaiwallahs* in conversation, or in jokes about how people made presumptions about their nonwhite friends or spouses being maids or nannies (I myself had such jokes directed at me both during my previous research in Dubai and during this research in Doha). Expatriates also deployed culture talk about the backwardness of Qatari traditions or even Islam to explain the inequalities around them.[16] Meanwhile, they expressed pleasure at the comforts of Doha life, the Western amenities available to them, and the safety and family-friendly environment of the city and the compounds in which they lived.[17] Colleagues they spoke with before arriving told them, and they readily believed, that they should not do anything to rock the boat because of Qatar's authoritarian government and nontransparent policing. Interestingly, I found that this belief never changed for most of my interlocutors regardless of how long they lived in Qatar, even those who claimed that they enjoyed unfettered academic freedom and had never experienced repressive state power.[18] Because they thought of themselves as temporary guests in the country, they trafficked in a discourse of respect for their hosts, and they attributed Qatar's monarchial and nondemocratic government to essentialized and often Orientalist representations of Qatari culture, thereby both recuperating a liberal/illiberal binary and also legitimizing Qatari state power.[19]

My interlocutors were also troubled by the country's dismal labor conditions, which tested their liberal values; but, as several pointed out to me, given an illiberal and repressive state, what could they possibly do to produce change? Some entirely exempted themselves from complicity in the system, employing nannies and maids they claimed to treat better than the Qataris, who they blamed for labor abuses.[20] Only a few mentioned the similarities between Gulf hierarchies and those in so-called liberal contexts, noting the exploitation of undocumented workers in the United States, for example. Expatriate discourses around labor conditions often highlighted their own lack of privilege as noncitizens, the expectation that they too were transient subjects, and the belief that power was more repressive in the Gulf than in supposedly liberal places like the ones they considered home. They believed they were more egalitarian, and thus superior to Qataris and other non-Westerners. Thus the process of migrating made them more liberal, for they constructed their subjectivities as embodying different values than the ones they understood to be circulating there.[21]

Whereas in the United States, some white faculty are still reluctant to discuss race—even in the academy, where conversations about race and diversity are common—colleagues in Qatar were conversant in race and culture talk. First, the question "Where are you from?" was standard—because the majority of people were from elsewhere, it was one of the first things that people asked when introducing themselves, and there was no offense built into it. Race, migration, intermarriage (especially since this was an accepted practice among many Muslims), and citizenship were conversational topics and not overly intimate for most people. In the classroom, faculty could not avoid these topics, as they were expected to perform and explain their own "Where are you from?" and they often expected students to do the same, as did students of each other. So while white faculty and staff might have exempted themselves from the civilizational aspects of their pedagogy, I rarely found that they were uncomfortable naming themselves as white or Western. The naming of whiteness actually worked to make unnamed forms of white supremacy even more invisible and insidious. It allowed liberal whites to ignore deeper forms of racial privilege by enacting liberal antiracist subjectivities.[22] Liberal whiteness relegates the white supremacist roots of Western intellectual concepts to the past, eliding how white supremacy continues to animate liberalism's present. This leaves room only to name overt and particular instances as racist, not structures or climate. In Qatar's expatriate worlds, the traffic in this kind of post-racial whiteness played out through cultural relativism, that most humanist of colonial products: as respect for Qatari culture and difference (a difference that was always inherently inferior) that allowed for guilt-free enclaving and segregated sociality, but without having to name them as such. White expat/experts were after all not *those* racists—the ones burning crosses or denying the Holocaust—but rather humanists who formed their identities through the discourses of multiculturalism circulating within the academy and global capitalism.

Stigma and Stagnation

Whiteness operated not only as a marker of privilege in Qatar but also as a particular form of labor. For faculty, it could also be a source of stigmatized labor as one moved away from the metropolitan centers of academia. There is very little ethnographic scholarship on middle and upper-class migrants to the Arabian Peninsula, particularly Europeans and North Americans, and in this scholarship they are rarely considered as laboring subjects. The limited accounts that address the work experiences of expatriates in the Gulf and challenge the male South

Asian construction worker as archetypical Gulf migrant also understand migration primarily through market fundamentalism and *homo economicus* rationality.[23] In the process they elide how intimacies, affects, and identities generate and are generated by migration and residency in the Gulf, specifically those connected to histories of race, imperialism, and Indian Ocean connectivity. In contrast, I suggest an approach to foreign residents' lived experiences that asks why labor becomes the primary defining feature for some migrants but not for others. This requires acknowledging that *no* person is reducible either to their labor or to their leisure/consumption. Field research among all migrant groups, then, should be attentive to the complexities of migrant desires, community building, and modes of both leisure and work. This kind of research is especially scarce among so-called expat populations. For example, while there has been significant negative media coverage of the afterhours lives of Westerners in the Gulf, particularly aimed at excessive drinking, heterosexual sex practices, and nightclub life, little attention has been paid to how these groups produce vibrant spaces of socialization and intimacy that counterbalance the work regimes that define much of their everyday existence.[24] Nor is there much critical attention given to how modes of governance in the Gulf create spaces of containment for well-paid expatriates and encourage only certain expatriate groups to perform heteronormativity through nightlife behavior on the one hand, or nuclear family structures, on the other, based on ethno-racial hierarchies of pay benefits, which include spousal and family allowances, solo accommodations, and/or the ability to purchase alcohol only for a privileged few.[25]

I found that Western employees in Education City were subject to continuous job insecurity even though they lived luxurious lifestyles in comparison to their US-based counterparts. Faculty and staff across all universities, disciplines, and job titles experienced this insecurity, regardless of time spent in Qatar or tenure status. This was due to a number of factors. The first was expatriates' status as foreign residents whose visas were tied to their employment. If for any reason they were asked to leave Qatar or not allowed back in, their employment would effectively be terminated. The stern advice given to them to heed Qatari laws and customs, but without much more detail on what this meant—especially when expatriate lifestyles in Doha did not diverge much from what they would be in the West—left people with generalized anxiety and led them to rely more on urban legends and essentialized notions of culture rather than gather their own information about legality and illegality, or even work off of their lived experience. A handful of faculty I met had tenure at their home campuses and had decided to come to Doha for a short while before either retiring or going back, but almost all hiring was done directly by the branch campuses. Many faculty members took positions in Doha after failing to get a job in North America or Europe. And many faculty positions were billed as tenure track, but there was no actual way to ensure permanence for expatriates, who could not gain access to citizenship or permanent residency. Instead, most tenure-track hires in the branch campuses were on rolling contracts. This meant that the tenure candidate went through a review process akin to tenure, with comparable standards and often involving home campus personnel. If successful, they were promoted to the associate professor level and would not have to go through review again—their contract would just be automatically renewed. This process, however, did not protect the faculty member from Qatar Foundation, which was responsible for issuing visas, or from the government of Qatar, which could deny entry at the airport or initiate deportation for any reason. I also found that many, though by no means all, faculty felt they had less autonomy under their branch campus superiors than they would in the United States: they were sometimes expected to be in Doha during the summers (a few had to teach), and work expectations that were laid out upon hire were increased with no real recourse. Although research standards were at or close to those of the home campuses, research opportunities and time were not as valued. The lack of true tenure, mingled with ambient concerns about restricted speech and academic freedom, led to greater insecurities about their careers and longevity in the Gulf.

Staff members faced different challenges: departments were subject to constant restructuring of positions and redistribution of personnel, and new directives from Qatar Foundation and the home campuses, along with budget cuts, often left everyone scrambling to comply within short time frames. Many mid-level administrators were embedded not in careers but rather in repetitive labor that was packaged as a form of expertise they brought to Doha that the branch campuses would supposedly not be able to find locally. This was certainly the case with Margaret, who was earning about 30–50 percent more than she would for a similar university position in the United States, and did not have to pay taxes, housing, or transportation costs, or even to fly back to North Carolina to visit her family every year. She had paid off her college loans in the first couple years she was in Doha, and she carried no credit card debt. Although she was living an economically comfortable life and saving for the future, Margaret was not satisfied with her work life. She did not feel adequately challenged or appreciated in her position, and she had not received a raise in over two years. She felt that less qualified people were consistently recruited directly from the United States for positions above hers, while she stayed at the same pay grade and position. Moreover, she was deeply bored with the administrative tasks that she was asked to do every day, tasks that made her feel more like she was a secretary than a human relations officer, despite her title, her master's degree in education, and her experience in American academia. She frequently took on new responsibilities and started new programs just to exercise her intellectual curiosity. She even sat in on a few of my classes the summer we met in order to learn more about anthropology while she worked on her own research paper.

Critics in the United States have attributed these problems—lack of recourse, fear of deportation, no real tenure system—to the illiberal and authoritarian Qatari state and its nontransparent and uneven treatment of foreigners. It was only when the state determined that you messed up badly enough that your lack of rights became visible; until then you were in a Faustian bargain.[26] Actors within the branch campuses reinforced these ideas by suggesting the Qatari state had the ultimate authority over employment. This was incorrect and obscured the logics that animated the American university's neoliberal and imperial motivations. The home campuses operated as corporate entities in the Gulf, engaged in limited liability agreements with the Qatar Foundation. Both were nonprofit entities—the Qatar Foundation was also public, as were Texas A&M and Virginia Commonwealth. But their agreements clearly outlined that the American university, through its branch campus, was directly responsible for the everyday management of all faculty and staff, including their termination. It was also responsible for setting curricula, admitting students, and engaging in community outreach.[27] As with most business partnerships in the Gulf, the noncitizen owner of the American branch campus was the on-the-ground *kafeel* that produced the conditions of precarity and exploitation, often for compatriots, that direct state sponsorship would likely have prevented or at least dampened, according to the very migrant rights activists who criticize projects like Education City and NYU Abu Dhabi.[28] Treating migrant labor as a category that did not include all of the employees of Education City allowed branch campuses to take a problem endemic to all levels of the academy and pass it off as the product of a supposedly illiberal state. With operating costs, consulting fees, and incentives coming directly from Qatar Foundation, branch campuses could have ensured much better working conditions and job security across the board. There were profits to be gained for them in not doing so, ones that resonated quite well with home campus systems, such as the growth in adjunct labor, the reliance on international student tuition, and long-standing entanglements between the academy, the state, the private sector, and imperial interests.[29]

My own journey to work in Doha for the first time in 2010 illustrates some of these contradictions of the branch campus, its role as a *kafeel*, and the fractured and incomplete nature of the liberal project. I had a contract to be a visiting assistant professor in the Liberal Arts Department at Texas A&M Qatar, to be held with my main campus tenure-track position as a short-term joint appointment. However, I was a unique case—most faculty and staff were hired directly to Texas A&M Qatar and did not hold joint appointments. For faculty and staff relocating to Doha from the United States, salaries were set according to equivalent positions in Texas; however, they also came with a Qatar incentives package that included a 30 percent salary bump, housing, business-class flights, and other benefits. In addition to listing my salary and work expectations, my contract stipulated that:

As a condition of employment, you shall abide by all Texas A&M University System Policies and Regulations and all University Rules. You also are expected to abide by the applicable laws and regulations of the State of Qatar and to respect the cultural, religious and social customs of Qatar. Your failure to abide by such applicable laws, regulations and customs may be considered a material breach of this offer letter, subject to termination by the University at its sole discretion.

No further information was included about what laws, regulations, or customs were applicable. I was also given specific instructions on what would be expected from me in Qatar, including on immigration procedures, how to get a driver's license, and medical insurance coverage information. My immigration procedures listed that, in order to establish residency in Qatar after arrival, I would be required to submit to "a medical examination, including a blood test and chest X-ray," a background check, and fingerprinting; I also would need an "exit/entry permit," approved by Qatar Foundation, every time I wanted to travel out of Doha, paperwork that took up to one week to process.[30] Since immigration was the first thing you had to do in Doha, your first contact with the bureaucracy of employment was with the state, and it could take several days of waiting in lines and interacting with different bureaucratic offices around the city to complete. These processes were interwoven into one's employment expectations, thus the state and the workplace did not feel distinct; employees were left feeling dependent on both. I was instructed by the Liberal Arts Department's administrator at Texas A&M Qatar to wait at a bus stop in Education City the morning after my arrival in Doha in order to get my medical tests. There, I joined several other Qatar Foundation employees on a small bus that took us to a hospital even further out of town. Chatting with those closest to me, I met two faculty members from Georgetown who had just arrived on three-year contracts, an events coordinator for the new multimillion-dollar horseracing stadium, a Student Affairs employee relocating from my main campus, and a postdoctoral student who was starting a one-year position at Weill Cornell Medical School. When our bus arrived at the facility, we were met by a young Qatari man, an employee of Qatar Foundation, who spoke to the guards at the hospital in Arabic so that we could bypass the long lines of construction workers waiting outside.

In addition to the bureaucratic hurdles of immigration and visa processing, the labor I performed required a certain embodied subjectivity and the ability to manage and work with the uniqueness of Texas A&M Qatar's student body in ways that were new to me, having never taught outside the United States. I was constantly aware of my amorphous charge to "abide by the applicable laws and regulations of the State of Qatar and to respect the cultural, religious and social customs of Qatar," and so I chose my clothing carefully to make sure it was not too tight, short, or revealing. I regularly came to campus with a shawl to drape over my shoulders, and I consciously emphasized my American accent and asserted my positionality as a US-trained anthropologist in order to maintain authority in front of my classroom. In this way, although I am not white, I attempted to perform a symbolic or geographic Westernness that established my expertise. The classroom experience also meant managing gendered, classed, and ethno-national interactions with my students, and between different students, all of which I was still learning, even though I had lived in the Gulf before. In addition, I practiced self-censorship and constantly worried about projects I was assigning, if I was pushing students too far outside their comfort zones, and whether I was successful as a teacher. These were not unusual concerns; they were ones that I had in College Station as well, although they manifested around different topics and interactions. Both spaces required me to self-regulate as well as to produce my identity in relation to my students and the normative college culture. At Texas A&M's main campus, for example, I was constantly aware of how, as a woman of color, my students often took my lectures about race or gender as personal opinion rather than as fact, as they might if the information was relayed by a white male professor. At the branch campus, students accepted my expertise more readily, but I had an added level of insecurity in that my stay in Doha was contingent upon not violating cultural standards that I still did not understand, and which I knew were being conveyed to me in suspect ways by my colleagues. I wondered if I would have been as aware of their coded language if I was not a researcher of the Gulf, if I was not South Asian in a country where South Asians experience so much racialization, or if I was not an in-between subject who regularly experienced marginalization at my home campus.

Most of the faculty in Education City were there more permanently, many with family members to support. Thus they had reason to feel more insecure about their jobs than I did. Many professed a deep belief that they could get kicked out of Qatar at any time; yet they discussed this openly, did not change what they said or did in the classroom or outside it, and held rather essentialized views of Qataris. Other faculty members criticized their employers, telling me that campuses squeeze employees in order to placate Qatar Foundation and home campuses, especially during contract renegotiation—while I was conducting research for this project, several of the campuses were renegotiating their ten-year contracts, so this was a common topic of discussion over drinks and at dinner parties. At Virginia Commonwealth, for example, soon after contract renegotiation, the university switched from three-year to one-year contracts, creating enormous job insecurity for faculty, many of whom had been there for several years. In addition, the administration was trying to increase research output in order to hit newly defined performance indicators, which would supposedly increase the management fee paid to the main campus. However, with a 3/2 teaching load (the highest in Education City) and as an arts campus with mostly MFA-holding faculty, the faculty had not yet received clearly defined research guidelines. A colleague I interviewed there was livid about this, telling me that it had nothing to do with Qatar but was rather about administrative greed and lack of care for the faculty who had struggled through the startup phase of the branch campus. These examples highlight how exploitative systems of academic labor were easily perpetuated in conjunction with the kafala system and white liberalism. Not only were faculty, including myself when I first started teaching and researching in Education City, rather depoliticized within this context, they also internalized many of the criticisms branch campuses and Gulf states were receiving at home.

Western expatriates, and faculty in particular, also faced stigmas from their metropolitan peers, even though their decision-making practices around employment were not that different. Many downplayed the economic motivations for coming to Qatar because those at home either implicitly or explicitly made them feel like their reasons for taking branch campus jobs were somehow impure due to the financial gain and benefits they received.[31] Often, these stigmas revolved around presumptions peers had of the Gulf as an illiberal place where people did not have freedom. Many expatriates found themselves in a position, therefore, of having to justify living and working where there were human rights violations, particularly around migrant labor issues.[32] In their criticisms, faculty in the United States presented themselves as not complicit in capitalist exploitation, even though they, like all academics, were also laborers. The stigmas levied by metropolitan academics also did not interrogate the imperial location from which they were able to create a site of liberal purity/piety for themselves and cast moral aspersions on the decisions of their peers, whose intellectual labor was immediately less valuable because it emerged from the satellite campus. The experiences of nonwhite and Muslim faculty, who did not neatly inhabit the subject positions offered by liberal academia's home spaces, and who in many cases chose to come to Qatar over tenure-track positions in the United States, called into question the idea that metropolitan universities were more liberal and egalitarian than their Gulf counterparts, offering openings to think about how each site might speak to the other without creating hierarchies of value or trafficking in a false binary of liberal/illiberal.

"It's the Same Water"

Ramzi, a Middle East studies specialist, was only in his third semester of teaching in Education City when I walked into his office and started browsing his impressive collection of books in several languages. Both he and his wife had left tenured positions at a reputable research university in the Midwest to come to Qatar, positions they had struggled for several years to secure at the same university. He was Arab-American; his wife, a journalist, was a naturalized citizen from Iran. They had both been familiar with the Gulf before deciding to pursue a move to Doha: he had lived in Dubai for a couple years before graduate school, and his wife's parents had worked in Qatar when she was a child. Qatar was geographically close to their aging parents, cosmopolitan, and offered the ability to raise their son in a Muslim-majority country. Even though they were not practicing Muslims, they were concerned about the messages their son received in the suburban white community where they lived. He was beginning to absorb and experience white supremacy and right-wing Christian attitudes from his schoolmates. Ramzi recounted to me one particular incident where his son had come home from school and asked if God was white; his classmates had been talking to him about his skin color and telling him that God was white like them. This incident particularly shook Ramzi and his wife, and they realized that it was just going to get worse from there. Ramzi was also intellectually interested in teaching his expertise to people from the region. In Qatar, he told me, he had the opportunity to teach more nuanced versions of Islamic history than the Wahhabi state one, and to discuss Middle East politics in more sophisticated ways than at his previous institution. The students were cosmopolitan and aware of the news, and even the more dogmatic Muslims were not even that dogmatic; you could challenge them or give alternate perspectives and they would listen. He felt that this was partly because he was coming from the inside rather than the outside—even though it absolutely felt like an American university, "there are more like minds here."

Ramzi's experiences as an expat/expert might seem incongruous with the narrative I have been constructing in this chapter about ethno-national labor hierarchy, racial segregation, and the whiteness of expertise. He was hired by his institution as a senior faculty member in order to increase diversity—branch campuses struggled with their faculty diversity numbers as a metric of success just as they did at home—as well as to teach courses that addressed growing student desire for more world and regional focus, a curricular shift that Qatar Foundation also promoted. Ramzi presumably accrued the same expatriate pay rate and benefits as his white peers, and he lived a similar enclaved lifestyle, with a nanny to take care of his child, free schooling at an international K-12 private school, business-class flights back to the United States, and luxury accommodations in a gated community of villas. He did not tell me if his wife had procured a professorship in Education City, an omission that was pretty glaring given how much I learned about his family in our time together. The two-body problem of employing an academic couple in a small place like Education City was much more difficult to navigate, and the privileging of patriarchal family structures in pay and benefits packages made it expected that the spouse who left their job to come to Education City would be the wife.[33]

Ramzi and I quickly moved out of interview mode and established an intellectual connection over my project and the initial arguments I was forming. I brought up the criticisms from some US-based academics that these were missionary or imperial endeavors. He told me that he had seen some of that among the faculty, that there was definitely a camp that was Eurocentric in what they taught and had stereotypical views of *khaleejis*, but that even in his short time in Doha, he had found that more and more faculty "know that the stereotypes are rubbish." The branch campuses were also setting the bar higher by hiring more informed faculty who were interested in the region or had connections to it. I found this to be the case in my faculty interviews as well. Every year as I went back for fieldwork, I found more tenure-track faculty, postdocs, research assistants, and graduate students conducting fieldwork; even many adjunct lecturers were in Education City because they had active research agendas in the region, were learning Arabic, were practicing Muslims, and/or had grown up or had family in the Gulf or Middle East. While at one time faculty positions in Education City were not difficult to obtain or considered especially coveted jobs, some of the more prestigious institutions received upward of one hundred applications for tenure-line positions, especially after the 2008 economic recession. I met faculty who had turned down offers at top research universities in the United States or Canada to take positions in Education City; who had left tenured positions, like Ramzi did, to take senior faculty or administrative roles; or who had come from the main campus for a short stint and decided they did not want to go back. Several faculty and staff whom I met had actively sought out positions in Gulf universities. These were folks who most often occupied in-between subject positions: they were both insiders and outsiders to the US academy and to the native spaces that they studied, or, in the case of Qatar, to the space where the university had expanded.[34] These interlocutors related wanting to be in the Gulf for personal reasons: they were most often Arab or *desi*, had lived in the region before, and now were interested in raising their children away from the racism and Islamophobia of the West, or in being closer to family or to cultural and religious roots. Doha for many felt like a comfortable mix between the West and either South Asia or the Middle East. This did not mean it was without problems, however. There were residency and job insecurities, as I detailed above, and similar structures of whiteness prevailed in branch campuses as in metropolitan workplaces. I heard varying accounts from non-Western or nonwhite faculty and staff about their experiences in Education City. Some felt they were not receiving the pay and benefits packages that Westerners received, while others felt that climate issues did not exist to the same degree and that they were paid fairly.

Even within inequality, there were benefits to be gained. As Ramzi noted, the intellectual pleasures of teaching in Doha could not be matched in the United States. The small, diverse classes offered in Education City provided pedagogical development, which encouraged faculty to stay. However, top-down understandings of branch campuses solely as arms of neoliberal profit or colonial replication made it difficult for the experiences of these in-between academics to be heard and taken seriously by US-based critics. Their pleasures in the Gulf may indeed have included the pleasures of enclaving and elite privilege, but they also highlighted untenable situations at home, some of which included the problems of being migrant laborers. International faculty in the United States were not exempt from the precarious situations that international students faced. In addition to racism and rising Islamophobia, international adjuncts and postdocs dealt with constant visa worries and legal fees, were disqualified from certain jobs if they were not already on work visas, and had added hurdles to tenure and promotion even if they did manage to obtain permanent residency. The subject who can claim to speak from the space of liberalism is therefore marked by privilege and comfort—that of citizenship status and of not being a migrant worker at home in an institutional space that had a growing migrant labor problem. This privilege did not just surface when the university exceeded the territorial borders of the United States. Additionally, the ways that nonwhite and non-American faculty expressed comfort and discomfort called into question the idea that metropolitan home spaces were liberal in the first place. Their experiences of these supposedly liberal spaces as unwelcoming and marginalizing (even for those who had the privilege of citizenship) were not taken into account when academics questioned motivations for their peers taking jobs overseas or dismissed globalized higher education as a failure or crisis of liberalism.

My conversations highlighted how those who experienced the metropole as unable to live up to its own claims were able to see supposedly illiberal spaces like Qatar as both contiguous and fraught in ways that their white counterparts usually could not. Describing her experience of relocating to Qatar, one South Asian American professor said, "Certainly this is not your typical American classroom," referring to the immense diversity of her students in Education City; but at the same time, she added, "I do not feel like a fish out of water. It's the same water." This professor also taught about Islam and the Middle East regularly. In her four years in Doha, she had noticed a rising conservatism among certain segments of the Qatari citizenry, aimed at state reforms and at Education City and some of its programming. But the only resistance she had ever faced to her work was from the main campus: when she brought a pro-Palestinian speaker to campus, a Zionist faculty member from the main campus complained to her department head and the main campus dean. What that faculty member did not note, she told me, was that she had also brought two Israeli speakers to campus during her time in Doha, something that would have created a lot of blowback in other Gulf countries, but not a single Qatari or any other student or faculty member had ever complained.

Conclusion

Labor camps and worker compounds segregate migrant populations by class, race, gender, and nationality. They allow for the policing of perceived threats to security and to sociocultural and religious values by reducing mobility and increasing surveillance of different groups of noncitizens. The camps I have discussed in this chapter were not, as most readers have come to expect, full of construction workers from South Asia imported to rapidly build the infrastructure that Qatar's petrowealth demanded. Rather, they were designed as comfortable, even luxurious, places of work and residency. Expat/expert lives in the Gulf could also be explained in terms of the geographies and technologies of the camp. Their nationalities in many ways defined their mobility and opportunities in Doha, as did their Western professional accreditations, their English-language skills and—to a large extent—their whiteness. Additionally, sites of white/Western privilege and expat consumption and production cordoned off this population in relation to other groups of residents. Although they were represented in state and commercial discourses as cosmopolitan consumers, these migrants were effectively in Qatar to perform a particular kind of labor, one that relied less on skill and experience and more on embodied dispositions and performances that were legible as expert within the ethno-racial hierarchies of Gulf residency and the American academy.

Conclusion

Anthropology and the Educational Encounter

Outside the Sidra Medical and Research Center, a massive building devoted to prenatal and women's health that seemed to have been under construction forever, were fourteen giant statues depicting stages of fetal development from conception to birth, commissioned by Sheikha Mayassa bint Hamad al-Thani, chairwoman of Qatar Museums and sister of the emir. Designed by the controversial British artist Damien Hirst, the statues—along with their rumored twenty-million-dollar price tag—caught international media attention for their boldness in showing the naked human form in a conservative Islamic country, as well as for what was billed as yet another over-the-top expenditure that did not make aesthetic or practical sense for Doha's urban development. (See Image 4.) A reporter for the *New York Times*, describing the installation, wrote: "Even for a Persian Gulf country that is aggressively buying its way into modernity, this installation takes official acceptance of Western art to a new level. Local women still adhere to centuries-old Islamic traditions, wearing the abaya, a long cloak, and niqab, or face covering; images of women are routinely censored in books and magazines. Even the representation of the human form is unusual."[1]

Shortly after the public unveiling of the Hirst statues in 2013, collectively titled "The Miraculous Journey," they were re-covered by large white cloths. This is when rumors began among my colleagues about why the statues were "shrouded": "There must be some major backlash against Mayassa; she's gone too far this time," said some. "These babies remind me of those aborted fetus images I used to see on campus back home that the pro-life groups would bring," said others. "It is haram to

IMAGE 4. Photograph of "Miraculous Journey" by Damien Hirst in front of Sidra hospital construction site, April 2014. Source: Alexey Sergeev, asergeev.com. Reprinted with permission.

display the human body in Islam," I also heard. Others felt the covered babies were creepy because they seemed dead—it would be better to just show them. The Qatar Foundation's official reason for covering them: to protect them from construction dust. While other public art in Doha has stirred controversy among Qataris, these statues seem to have gone relatively unquestioned.[2] Qatar Museums still highlights the statues on their web page, and there have been no attempts, as far as I know, to remove them or move them to a less prominent position on campus.

The reactions by Western academics, who comprise the majority of the professoriate within Education City's American branch campuses, highlighted their own entry into seeing fetuses: through pro-life vs. pro-choice debates on college campuses for the most part—a visual reality that was not part of campus culture in a country where abortion is illegal and absent from public discourse. In addition, childhood is not publicly sexualized, so the nude form of an unborn, developing baby was relatively disconnected from adult bodily display. Circulating ideas about what was haram, particularly around gender and women's bodies, also highlighted the gatekeeping and culture-making practices of Western experts and consultants, and were not necessarily connected to scholarly Islamic debates or Qatari everyday practices, as I have explored in earlier chapters of this book. In addition, my colleagues' watercooler conversations and the international media coverage of this art installation, which tended to converge, included judgments about choices made by Qatari leaders, judgments that implied a proper development trajectory for the country—a proper way to balance tradition and modernity within that trajectory—and implied that Qatar (an elusive yet unified state actor) was failing at both. What would make more sense, after all, for a women's hospital in a country focused on increasing the birth rate among citizens and reducing miscarriages and birth defects, than statues depicting a healthy (and male) developing fetus?

The title of this concluding chapter speaks to Talal Asad's important volume exploring the history of anthropology as a way of knowing about the other, in which he argued that British anthropology's post–World War II turn away from holistic functionalism to more specialization, which coincided with so-called primitive societies becoming postcolonial nation-states, was not a calculated and reflexive move away from the imperial logics that shaped European academic knowledge practices but rather a naturalization and universalization of those fundamental understandings of difference.[3] To claim that the discipline changed because the world changed did not question the inherent assumptions upon which ideas about non-European people were founded; rather, it allowed those ideas to proliferate as the discipline grew and gained more academic legitimacy. Asad's call for a decolonization of anthropology was therefore not just about anthropology but about Western epistemology in much broader academic and nonacademic forms, which influenced and in turn were constituted through ethnographic encounter. Building on Asad's important intervention, this book has explored how the American academy and its disciplines have normalized traditional anthropological modes of understanding culture as bounded and tethered to place in order to address diversity and difference. The anthropologization of difference in higher education—especially as universities globalize into locations that are considered the West's others—was also central to the branch campus as a space of encounter, where both Qatar and America were (re)constituted along with ideas of liberalism, illiberalism, gender, nation, ethnicity, class, sexuality, and religion. The faculty and administrators within Education City, even though they tended to be more positively oriented toward the project than their US-based counterparts, reduced Qatariness to fixed notions of culture and religion—ironically becoming themselves producers of difference through their gatekeeping practices. This was evident in the explanatory frameworks that many of them deployed to understand the Hirst statues and their shrouding—the word most often used to describe their re-covering, which both implied death and evoked an exotic other, as well as the Orientalist gaze on the veiled female form. Culture and religion, I found, were not easily thought or taught as flexible in branch campuses, just as they were not at home, despite the language of diversity and multiculturalism that pervaded both spaces. And they were ongoing threats to liberal success.

What counted as failure and threat, and to whom, and how Qatar Foundation responded to criticisms, primarily from segments of the citizenry that felt left out of knowledge-economy development, is where I end this book. I do so by examining the changes that occurred around the formation of Hamad bin Khalifa University (HBKU), the umbrella national institution that during my research began to encompass the branch campuses, research centers, and new local institutions opening in Education City, including the Sidra Medical Center.[4] HBKU's formation reconfigured space within the Education City compound and changed my everyday mobility within it, as it did my students' and colleagues'. I explore these changes in order to consider how anthropological categories of difference and the university's approach to incorporating oppositional politics migrated along with American institutions, disciplinary formations, faculty, and administrators. While such changes may appear to some as failures of liberal education in an illiberal space, I argue that they highlight the openings a Qatari American university might provide for new imaginaries of pedagogy and decolonized knowledge production.

Nationalizing Education City

During the years that I conducted research for this project, I saw public debates simmer to the surface among Doha's residents about the pace and scale of development, the contours of Qatar's national branding, and who modernization actually serves. These debates took place in Arabic and English newspapers, on television and radio shows, on university campuses, and within social media forums. Education City might not always have been the direct topic of conversation, but the Qatar Foundation understood that conversations about the country's future connected to this space as an ideological, economic, and material project. As such, the Foundation spent considerable effort and money shifting both its rhetoric and its built environment since the inception of the project to better address local stakeholders.

Originally a "collection of individual buildings that are differentiated by a variety of architectural expressions,"[5] Education City's built environment was marked by a lack of cohesiveness and inattention to use-value for students and staff. Its touted sustainability efforts, similarly, were more about international branding than actual environmental impacts, similar to other green projects in the Gulf.[6] The campus was also an elite enclave gated off from the rest of Doha, governed as a free zone where some of the laws in force in the rest of the city were relaxed.[7] Several of my early student and alumni interviews reflected a sense of not knowing many people outside one's university building, for the branch campuses felt rather atomized. Local controversy also began to build about Education City being inaccessible, both physically and academically, to the citizens it claimed to serve. This pushback, which intensified around the time of the Arab revolutions, led to state responses in other areas, such as doubling (or more) public sector salaries, instituting mandatory military service for men, removing alcohol from the

Pearl freehold complex, slashing the Qatar Foundation's budget, and increasing funding to the national public Qatar University.[8] In response to these criticisms, Qatar Foundation's planning and programming changed considerably, as did to a lesser degree that of the branch campuses. Parts of the campus were closed to car traffic to create more pedestrian- and bus-friendly corridors for students, and more greenways were built. Attempts to engage the wider community could be seen in the removal of security checks and ID requirements at gates to the compound, which took place in late 2014. Meanwhile, branch campuses and some newly opened local institutions started offering more community-based programming and courses that were regionally focused.

Perhaps the most representative of these changes was the rebranding of Education City as Hamad bin Khalifa University, a national university that encompasses the educational and research institutions in Education City, including the American branch campuses. I first learned about HBKU when I was beginning my research in 2010. At that time, there were rumblings about a potential "local university restructuring" among my colleagues, but there seemed to be little concern about the impact it would have on the functioning of day-to-day academic life. By the time I was finishing this project in fall 2014, HBKU had become more centralized, and its bureaucratic presence was palpable in Education City. The new initiatives and institutions launched by Qatar Foundation under the HBKU name were met by resistance and insecurity from branch campus administrators, who felt that their institutional independence was under threat, particularly since many were undergoing contract renegotiation with Qatar Foundation under tighter budgets. The formation of HBKU and the positioning of the branch campuses under its umbrella represented a solid move toward nationalization and away from the "best international brands" approach that Qatar Foundation had started with twenty years earlier. The website for Education City also reflected this turn to the local and to Qatari heritage and culture, most recently in 2016 with rebranding, a new strategic plan, and a new logo and tagline for HBKU that focused on heritage and directly mirrored the language of the *Qatar National Vision 2030*.

The first building to carry the HBKU name was the Student Affairs building, which completed construction in 2011. By 2014, HBKU Student Affairs had hired several administrators, including a few Qataris, and was up and running with its own programming as a vibrant space that brought students together, thus making branch campus Student Affairs officers wonder about redundancy and how to work with and across this new format. Local institutions, such as the Qatar Faculty of Islamic Studies and the Translation and Interpretation Institute were pulled under the HBKU umbrella. HBKU is modeled upon a research university and had begun offering its own master's and postgraduate degrees in 2014, some in collaboration with branch campus faculty; more were in the planning stages. The university had also hired research faculty directly, not through any of the branch campuses or other institutions, and funded them through lucrative Qatar National Research Fund grants, even though these faculty had no research or teaching programs yet in operation.[9] The newly opened Qatar Faculty of Islamic Studies building, in one of the prime locations in Education City, showcases the shift away from the secular liberal enclave environment that Qatar Foundation originally intended. The building draws from Arabic architecture and is covered with Islamic script. It also includes a large mosque that is open to the public for Friday services. The institution itself, an indigenous and nonsecular graduate school, also highlights efforts by Qatar Foundation to move away from relying solely on foreign institutions and liberal education. In planning for the Qatar Faculty of Islamic Studies, Qatar Foundation aimed to replicate a traditional madrasa, where learning and worship took place in one space.[10] As one person told me, the new initiatives were all aimed to create a system "skewed to force people to study more about Qatar." The focus on Qatar and Qataris was also reflected in changes in scholarship and grant mechanisms, some of which were available either only to citizens or to local scholars.

For many Western expatriates, however, daily life in Education City did not feel as open or as accessible as before. In 2014, when I arrived in Doha after a two-year hiatus to complete fieldwork, I had to contend with these new changes, which on the surface might indicate the very failure of liberal social engineering in so-called illiberal space that the cautionary critiques of American university partnerships in the Gulf foretell. That semester, I was a visiting assistant professor at the Qatar Faculty of Islamic Studies, where I was the only non-Muslim woman employee, and the only woman faculty member. My role as a faculty member (and my non-Muslim and South Asian female body) required disciplining into an institutional identity that defined itself directly against the branch campuses, which were read as both secular and Western. As I mentioned in Chapter 2, I was told after starting my position that I was required to wear hijab. When I shared my experiences with my American branch campus colleagues, they were often shocked, and asked me how I could tolerate such a violation of my rights. They then used my experiences as evidence of Qatari backwardness in conversations with others, folding them into the civilizational narratives that underpinned many of their understandings of the role of their universities in the Gulf and of what constituted Qatari culture. These were the anthropological self/other binaries that my students and I were unpacking in the classroom and that critics of American university globalization relied on to challenge the existence of those classrooms. Nevertheless, I still had to think through what it meant to negotiate my bodily movements within Education City—at work, I was constantly policed by staff and faculty, yet my students were attuned to anti-colonial politics in ways that exceeded those of students in American university classrooms, even those in branch campuses. In our anthropology of the Middle East class, for example, they were quick to understand Edward Said's *Orientalism*, not only applying it to the Middle East and North Africa region but also using it to compare the contemporary experiences of Gazans with those of African Americans. In branch campuses, I felt more comfortable because they resembled my academic home spaces in the United States; yet these were in many ways white spaces, where expertise mapped onto white bodies, and white colleagues practiced social segregation and often made disparaging comments about Qataris and other nationals, reminding me not only of how American liberal academia is racist but also of the traces of British and American colonial divisions that underpinned Gulf ethno-racial labor hierarchies. My experiences of moving between spaces that increasingly embodied different epistemologies, gender norms, and social expectations highlighted not the failures of liberalism, as they did to the majority of my colleagues, but rather revealed the archival nature of the university, especially as it became more embedded within the local context.[11]

Archiving Contestation

The post–civil rights US university has reassembled itself by archiving the oppositional social movements and alternate forms of knowledge of the 1960s–80s in ways that depoliticize and contain difference.[12] The archival university labels and incorporates difference through the language of diversity, rendering it apolitical, digestible, and a metric of liberal success— part of the university's universal progress narrative. This is why it is not surprising for those of us who work in US universities to sometimes find ourselves in buildings where philosophy and women's studies, or Classics and ethnic studies—disciplinary formations that are not just incommensurable but speak to one's historical annihilation of the other—to be housed nicely together, sharing space and students, participating in projects of interdisciplinarity and global education, the buzzwords of today's university growth initiatives. At my current institution, I recall sitting on the International Affairs advisory committee, trying to explain why a Europe concentration that included Greek and Roman mythology and traditional art history courses could not possibly fulfill the function of a global citizenship project, to a room of mostly blank stares; at the Texas A&M home campus, I remember listening with my mouth open as the Department of Anthropology actively discussed, in all seriousness, a merger with Classics: questions about how such a merger would fit with cultural anthropology's decolonial agenda, which included joint appointments in

Africana studies and women's and gender studies, were dismissed or met with hostility. Such is the nature of the archival university.

I would suggest that the postcolonial university is even more a site of archive than its metropolitan counterpart. We should indeed consider American branch campuses in Qatar postcolonial, in that they are part of a postcolonial state's attempts at building an indigenous education system, and in that the students they serve are Qatari or come from other postcolonial contexts. They are, of course, as most postcolonial sites, also spaces of ongoing and uneven imperial encounter. In 2014, my interlocutors were very concerned about what they read as a backlash against Education City by conservative elements of Qatari society, some of whom were inside the new administrative scaffolding of HBKU. For my Western colleagues, attacks on coeducation, which they saw as foundational to liberal education, and which many of them either implicitly or explicitly linked to their civilizational understandings of Qatari Muslim culture, signaled a major step backward in the gains they had made, and thus highlighted the fragility of the entire system of the branch campuses. I argue, however, that this backlash was an example of the university's capacity to archive oppositional politics, while also opening moments for questioning the moralities associated with liberal education's progress narratives.

I discussed in Chapter 3 how when I arrived in 2014 to complete fieldwork for this book, Qatari women on a charity trip to the Amazon had just returned home after being chastised on social media for not wearing their hijabs and for being photographed hiking with men. This incident had caused concern among Student Affairs staff about upcoming mixed-gender trips. A couple trips had been cancelled already, or changed, in case of similar responses from community members. That year, an annual Halloween event, which included a haunted house cosponsored by Northwestern and Texas A&M, was not approved by HBKU administration, and this came up in some of my student interviews. Halloween, apparently, was un-Islamic, and the haunted house would put men and women in too close proximity in a dark space to be respectable. Thus the event's name had been changed, the date had been moved from October 31st to the following week, and men and women would now enter the haunted house (which would no longer be referred to as haunted) separately. Other incidents I heard referred to as backlash were security guards enforcing curfews on the mixed-gender spaces of dorms, where no curfews were actually in place, and of Education City's new local reputation as Sin City due primarily to supposed transgressions on Qatari women's morality as a result of mixing with men. One student at Northwestern even told me that her request to have a fundraising (halal) hotdog-eating contest in 2013 was denied by the administration as inappropriate, although administrators would not openly claim that this was because of potential sexual connotations.

Faculty, staff, and students at branch campuses all related to me that policies and attitudes around heterosociality were increasingly unclear and more conservative since the inception of HBKU. While this was sometimes the case of branch campuses being proactively conservative, uncertainties around what counted as proper behavior usually occurred in the interstitial spaces between the branch campus buildings—those that were HBKU administered and therefore considered Qatari or local, and not American. Student housing, for example, was one site where these tensions played out, as student housing fell directly under HBKU administration. While men and women used to be housed in the same complex (though in different buildings and without access to each other's residence halls), the newly opened men's dormitories had essentially segregated residential life to opposite sides of campus. While geographically more difficult, the Department of Residential Life still held mixed-gender events, and the social spaces and dining halls in the dorms were open to all members of the community, including staff and faculty. The security that patrolled the dorms, however, did not necessarily understand or conform to what public safety would look like on an American college campus, and often took a punitive rather than paternal approach to student behavior. Thus students would get arrested for things that they would not if they were under the umbrella of American institutions, such as drinking or public displays of affection. This made international students, who populated the dorms, even more precarious, because if they were kicked out of housing or arrested, they were effectively no longer able to go to school because they could not afford to rent apartments in Doha. They might also face deportation.

I met with the head of Residential Life one morning in November 2014 to tour the new men's dormitories and ask about rumors of new curfew enforcement, especially around mixing. He told me that while there was ongoing conversation in his office about whether there ought to be a curfew, the incident of men getting kicked out of female dormitories that had sparked the rumors was due to one security officer's individual decision; it was not a new official policy. I asked how that could be: a security officer is probably not empowered to make such a decision. As vulnerable migrant workers, it would be hard for security guards on campus, who tended to be Filipino or Kenyan, to exercise authority over students. He told me that when such punitive actions took place, guards were usually following directives from higher management, who were mainly Qatari or Arab. This explanation backed up the idea that Qataris were resistant to gender integration. However, development goals in Qatar and the Gulf states fundamentally revolved around a form of state-sponsored feminism, which explicitly centered the education of women and their entry into the workforce, to the extent that women comprised the majority of matriculated students in many colleges and universities and surpassed men in tertiary education. The Academic Bridge Program, for example, which I explored in Chapter 2, was a local institution inside Education City that was co-educational; unlike the branch campuses, it has met with no resistance from Qataris, even though most of its students come from gender-segregated public schools. The curriculum and programming are designed to bolster basic skills, especially in English, but also to give men and women an opportunity to learn to work together in mixed environments through clubs, group work, gender-integrated classes, and social events. Activities are designed, according to administrators and faculty that I spoke with, to "ease" students into coeducation while also helping them get into college.

Alanoud, a Qatari staff member at the Academic Bridge Program, explained that they were successful with Qataris because they created activities that were culturally appropriate. When planning activities, she explained, one should always ask what the aim is. Is it educational? The target should be to benefit the country, not to lose Qatari identity. As she emphasized, "Don't force them to be American!" The Academic Bridge Program, she said, focused much more on Muslim, Arab, and Qatari identity. She brought up recent Twitter complaints, for example, about how Georgetown had a large Christmas tree (we were meeting in December) but no *adhan* (call to prayer): "If you are preventing Islam, then why is there Christianity? Either have none, or all."[13] Alanoud reproduced state-sponsored feminism in our interview, noting that women were working harder and were more interested in education than ever, and that most of them were entering the workforce after graduation. However, her take on women's earnings was that they were disposable income, and that women were supported by men in their education and work aspirations. Women's education did not therefore include liberal feminist claims to rights and equality but rather was a part of constructing a patriarchal modern national femininity. A similar argument could be made for HBKU, which was shifting the structure of Education City and focusing in particular on creating an indigenous, non-Western university in Qatar, one that is able to include the branch campuses but does not model them.

Qatari families and HBKU middle managers did not seem to have the same anxieties about the Academic Bridge Program that they had about the branch campuses, the dormitories, and certain Student Affairs events. This was particularly interesting since my colleagues at the branch campuses pinpointed heterosociality as the primary reason for Qatari backlash to the Education City project and for the lack of Qatari students joining in Student Affairs activities. The perceived threat of the mixed campus, then, was not about mixing itself, which was inevitable and already existed in many parts of Qatar, but about maintaining an imagined community of Qatariness that was founded on a myth of particular traditional Muslim gender roles—ones that were defined precisely against the presence of the non-Muslim, non-Arab expatriate threat to tradition. This is why political opposition (read as backlash by my colleagues) and the concessions made to it manifested themselves on the bodies of Qatari women in particular; therefore, the pressures women felt to be appropriate, even as they were unsure what that meant, as I explored in Chapter 3, pervaded the branch campuses in ways they did not in the Academic Bridge Program. The critiques of Education City—through the discourse of gender threat—contained within them anti-imperial sentiments that were too readily dismissed as part of conservative or backward ideas about culture. This could explain the policing I experienced within the Faculty of Islamic Studies—as a particularly placed expatriate non-Muslim expert, but also as a South Asian brown-bodied female who could be disciplined in certain ways but not in others (my pay and benefits, for example, were probably higher than many of my colleagues who did not hold American passports).

The changes in Education City were quite ordinary reflections of how institutions incorporate political contestations and calls for greater representation. Rather than producing a more fractured landscape of higher education, it is in these dissonant moments where we can see how archival logics were able to incorporate seemingly incommensurate political projects, through the use of anthropological categories of difference. The amalgam Qatari American space of HBKU is not proof of the failure of liberal education in illiberal space, or evidence that globalizing the American university is an extension of crisis; rather, it is within the framework of liberalism's own logics. It offers a space of potential openings from which we can critique our categories of knowledge, especially around culture, and how culture is used within debates about global education, Gulf exceptionalism, and anthropology. American institutions are passing into places where they engage different publics, and in the process of their localization the concept of education and its meanings are perhaps reconfigured. In Qatar, these universities were more public in certain ways—free to nationals and almost akin to "need blind" for foreign residents and international students due to their financial aid structures, although these were shifting, as I explored in Chapter 4. But these branch campuses were also set up as corporations in the Gulf, with CEOs, in order to transfer money back into US state institutions, asking us to rethink what a public university and state sovereignty mean in a place like Texas or Virginia, and what transnational neoliberalism can offer and what new challenges it brings for faculty and students in terms of funding, academic containments, student and faculty demographics, and encounters with American empire.[14]

Speaking Back

I was finishing this book through the 2016 election cycle and the first few months of the Trump administration. During that time, I watched many of my colleagues and friends discuss the state of the United States on social media through parallels to Nazi Germany and fascism, or to African and Middle Eastern dictatorships, lamenting an end to liberal democracy, as if the roots of illiberalism were not planted in the very soil of the settler colonial racial states of the New World, and as if the groundwork for Trump's nativist executive orders and domestic state terror were not laid by the Obama, Bush, and Clinton administrations. Natalie Koch has referred to this discourse as "Orientalizing authoritarianism," importing it from elsewhere in order to perpetuate US exceptionalism and illiberalism as exception, scripting Trump into accepted and knowable frameworks of imperial America.[15] I also witnessed a collective grief from white feminists following the election on November 9, 2016, which sparked fissures and debates within academic and nonacademic feminist spaces about the absence of liberal feminism from activist movements like Black Lives Matter, NoDAPL,[16] and immigrant and Muslim rights struggles in the lead up to the election—conversations and contestations that made intersectionality a concept that many more people are now thinking with in forming their political stakes. Watching the Women's March in its last days become a more inclusive space that rippled globally, and then seeing taxi drivers strike at JFK and other airports while well-to-do lawyers scrambled to prepare motions and offer legal aid after the executive order that banned travelers from seven Muslim-majority countries, inspired hope in solidarity politics that pushed against identity and ideology, challenging many to move into previously unknown modes and vocabularies of mobilization and belonging. It is here, in the known and unknown epistemologies of encounter, subjectification, and difference, that I have always found this project and my role in it to reside; and this moment of American liberal crisis and imperial reinvigoration, while not at all exceptional, provides an interesting point of departure from Qatar and its branch campuses.

Academic and intellectual critiques of the American Left's response to Trump were well and good, but embodied existence at my PWI (predominantly white institution), especially after students started becoming increasingly frightened for themselves and their families, was a different thing. I began having temporary escape fantasies to the warmth and comfort of the Gulf, which started to solidify into questions about serious alternate academic possibilities for the first time in my career: What would it be like to work in a Gulf university, where my colleagues actually get paid livable wages, where they do not think of evenings and weekends as "publish or perish" time but instead enjoy leisure and family, where higher education is funded as a public good so they have the resources to take their students on trips to neighboring countries or to conferences, where I would have research funding and proximity to my field sites, where I would not always stand out demographically? I explored some of these reasons for Muslim and nonwhite faculty taking jobs in the Gulf in Chapter 5. I think it is not a small thing to highlight here that Dubai was the first city I ever lived in, as a PhD student in my thirties conducting dissertation research, where I woke up one day and realized that I had been moving through life without having to think about the brownness of my body, a feeling I had never felt before. Dubai and Doha, of course due in large part to my class privilege and my Western passport, but also because of their Muslimness and large South Asian populations, were for me spaces of cultural familiarity and relative gender safety in public space. I found deep comfort in them—they were home spaces in ways that Pennsylvania, Texas, or almost anywhere in the United States could never be—despite the different challenges and restrictions I faced there. And although academics may be rightfully suspicious of both the neocolonial and neoliberal aspects of the transnational American university, I think they have to be equally, if not more, suspicious of what writing branch campuses off under grand narratives of neoliberalism and crisis recuperates and erases. For many in the US academy, the answers to the violences of liberalism and democracy might lie in the elsewheres and in the imaginaries, intellectual communities, and home spaces, however fraught, that they offer.

The forms of belonging and exclusion taking place at universities in Qatar, as I hope I have brought to life in this book, were diverse and varied between students, between classrooms, and between universities. It was impossible to paint them with one stroke, just as it is impossible to paint our own home institutions this way or to make the mistake of thinking that somewhere out there an idealized university form both exists and is potentially mobile. For the upwardly mobile local expats I introduced in Chapter 4, for example, university experiences were not simply about neoliberal consumption of educational services; rather, they increasingly included emerging claims to civil rights and diasporic citizenship. For the young Qatari women in my Texas A&M classroom, modernization brought new opportunities as well as reassertions of parochial understandings of who can claim rights to the country and its future. The identifications and interactions enabled by the American branch campus may be changing the face of belonging in places like Doha even as they produce scholars who can engage the very debates within which they are imbricated. Like postcolonial academics, who were also products of Western educational systems and significantly changed the landscape of the American academy in the 1980s and 1990s, these students can produce new approaches to questions of knowledge production, history, racialization, and power. The enormous activism across the Arab world that coincided with the span of this research project, along with the great devastation that the region has faced, represents young people in these countries questioning, challenging, and redefining state responsibility, freedom, citizenship, global power, and the very concept of the human. If the conversations many of us want to have about the state of higher education are rooted in questions about which practices, infrastructures, and institutions constitute public good, then youth in the Middle East are compulsory interlocutors. Because we have scripted, and continue to script, the limits of our publics on their futures.

Notes

Introduction

1. This book focuses on Qatar as well as the broader context of the Gulf Cooperative Council (GCC) countries: Qatar, Saudi Arabia, Kuwait, the United Arab Emirates, Oman, and Bahrain. I use the terms Arabian Peninsula, Gulf, and Gulf states relatively interchangeably (with the acknowledgment that Yemen is often left out of these groupings). GCC countries share history and some political, economic, and cultural features while also remaining distinct in other ways. The ongoing "siege" of Qatar by a Saudi-led coalition of countries in 2017 highlighted how this is not a uniform region of the world. I am invested in locating Qatar and the Gulf states within broader scholarly framings, including the Persian Gulf and Indian Ocean.

2. Cross-cousin marriage (father's sisters' children or mother's brothers' children) is common in the Arabian Peninsula. Cousin marriage (cross- and parallel) is also relatively normalized among some South Asian and Arab diasporic communities.

3. After Qatari independence in 1971, there were people who refused citizenship or were not able to access it. These people are referred to as *bidoon*. Within contemporary framings, *bidoon* are treated as those without nationality and sometimes as undocumented migrants. However, most are indigenous to the Arabian Peninsula.

4. Even though the faculty member hired into that position has since left, sociology is offered as a course in Liberal Arts, and the curriculum in general is more diverse than it was eight years ago.

5. Notable ethnographic research on Gulf branch campuses includes Tanya Kane, "Transplanting Education;" Marjorie Kelly, "Issues in the Development of a Gulf Studies Program;" Mary Ann Tetrault, "Identity and Transplant"; and the articles in the *Journal of General Education* 63, nos. 2–3 (2014).

6. Many of the main lawns are Astroturf.

7. The gates of the compound are no longer closed to the public, a change that occurred in late 2014 in response to criticisms from Qatari citizens, who

felt the campus was inaccessible. I go further into the resistance to Education City in the book's chapters, especially in the Conclusion.

8. Gulf urban planning, especially when it is outside of the municipal city borders, has often revolved around such themed mini-cities, which are often gated and also operate with relaxed laws akin to what Aihwa Ong has referred to as zones of differential sovereignty. Ong, *Flexible Citizenship*.

9. 2016–17 figures from *NAFSA: Association of International Educators*, http://www.nafsa.org/

10. *Global Higher Ed* blog: http://www.globalhighered.org/

11. Nick Anderson, "Northwestern Professor"; Seyla Benhabib, "Why I Oppose Yale in Singapore"; Ariel Kaminer, "N.Y.U.'S Global Leader"; Ursula Lindsey, "Qatar Sets Its Own Terms"; Ian Wilhelm, "Duke Faculty."

12. Virginia Aksan, "How Do We 'Know' the Middle East,?" 9–10.

13. Andrew Ross, "Human Rights." Ross and two other members of an activist group called Gulf Labor were prevented from entering the UAE in 2015.

14. Similarly, Seyla Benhabib, opposed to her home campus, Yale, opening a satellite in Singapore, suggested that "experiments in democratic education are best performed within genuinely open, multicultural and multi-faith democracies, such as India, rather than in the artificial, boutique-like security of places like Singapore or Abu Dhabi." Benhabib, "Why I Oppose Yale in Singapore."

15. Gary Wasserman, *Doha Experiment*, 223.

16. See also Natalie Koch, "We Entrepreneurial Academics."

17. John Agnew, "Territorial Trap."

18. For a discussion of translocal encounters, see Mei Zhan, *Other-Worldly*, 6–7. Betty Anderson, *American University of Beirut*, and Jonathan Lyons, *House of Wisdom*, discuss the knowledge exchange with the Middle East that impacted Western understandings of liberalism.

19. Neha Vora, "Unofficial Citizens"; Vora, *Impossible Citizens*.

20. See e.g. Ralph Litzinger's astute critique of Duke's Kunshan campus. Litzinger, "Going Global."

21. In the published version of Professor Aksan's MESA Presidential Address, for example, there is a rebuttal by Professor Mehran Kamrava, then acting dean of the Georgetown School of Foreign Service in Qatar and director of the school's Center for International and Regional Studies. Kamrava, "Response to MESA President." Kamrava highlights several incorrect statements in her speech, noting first that the branch campus delivers the exact curriculum as the home campus in Washington, DC, including courses like the required Problem of God, which is sometimes taught by their resident Jesuit priest, along with his disappointment that the president of MESA would discredit a project she has never visited or bothered to learn much about. In my own interactions with Professor Kamrava, I asked him if being Iranian posed

any difficulty in Qatar, and he said never. He was very happy there, publishing controversial work, including on the royal family, and bringing speakers on a range of topics, such as the Arab Spring, the GCC's relationship with Iran, migrant labor rights, Qatari women's rights, and Palestine/Israel. He found himself defending his work more to colleagues in the United States than to Qataris. This was a familiar story.

22. See also Neha Vora and Natalie Koch, "Everyday Inclusions"; Natalie Koch, "Orientalizing Authoritarianism."

23. Similarly, India, where Seyla Benhabib suggested we focus internationalization efforts rather than Singapore, and which is technically the largest democracy in the world, used antiquated colonial-era sedition laws in 2016 to violently crack down on student protestors and censor their speech. In addition, the rise of the religious right-wing Hindutva movement, which has intensified under the Modi administration, has led to all sorts of rollbacks of secularism and multiculturalism, as well as a drastic spike in Islamophobic violence and targeting of journalists.

24. For NYU student coverage of the first visa denial, see Mark DeGuerin and Amy Rhee, "Lack of Academic Freedom," *NYU News,* October 2, 2017: https://www.nyunews.com/2017/10/02/lack-of-academic-freedom-plagues -nyu-abu-dhabi/. For a response to NYU New York's portrayal of their campus, see Tom Klein and Kristina Stankovic, "Letter from the Editors," *The Gazelle,* October 7, 2017: https://www.thegazelle.org/issue/121/letters/letter -from-the-editor-response-to-wsn.

25. Pascal Menoret, "Imperial Liberal University"; Joseph A. Massad, *Islam in Liberalism.*

26. Bill Readings, *University in Ruins.*

27. Ibid., 9–10.

28. Philip Altbach, "Globalisation and the University"; Burton Bollag, "America's Hot New Export"; Ann I. Morey, "Globalization"; Mary Poovey, "Twenty-First-Century University."

29. See also Clyde Barrow, *Universities and the Capitalist State.*

30. Readings, *University in Ruins,* 171.

31. Drawing from her research in Italy, Lilith Mahmud similarly writes: "The Masonic experience illustrates two key points about liberalism: first, that being liberal in the Occidentalist sense is an aspiration, not a fact, and it takes a painstaking labor of self-cultivation to naturalize it as a Western trait, and second, that widespread and systematic instances of illiberalism within Euro-American societies are coded as exceptions that only prove the rule." Mahmud, "We Have Never Been Liberal."

32. Janet Roitman, *Anti-Crisis.*

33. Craig Steven Wilder, *Ebony & Ivy.*

34. David Wallace Adams, *Education for Extinction*; Wilder, *Ebony & Ivy.*

35. Lisa Lowe, *Intimacies of Four Continents*.

36. Roderick Ferguson, *Reorder of Things*.

37. The modern university was not a project of enforced secularization, however, but one in which the relationship between science and religion was openly discussed. It was not until specialization into disciplines with very narrow research foci that the relationship between scientific knowledge production and religious inquiry was severed. Jon Roberts and James Turner, in *The Sacred and Secular University*, trace the slow and incomplete way that alignments between science and religion (science being a way to access supernatural agency) were replaced by specialized and unending scientific inquiry, which took as foundational Nature's agency. In the process, larger questions about humanity, morality, and divine law became less central. Interestingly, the triumph of secularism that we peg to Western liberalism and Darwinian and other scientific thought occurred first at the American University of Beirut, where Arab medical faculty and students revolted against the censorship of Darwin by American university leaders about 100 years before these debates changed the tenor of the metropolitan American university. Anderson, *America University of Beirut*.

38. Piya Chatterjee and Sunaina Maira, *Imperial University*, 7.

39. Anderson, *American University of Beirut*; Victor Bascara, "New Empire, Same Old University?"

40. Ferguson, *Reorder of Things*.

41. Christopher Newfield, *Unmaking the Public University*.

42. For an excellent overview of the links between universities and Cold War politics, see Hugh Gusterson, "Homework." After World War II, universities across the United States became more openly nationalist, investing in (and receiving federal funds for) the production of democratic, patriotic citizen-subjects. This included the GI Bill of 1944, which greatly expanded the reach of higher education to include veterans, but also entangled the university even more in militarism. Title VI of the National Defense Education Act, passed in 1958, funded language and culture programs in areas strategic to Cold War interests, creating the traditional geographic areas we still use today in determining anthropological and other expertise. See US Department of Education, "The History of Title VI and Fulbright-Hays: http://www2.ed.gov/about/offices/list/ope/iegps/history.html. Zachary Lockman, in *Field Notes*, however, has argued that the story of area studies is more complicated than "Cold War" narratives reduce it to. Faculty were interested in area studies theories and methods well before World War II, donor organizations played a large role in getting them off the ground, and US national interests, while central and important, were part of a longer and more complicated set of entanglements.

43. Cold War programs coincided with a vast increase in international student recruitment and the development of scholar exchange programs such as

Fulbright, both intended to display an anti-colonial face domestically and internationally, and to impart liberal capitalist subjectivity on foreign elites as a form of soft power.

44. Ferguson, *Reorder of Things*; Robyn Wiegman, *Object Lessons*.

45. Chatterjee and Maira, *Imperial University*; Kathleen Hall, "Science, Globalization, and Educational Governance"; Renato Rosaldo, "Cultural Citizenship and Educational Democracy"; Charles Taylor, "Politics of Recognition."

46. Sara Ahmed, *On Being Included*.

47. Ibid.

48. Karen Brodkin, Sandra Morgan, and Janis Hutchinson, "Anthropology as White Public Space?"; Gabriella Gutierrez y Muhs et al., *Presumed Incompetent*; Guofang Li, Gulbahar Beckett, and Shirley Geok-Lin Lim, *"Strangers" of the Academy*; Tami Navarro, Bianca Williams, and Attiya Ahmad, "Sitting at the Kitchen Table."

49. Ellen Schrecker, *No Ivory Tower*.

50. Lara Deeb and Jessica Winegar, *Anthropology's Politics*; Steven Salaita, *Uncivil Rites*.

51. As Lara Deeb and Jessica Winegar have noted, about 40 percent of anthropologists of the Middle East and North Africa are "region-related," and they face high levels of microaggressions, surveillance, and discrimination, including pressure to reproduce American imperial agendas, particularly the "compulsory Zionism" that is promoted by administrators, students, and donors. Deeb and Winegar, *Anthropology's Politics*.

52. "The metaphor of reflection," according to Roderick Ferguson, "enables Marxism to commit itself once again to forms of universality and abstraction that ultimately marginalize the autonomy and significance of minority difference and culture." Ferguson, *Reorder of Things*, 81.

53. Newfield, *Unmaking the Public University*.

54. Janet Roitman argues, for example, that "the crude idea of a generalized and always effective neoliberalism occults the ways in which state agencies and infrastructures are crucial to the establishment of markets and economic practice." Roitman, *Anti-Crisis*, 57.

55. Tami Navarro, "But Some of Us Are Broke."

56. Weigman, *Object Lessons*.

57. As Sara Ahmed has written on her blog, for example:

> critiques of neoliberalism can also involve a vigorous sweeping: whatever is placed near the object of critique becomes the object of critique. For example, my empirical research into the new equality regime taught me how equality can be dismissed as a symptom of neo-liberalism, as 'just another' mechanism for ensuring academic compliance . . . They can then enact non-compliance with equality *as a form of resistance to bureaucracy*. Equality becomes something

imposed by management, as what would, if taken seriously, constrain life and labour. Whilst we might want to critique how equality is bureaucratised, we need to challenge how that very critique can be used to dismiss equality . . . [how] an idea of universal knowledge or universal culture can be so *thinly disguised* as a critique of neoliberalism and managerialism.

https://feministkilljoys.com/2015/06/25/against-students/ (accessed January 17, 2017).

58. Because of this strong sense of school spirit, Texas A&M students are often second-, third-, and even fourth-generation Aggies, and the alumni fund of the university is one of the largest in the United States, contributing to why the university's endowment ranks so high.

59. Silver Taps is a monthly tribute to Aggies who passed away while enrolled in the university, while Muster is an annual event to honor "absent" Aggies—those who have fallen, usually within the context of military engagement.

60. Timothy Mitchell, *Carbon Democracy.*

61. John Chalcraft, "Monarchy, Migration and Hegemony"; Calvert W. Jones, "Seeing Like an Autocrat"; Menoret, "Imperial Liberal University"; Mitchell, *Carbon Democracy*; Robert Vitalis, *America's Kingdom.*

62. Lyons, *House of Wisdom.*

63. Amira Sonbol, *Gulf Women.*

64. Miriam Cooke, *Tribal Modern*; Benjamin Smith, *Market Orientalism.*

65. Saba Mahmood, "Secularism, Sovereignty, and Religious Difference."

66. Jocelyn Mitchell, "Beyond Allocation."

67. Mitchell, *Carbon Democracy.*

68. George Katodrytis and Kevin Mitchell, "Gulf Urbanization"; Karen Exell and Trinidad Rico, *Cultural Heritage in the Arabian Peninsula.*

69. Steffen Wippel et al., *Under Construction.*

70. Lieba Faier and Lisa Rofel write that encounter ethnographies "explore how culture making occurs through unequal relationships involving two or more groups of people and things that appear to exist in culturally distinct worlds." Faier and Rofel, "Ethnographies of Encounter," 363.

71. Faier and Rofel, "Ethnographies of Encounter."

72. Anderson, *American University of Beirut.*

73. Ibid.

74. Sheikha al-Misnad, *Development of Modern Education in the Gulf.*

75. Mary Louise Pratt, "Arts of the Contact Zone."

76. While Mary Louise Pratt's *Imperial Eyes* focuses on European colonialism, in the so-called "New World" but also in Africa, I think this concept is quite useful for understanding and unpacking the internationalization of American higher education in the contemporary moment as well, and its importance to new, postcolonial, and self-described modernizing states.

77. Pratt, "Arts of the Contact Zone," 34.

78. Pratt calls them "autoethnographies." She illustrates with one text in particular, a 1,200-page letter, *Nueva Coronica* (New Chronicle), written by an Andean named Guaman to the king of Spain in the fifteenth century. Guaman writes in the style of colonial bureaucratic reports; however, his text and illustrations describe a new Christian world with Cuzco at the center, and he writes a new genesis in which Andeans emerge as the descendants of Noah. Combining both Andean and Christian symbolism, he merges metropolitan and indigenous content to reflect conquest back to the Spanish as well as to the Andeans themselves, in order to make sense of the new codes and meanings that come out of the asymmetrical encounters of colonialism.

79. A short tagline, "Unlocking human potential," and Qatar Foundation's Sidra tree logo can be found in the corners of full-page ads inviting us to think. (The Sidra tree is native to the Arabian Peninsula and is associated with knowledge.)

80. *TheFoundation* magazine 9, no. 32: https://cdn.qf.com.qa/app/media/download/1037.

81. Qatar in the twenty-first century is of course not South America under Spanish conquest, and the differences between them matter in terms of understanding what a contact zone might look like in global space-time, where information is so immediately available (Pratt was discussing a written text that might have slipped past European audiences altogether). Encounters have been layered over centuries of collaboration to make any "local" impossible (and problematic) to recuperate, and the amounts of wealth in the Gulf and geopolitical entanglements between the region and other states make claims of imperialism more fuzzy.

82. Ali Khalifa al-Kuwari, *People Want Reform*.

83. Traditional/modern do not map easily on to Qatar's spaces, state projects, or residents' actions and politics. National dress is thoroughly modern, and until state formation Gulf "nationals" wore all kinds of clothing from many parts of the world.

84. Men were also targeted by the campaign for wearing tank tops and shorts, but in lesser numbers.

85. Lila Abu-Lughod, *Do Muslim Women Need Saving?*; Joan Scott, *Politics of the Veil*.

86. Vora and Koch, "Everyday Inclusions."

87. Donna Haraway, "Situated Knowledges."

88. I conducted over 100 formal semi-structured interviews with students, faculty, and staff over 14 months of fieldwork between 2010 and 2014, and had dozens of additional informal conversations. My research was approved by the Institutional Review Board at Texas A&M from 2010–2012, and by the Institutional Review Board at Lafayette College from 2013–2015. In Doha, new

Institutional Review Board procedures were continuously being implemented at different institutions, and I tried to keep up with them as I learned about them. I had approval from Texas A&M Qatar for my research in 2012. When I returned in 2014, I learned that Georgetown had centralized approval for Education City, so I obtained approval from their research office. About midway through my project, I learned from Carnegie Mellon Qatar that I was not allowed to conduct research among their students without an IRB approval from them, and that they did not give IRB approval to non-Carnegie Mellon faculty, so I stopped interviewing their students on their premises. Throughout the book, I have given my interlocutors pseudonyms as well as changed some identifying features, including at times branch campus affiliation.

89. Vora, *Impossible Citizens*.

Chapter 1

1. Rehenuma Asmi, "Cultural Translation"; Asef Bayat, "Transforming the Arab World"; Kris Olds and Nigel Thrift, "Cultures on the Brink"; Aihwa Ong, *Neoliberalism as Exception*.

2. *Qatar National Vision 2030*.

3. Rosemarie Said Zahlan, *Creation of Qatar*. Similar initiatives—Saudization, Emiratization, Omanization, etc.—exist in all of the Gulf Cooperation Council countries.

4. Women who marry Qatari nationals can naturalize but risk losing their citizenship upon divorce. Some long-standing Arab immigrants who are Muslim, speak Arabic, and have political influence have also been able to naturalize. Some other exceptions are made to the citizenship laws, such as for players on Qatar's sports teams. Citizenship, meaning carrying the Qatari passport, is also not the same as nationality, which grants more privileges, and was in place before Qatar became independent in 1971. The laws around citizenship have changed since the inception of the modern state; currently there is discussion about whether to make permanent residency available to long-standing foreign residents who have made significant contributions to the country.

5. George Katodrytis and Kevin Mitchell, "Gulf Urbanization."

6. Neha Vora and Natalie Koch, "Everyday Inclusions."

7. Timothy Mitchell, *Carbon Democracy*. See also Robert Vitalis, *America's Kingdom*. Imperial economic interests were inseparable from ideological ones, producing the idea that "self-determination" and "development" were naturally aligned with some populations and not others by utilizing racial and ethnic logics.

8. Mitchell, *Carbon Democracy*, 137.

9. Vora and Koch, "Everyday Inclusions."

10. Christopher Davidson, *Dubai*; Allen J. Fromhertz, *Qatar*; Mehran Kamrava, *Qatar*.

11. For an excellent analysis of how economic reductionism impacts Gulf migration literature, see Attiya Ahmad, "Beyond Labor."

12. Many who fall under the kafala system of migration profit from it and are included in nation-building projects and statecraft, while many citizens, who are supposedly the beneficiaries of rentier wealth, are in fact not experiencing it as such. But kafala's marking as the source of Qatar's "modern-day slavery" has become yet another index of the country's unnatural wealth, backward culture, and illiberalism. I make this argument about the United Arab Emirates in Vora, *Impossible Citizens*.

13. John Chalcraft, "Monarchy, Migration, and Hegemony"; Ahmed Kanna, "Group of Like-Minded Lads"; Vitalis, *America's Kingdom*.

14. Jill Crystal, *Oil and Politics*. For a longer discussion of these tactics in Saudi Arabia, see also Vitalis, *America's Kingdom*.

15. Calvert Jones, "Seeing Like an Autocrat."

16. Miriam Cooke, *Tribal Modern*; Fromhertz, *Qatar*; Kamrava, *Qatar*; Kristian Coates Ulrichsen, *Qatar and the Arab Spring*.

17. Noora Lori, "National Security," and Lori, "Temporary Workers?"

18. Mandana Limbert, "Caste, Ethnicity, and the Politics of Arabness," discusses how contemporary understandings link Arabic and Arabness as part of a shared identity originating in the Arabian Peninsula. But Arabian Peninsula inhabitants did not understand Arabness in terms of language (their servants spoke Arabic, for example). It was about patrilineal purity and superiority (primarily in relation to servants). With the formation of the Gulf Cooperation Council (GCC), Arabness became more fixed, more racial, and elite. The GCC sees Islam and Arabness as the essential bonds between countries. But many elites did not speak Arabic at the time of state formation. There was new interest in Arabic language in order to cement social divisions and civic myths. Education policy in the GCC since 1975, for example, has focused on "Arabization": these are policies aimed at exclusion. And this Arabness has been projected onto the pre-oil past.

19. Amelie Le Renard, *Society of Young Women*, discusses this form of classification or designation as "national distinction," translating from the Arabic *khuṣūṣīya*. I also use designation and classification, which are more legal terms, in keeping with the usage of the original word. A conversation with Fahad Bishara helped to clarify this translation.

20. Jane Bristol-Rhys, *Emirati Women*; James Onley, "Gulf Arab Headdress"; and Fatma Al-Sayegh, "Women of the Gulf," all discuss the heterogeneous forms of pre-oil and pre-independence dress in the Gulf.

21. Benedict Anderson, *Imagined Communities*; Chalcraft, "Monarchy, Migration, and Hegemony." See also Farah al-Nakib, *Kuwait Transformed*; and Ahn Nga Longva, *Walls Built on Sand*, who make similar arguments for Kuwait.

22. Pamela Erskine-Loftus, Victoria Hightower, and Mariam al-Mulla, *Representing the Nation*.

23. Mohammed Alsudairi and Rogaia Abusharaf, "Migration in Pre-Oil Qatar"; Karen Exell, "Locating Qatar"; Natalie Koch, "Is Nationalism Just for Nationals?" See also Sarina Wakefield, "Heritage, Cosmopolitanism and Identity," on Abu Dhabi.

24. John Crist, "Innovation in a Small State."

25. *Human Development Report 2016*, Qatar: http://hdr.undp.org/sites/all /themes/hdr_theme/country-notes/QAT.pdf. It is unclear how many nonnationals, if any, are included in the population data. Given how high the rankings are for GCC countries, and my arguments above about how academic research tends to map belonging on to citizens alone, I would presume that low-wage migrant workers are not included in these data, especially if "households" are the primary unit of study.

26. Ministry of Development Planning and Statistics Report, I: https:// www.mdps.gov.qa/en/statistics/Statistical%20Releases/Social/RAndD/2012 /RD-Survey-2012-2013-En.pdf.

27. Nick Anderson, "Texas University Gets $76 Million Each Year to Operate in Qatar, Contract Says," *Washington Post*, March 8, 2016: https://www .washingtonpost.com/news/grade-point/wp/2016/03/08/texas-university-gets-76 -million-each-year-to-operate-in-qatar-contract-says/?utm_term=.e241cf 91d36a#contract.

28. Tom Finn, "'Social Curse' of Huge Personal Debt Raises Worries in Wealthy Qatar," *Reuters*, March 3, 2016: https://www.reuters.com/article/us -qatar-debt-doha/social-curse-of-huge-personal-debt-raises-worries-in -wealthy-qatar-idUSKCN0W51UC.

29. This has become even truer for Syrian, Iraqi, Libyan, and other students who effectively have no stable countries to even consider "returning" to after graduation.

30. Natasha Ridge, *Education and the Reverse Gender Divide*, 36.

31. Ibid., 37.

32. Ibid., ch. 5; Ulrichsen, *Qatar*, 164–65.

33. Ulrichsen, *Qatar*, 164–65.

34. Mohanalakshmi Rajakumar et al., "Education, Marriage, and Professionalization."

35. John Chalcraft, in "Monarchy, Migration, and Hegemony," writes of nationalization programs and their effects:

> It may be that nationalization programmes, and the flurry of conferences, panels, lectures, press articles and discussion that surrounds them, while making little difference to the composition of the workforce, do repeatedly affirm the unity of nationals against foreigners, ingrain the interpellation of migrants as demographic and cultural threats, and provide an important justification for

the patronage-enhancing policy of the rotation of 'guest-worker' migrants: if migrants are supposedly to be replaced, sooner or later, by nationals, there need be no provision for their assimilation. (27)

36. Bayat, "Transforming the Arab World," 1231.

37. Fida Adely's work in Jordan, *Gendered Paradoxes*, considers how development discourse, like colonial discourse, sees Arab and Muslim women as oppressed due to family and community, and education as the solution to their oppression, because it will afford them autonomy. But this narrative is based on Western women's experiences. In contrast, the Jordanian women she interviewed included family and country in their definitions of progress. There is a teleological assumption in development discourse that education delays family, allows entry into the workforce, and leads to women's liberation. But higher education among Jordanian women was not necessarily connected to desire for careers; instead, it was seen as a way to be more secure. Sally Findlow, "Women, Higher Education and Social Transformation," identifies a similar "feminist-internationalist policy orientation" in higher education in the UAE and the Gulf.

38. Asef Bayat writes:

The combination of such social and political conditions has more than ever reinforced, in the mainstream media and academic circles in the West, the already prevalent idea of "Middle Eastern Exceptionalism"—that kernel of the Orientalist paradigm. Thus, in comparison with its counterparts in the developing world, the Middle East—in particular the Arab world—is often viewed as something very different, a 'unique' cultural entity which does not fit into conventional frames of analysis. Policy personnel in the West, notably the US, call for an urgent change in the region, and yet believe that change will not come from within, but from without, and by force. (Bayat, "Transforming the Arab World," 1226)

39. Gary Wasserman reproduces much of this language in *The Doha Experiment*, as do the Georgetown main campus deans that write endorsements for it.

40. Initially called "Project Airforce," RAND was set up after World War II to conduct research related to US security interests. Today, half of its funding comes from the US Defense Department or other security concerns, and the other half from the public sector. It undertakes contract-based research in the United States and abroad.

41. Sohail Karmani notes how this plays out in Qatar and the Gulf specifically as "More English and Less Islam." Karmani, "English," 264.

42. Personal interview, former RAND employee, Oct. 2014.

43. Rehenuma Asmi, "Storytelling in Qatar," 42.

44. Asmi, "Cultural Translation," 14.

45. During my time in Qatar, I was left with the same impression through my conversations with students who came through independent schools and with parents (primarily Arab foreign residents) who were negotiating the school system.

46. Asmi, "Cultural Translation." For critiques of charter schools and neoliberal reform of K-12 education in the United States, see also Michael W. Apple, "Between Neoliberalism and Neoconservatism"; and Kathleen Hall, "Science, Globalization, and Educational Governance."

47. Rehenuma Asmi calls this a "close encounter," borrowing her term from Anna Tsing. Asmi, "Cultural Translation."

48. Our conversation recalled much of what Rehenuma Asmi found in her research.

49. It is common for foreign experts to be scapegoated in breakdowns in state-citizen relations. See Karen Exell, "Locating Qatar."

50. Sheikha al-Misnad, *Development of Modern Education.*

51. Ulrichsen, *Qatar.*

52. Tanya Kane, "Transplanting Education."

53. As Rogers Brubaker writes, "[c]ivic nationalism, characterized as liberal, voluntarist, universalist, and inclusive; and ethnic nationalism, glossed as illiberal, ascriptive, particularist, and exclusive . . . are seen as resting on two corresponding understandings of nationhood, based on common citizenship in the first place, common ethnicity in the second." Brubaker, *Ethnicity Without Groups,* 133. Civic nationalism, the purview of the West, is considered the more civilized and less harmful of the two; thus a moralizing distinction is built into the definitions of these supposedly distinct forms.

54. Vora and Koch, "Everyday Inclusions."

55. Koch, "Is Nationalism Just for Nationals?"

56. I was a reader for a funded Qatar National Research Fund grant in 2014 that was going to survey both national and nonnational residents of the Qatar National Museum before it opened in order to determine what forms of display would garner the best audience reception—clearly, government agencies understand that marketing the nation domestically includes marketing to foreign residents.

57. Sarina Wakefield argues that culture industries in the Gulf (using Abu Dhabi as her case study) are increasingly "elite-centered," disenfranchising certain citizens as well as low-wage migrants: "In Abu Dhabi the heritage narratives exclude the huge numbers of migrant labourers who make up a significant proportion of the population, favouring instead heritage presentations and narratives that are familiar to, but do not represent, the largely white-collar, middle-class Western expatriate workers." Wakefield, "Heritage, Cosmopolitanism and Identity," 110. Similarly, the authors in Karen Exell and Trinidad Rico's edited volume, *Cultural Heritage in the Arabian Peninsula,* discuss how

producing "global citizens" and producing national designation go hand in hand—nationals and elite visitors are taught how to consume cosmopolitan art and culture alongside purified ideas about native pasts. These pasts are also legitimized through international heritage bodies, and thus archaeology plays a large part in projects of nationalism.

58. Crystal, *Oil and Politics*, 163.

59. A non-exhaustive list of this work includes: Attiya Ahmad, *Everyday Conversions*; Andrew Gardner, *City of Strangers*; Amelie Le Renard, "Hierarchical Intimacies"; Mandana Limbert, "Caste, Ethnicity, and the Politics of Arabness"; Sharon Nagy, "Search for Miss Philippines Bahrain"; Vora, *Impossible Citizens*; Katie Walsh, "Negotiating Migrant Status."

60. Koch, "Is Nationalism Just for Nationals?"

61. In June 2017, a bloc of four countries led by Saudi Arabia closed air and water access to Qatar and changed travel, residency, and other policies in order to isolate the country and its citizen as well as noncitizen residents. This action comes out of long-standing political and economic tensions between the Gulf Cooperative Council countries. As of June 2018, the "siege" is still ongoing.

62. There are elites in Qatar who wield power but are not included in knowledge-economy branding, including Islamists who align with Muslim Brotherhood-leaning leaders like Yusuf al-Qaradawi, and a range of more secular nationalist intellectuals interested in democratic reform. See for example Ali Khalifa al-Kuwari, *People Want Reform*. These are some of the greatest sources of dissent from within the country against Education City and Western education reform more broadly, and Qatar Foundation has worked to address their concerns and fold them into its mission and planning.

63. Quoted in Mohanalakshmi Rajakumar, "Assessing the Rhetoric of Sheikha Moza," 128.

64. As Calvert Jones notes about the role of foreigners in contemporary education development in the UAE, "the new *civics* classes are themselves taught by British and American expatriates, hired to make creativity, individual empowerment, and critical thinking an integral part of being an *Emirati* citizen." Jones, "Seeing Like an Autocrat," 29 (emphasis hers).

Chapter 2

1. Although this was not the case with the faculty, which was much less diverse, as I explore in Chapter 5.

2. I discuss orientation activities in greater detail in Chapter 4.

3. Renato Rosaldo, "Cultural Citizenship."

4. Talking about student segregation at the University of Illinois, Nancy Abelmann described what she called an "intimate tension" between "ideals about a universal humanity in which people can become fully human regardless

of the contingencies of the likes of race, nation, and religion, and the life of particularities: family, race, community." Abelmann, *Intimate University*, 2. Her study focused on Korean and Korean American students, who make up a large proportion of the University of Illinois Urbana-Champaign campus and are for the most part not integrated into the rest of the student body. Factors like family, church involvement, language, and work made them appear to be choosing self-segregation.

5. Tanya Kane, "Transplanting Education," 177–257.

6. ABET is an industry-standard accreditation for university engineering programs provided by the Engineers' Council for Professional Development: www.abet.org.

7. Andrew Gardner, "Gatekeepers."

8. It is important to note here that I am discussing a problem of climate that does not necessarily encompass every action by every faculty member. Climate, however, is reproduced through inaction as well as through direct action.

9. Excerpt reproduced from an interview with Natalie Koch from 2016, with permission of the researcher.

10. Gary Wasserman discusses "hundreds" of books held by customs that were on Georgetown faculty syllabi as proof of a uniform Qatari authoritarianism and failure of the liberal education project. Wasserman, *Doha Experiment*, 182–84. However, he also speaks about the open access to e-books and the way that students were willing to work around individual customs officer's decisions, showcasing the heterogeneity of Qatari political opinions and decision making. In my conversations with multiple faculty members, over multiple years of teaching, and across all campuses, including faculty who teach politics, religion, and other potentially controversial courses, I never met someone who had more than a one-off issue with a book. And these instances are very rare.

11. Amelie Le Renard, *Society of Young Women*, 29–33.

12. Qatari men represented a very small proportion of Qatari students in Education City, and they were also outnumbered by Qatari women in higher education across the country. There were many reasons for this, such as the high salaries they could attain in the public sector with a high-school degree, mandatory military service (which was instituted in 2011), and the sense that women could improve their life circumstances through education much more than men could. Texas A&M, because it offered engineering degrees, which many families could tie directly to valued jobs in the country, tended to attract more Qatari men than other branch campuses.

13. Jane Bristol-Rhys discusses similar experiences among Emirati college students. Bristol-Rhys, *Emirati Women*, chap. 5.

14. Le Renard also discusses this sense of surveillance among other nationals in Saudi Arabia. Le Renard, *Society of Young Women*.

15. As Nancy Abelmann writes, "It makes no sense to categorically distinguish self-segregation from some sort of segregation proper." Abelmann, *Intimate University*, 3–4.

16. See Lila Abu-Lughod, *Do Muslim Women Need Saving?*

17. Karak is an Indian-style milky tea that is popular in the Gulf.

18. See Sara Ahmed's ethnography of diversity work in higher education, *On Being Included*, for an excellent overview of this argument.

Chapter 3

1. Vodafone's website for the trip, promotional information shared on the Qatar Foundation website, several individual Twitter accounts, and YouTube videos have since been taken down.

2. Elysia Windrum, "Charity Endeavor in Brazil Sparks Cultural Debate on Qatari Identity," *Doha News*, August 15, 2014: https://dohanews.co/female-qatari-youths-trekking-brazilian-amazon-causes-public-backlash/.

3. Alanood al-Thani, "Twitter Mobs and What It Means To Be Qatari," *Doha News*, August 20, 2016: https://dohanews.co/twitter-mobs-means-qatari/.

4. In the midst of this controversy, Vodafone's CEO, an Al-Thani family member, decided to withdraw the company's sponsorship of the project and take down the social media campaign associated with it. Joined by the production crew from the film company, Medidante, the team continued on their charity trip, staying in touch with concerned family members via phone as debates swirled in social media about what proper behavior for Qatari women should be. Elysia Windrum, "Qataris' Amazon Adventure to Continue After Vodafone Withdraws Support," *Doha News*, August 18, 2014: http://dohanews.co/vodafone-qatar-backs-charity-endeavor-result-negative-criticism/.

5. Ali Khalifa al-Kuwari, *People Want Reform*; Christian Coates Ulrichsen, *Qatar*.

6. Natasha Ridge, *Reverse Gender Divide*.

7. Like Amelie LeRenard in *A Society of Young Women*, I purposefully use the term *heterosocial* in this chapter in order to denaturalize this type of public space.

8. Worn primarily but not exclusively by national women in Qatar and other Gulf states, the abaya is usually paired with a shayla, a sheer black scarf, worn almost identically to a hijab. Wearing an abaya is also a fashion statement, and styles change frequently, although for more pious women, it represents modesty and is rarely adorned or cut close to the body. Some more conservative women will also cover their face with a niqab, or throw the end of their shayla over their face while moving from car to home. In Education City, women rarely wore a niqab.

9. Leslie Miller-Bernal and Susan Poulson, *Going Co-Ed*.

10. Many administrators went even further than gender integration to try to break up high-school comfort zones by distributing Qataris from the same independent and segregated high schools amongst the various orientation groups.

11. Lila Abu-Lughod, *Do Muslim Women Need Saving?* Lisa Kirchner's extremely problematic memoir about being one of the founding administrators at Carnegie Mellon is an example of this feminist yet racist missionary zeal. She writes, for example, about how she came to Qatar imagining herself as a role model for Qatari women, but then laments that "putting a good university in their backyard, however, eliminated the last good reason these women had to leave the country. Far from being a vehicle for liberation, I'd become a tool for oppression." Kirchner, *Hello American Lady Creature*, 63. And she is unabashed in her racism, especially toward Muslim and Qatari men, saying, "I was stunned when Michael Moore's *Fahrenheit 911* came to Doha. Much as I wanted to support something indie and something recent-ish, I didn't like the idea of watching a documentary about America's war on terror amidst a group of men clad in *thobes*." Ibid., 58.

12. The ongoing debates around TERF (trans-exclusive radical feminism) in both scholarly and activist spaces highlights how feminism still includes an investment in a biologically constituted homosocial female "public."

13. "In loco parentis" means "in place of the parent" in Latin. It is a concept used by members of university communities to debate the relationship between the institution and young college-goers.

14. Le Renard, *Society of Young Women*, 162.

15. Though, interestingly enough, it was often the president of Qatar University who articulated the more overtly feminist stance in public commentary.

16. Mehran Kamrava, *Qatar*, 163; Mohanalakshmi Rajakumar, "Rhetoric of Sheikha Moza," 139.

17. Rajakumar, "Rhetoric of Sheikha Moza," 131. Rajakumar does an excellent discursive analysis of Shiekha Moza's speeches, which I use to tease out this portion of my argument.

18. Other prominent Qatari women do this as well. See, e.g. Buthaina al-Ansari, *Qatari Women Before/After Oil & Gas*.

19. Ziba Mir-Hosseini analyzes this approach to Islam within modern Gulf states, in "Gender Rights."

20. See Attiya Ahmad, *Everyday Conversions*, for more on the role of housemaids in the social reproduction of Gulf citizens.

21. Amelie Le Renard's interlocutors also discussed the difference between 'ayb and haram, as custom versus religion. Le Renard, *Society of Young Women*, 62. They used this distinction to advocate for themselves within the family, using their rights in Islam to challenge patriarchal restrictions that were 'ayb.

22. Jane Bristol-Rhys discusses similar generational differences between Emirati college women in relation to their mothers and grandmothers in *Emirati Women*. For more on pre-oil Gulf cities, see Farah al-Nakib, *Kuwait Transformed*, and Hoda el-Saadi, "Women and Economy."

23. *Jāhilīya*, or Jahilia as Leila Ahmed refers to it, is the name of the society in pre-Islamic Arabia that the Prophet Mohammed was born into. It is portrayed as the time of ignorance in all available historical records, which reflects the Islamic redefinition of that time period. Ahmed, *Women and Gender in Islam*, 46.

24. Dukhan is an oil and gas field about eighty kilometers west of Doha.

25. *Ya'nī* is commonly used in Gulf-accented English. It translates to "I mean" or "that is to say" in Arabic.

26. *Yalla* means "Let's go" or "C'mon."

27. Mohanalakshmi Rajakumar et al., "Education, Marriage, and Professionalization," highlight several similar constraints that Qatari women have to maneuver.

28. Social capital, or connections.

29. There is a long history of Islamic feminism in the Middle East, primarily in Egypt, but these ideas circulate in the Gulf as well. Leila Ahmed, *Women and Gender in Islam*, chap. 9. Islamic feminists usually reinterpret passages of the Quran (as well as the Hadith and other texts) that have been used to claim women's inferiority to highlight less patriarchal readings. Some have even argued that Islamic feminism, as it roots its challenges to patriarchy in the home and the marital relationship, is even more radical than Western liberal feminism, which tends to focus more on the public sphere. See Margot Badran, *Feminism in Islam*; Sa'diyya Sheikh, *Sufi Narratives of Intimacy*, introduction and chap. 6; Azam Torab, *Performing Islam*, introduction; Amina Wadud, *Inside the Gender Jihad*. In addition, they argue that *shari'a*, *fiqh*, and other legal and scholarly traditions have implicit patriarchal bias since they were written by men within social conditions of gender inequality in which women were excluded from the production of Islamic knowledge. Sa'diyya Sheikh writes: "The limitations of discourse focused solely on rights is that it deals with the symptoms of inherited structures of patriarchal discourse without necessarily interrogating the nature and roots of the structures." *Sufi Narratives of Intimacy*, 222. Qatari women heard these arguments through their family members, the media, and sometimes in the context of the university. They were not uncommon in the Gulf states. See, e.g. Alessandra Gonzalez, *Islamic Feminism in Kuwait*. When I was drafting this chapter, a debate raged at Qatar University about a prominent Saudi feminist professor who had been teaching Islamic feminism in her Gender and Islam class for many years. Some online commentators called for her to be fired, while many others, students and faculty alike, supported her. Ursula Lindsey, "Women and Islam: A

Topic That Troubles," *Al-Fanar Media*, March 10, 2017: http://www.al-fanar media.org/2017/03/women-islam-topic-troubles. Islamic feminist ideas also circulate in the Gulf through women's *da'wa* movements, which are forms of consciousness raising that take place in homes or community centers. See Attiya Ahmad, *Everyday Conversions*, for an ethnographic look at *da'wa* movements in Kuwait.

30. For a discussion of "quiet encroachment" through women's everyday actions as a form of feminism in the Middle East, particularly Iran, see Asef Bayat, *Life as Politics*, chap. 4.

Chapter 4

Portions of this chapter were previously published in *Ethnic & Racial Studies*. See Vora, "Between Global Citizenship."

1. Neha Vora, "Free Speech and Civil Discourse."

2. Nada Soudy highlights this well in "Home and Belonging," in which she compares second-generation diasporic Egyptians in Qatar and the United States.

3. Neha Vora, *Impossible Citizens*, chap. 5; Vora, "Is the University Universal?"

4. Private interview with localexpat, November 2006.

5. *Desi* is a commonly used term for South Asian.

6. Kevin Gray, Hassan Bashir, and Stephen Keck, *Western Higher Education in Asia*; Ben Wildavsky, *Great Brain Race*.

7. Louis Althusser, "Ideology."

8. Some social citizenship benefits of the welfare state, as well as forms of Muslim charity, have extended to noncitizens since the founding of the Gulf states, highlighting how certain foreign residents have always been folded into citizenship structures. See Neha Vora and Natalie Koch, "Everyday Inclusions."

9. During my research this minimum was raised from QR 8,000 to QR 10,000 a month. (QR 10,000 is about US$2,750.)

10. A CDA was the equivalent of a resident advisor.

11. I discuss the Varkey Group and elite schools in the UAE, in Neha Vora, *Impossible Citizens*, chap. 5.

12. Tanya Kane discusses how certain Arab expatriates were receiving citizenship, including one of her interlocutors at Cornell Medical School. In an interview she had with Sheikha Moza, they discussed the possibility of all graduates from Cornell receiving citizenship in the future. Kane, "Education in a Globalized World," 277.

13. This might have been as employees on parents' businesses or it might have been because the rules were lax or their parents had *wasta*. I was unable to ascertain.

14. This program is now only open to nationals. It was originally open to foreign residents as well.

15. Vora, *Impossible Citizens*.

16. Tea carriers—these were staff responsible for serving coffee and tea and doing other odd jobs inside universities.

17. For a more in-depth exploration of journalism classes and how they foster critical thinking skills at Northwestern Qatar, see Mary Dedinsky, "Journalism and Scholarship."

18. I explore similar narratives of faculty and staff in Chapter 5.

19. I discuss "multiple logics of belonging" in greater detail in the introduction to *Impossible Citizens*.

20. For an exploration of how certain ideas and approaches become understood as global and others as vernacular, see Peggy Levitt and Sally Merry, "Vernacularization on the Ground."

21. Eng-Ben Lim, "Performing the Global University."

22. Ibid., 40.

Chapter 5

An early version of this chapter was previously published as "Expat/Expert Camps: Redefining Labor within Gulf Migration" in Omar Al-Shehabi, Adam Hanieh, and Abdulhadi Khalaf, *Transit States*.

1. In this chapter, I often do not specify names of universities, as it might compromise the identity of my interlocutors.

2. For more on expatriate homemaking, see Ruba Salih, "Shifting Meanings of 'Home'," and Katie Walsh, "'Dad Says I'm Tied to a Shooting Star!'"

3. My schedule as a faculty member was more flexible, although during summer sessions I was also on campus every day, teaching, planning lessons, and holding office hours.

4. Short-term employees (under a year), and some long-term ones as well, were usually put up in hotels or provided with furnished serviced apartments that had some hotel amenities, like a 24-hour front desk, on-site dry cleaning, and a restaurant. During my teaching appointments in Doha, I was always offered a serviced apartment. Full-time employees sometimes lived in apartments in high-rise buildings, or, most often, in villas within gated compounds around the city. Compounds ranged in terms of the amenities they offered, but could include restaurants with delivery service, grocery stores, day care, swimming pools, tennis courts, salons, and gyms.

5. In contrast, my social circle included a number of long-term South Asian (primarily Indian) expatriates and their families, who socialized primarily in each other's homes, and sometimes in bars and hotels. I also spent time in academic networks, which were multinational but predominantly Western and white.

6. There are no data readily available on the number of Americans or Westerners in Doha. The numbers from the American embassy do not distinguish between active military and civilian expatriates. The Qatar Statistics Agency (QSA) does not break down the non-Qatari population by nationality in its census data. Although Westerners probably make up a small percentage (less than 10 percent) of the overall population, they are ubiquitous within Education City, in many upscale housing compounds and in hotel bars and restaurants.

7. Lee Rensimer, "'Going Global'."

8. For a commentary on how "ethnocracy" reproduces Gulf exceptionalism, when similar patterns of stratification are visible in many parts of the world, see Neha Vora and Natalie Koch, "Everyday Inclusions."

9. These comments resonate with Bob Vitalis's work on American Aramco, *America's Kingdom*, and the justifications given for why white Americans deserved the luxurious housing and other amenities they received, and why other ethnic groups would not desire such accommodations, based on their presumed "culture."

10. Mohanalakshmi Rajakumar, "My American Academia."

11. Ahmed Kanna, "'Group of Like-Minded Lads in Heaven,'" and Anne Coles and Katie Walsh, "From 'Trucial State' to 'Postcolonial' City?" have explored how imperial forms of racial boundary policing impact the experiences of British and other white expatriates in the contemporary Gulf.

12. Ahmed Kanna, discussing Dubai but also the Gulf Arab states more generally, describes labor, space, and leisure as marked by "a neocolonial hierarchy which privileges Europeans and North Americans." Kanna, "'Group of Like-Minded Lads in Heaven," 612.

13. Ahmed Kanna recounts similar experiences among white expatriates in Dubai. On one occasion, a white Dutchman tells him that he would not move back to Holland because of the rise in immigrants there. Ibid.

14. Amelie Le Renard discusses similar conversations among her French interlocutors. Le Renard, "Hierarchical Intimacies."

15. I include myself in this group of expatriates, and have tried to address my own complicities and subject position in my overall scholarship and in this book, including during my stints as a visiting professor in Education City.

16. See also Kanna, "'Group of Like-Minded Lads in Heaven,'" and Pascal Menoret, "Imperial Liberal University."

17. Natalie Koch, "We Entrepreneurial Academics."

18. Gary Wasserman's memoir about teaching in Education City, *The Doha Experiment*, begins and ends by describing Qatar as fundamentalist, illiberal, lacking in freedom, and basically the opposite of the United States. His teaching experiences, however, seem to indicate that his daily life was rather ordinary and not much different from academic life in US classrooms.

19. Their vocabulary was not that different than many of my local expat students; however, local expat students used guest and host vocabulary instrumentally to find ways to advocate for change. Koch had similar findings among her faculty interviews in Qatar and the UAE. Koch, "We Entrepreneurial Academics."

20. See also Le Renard, "Hierarchichal Intimacies."

21. My findings resonate with Amelie Le Renard's work among Westerners in Dubai, where she explored how race was made through people's understandings of self in relation to others. Despite their practices, which were not much different from those of Emiratis or other expatriates, such as not paying housemaids on time or stereotyping other nationalities, Westerners narrated themselves as more egalitarian and sympathetic to labor rights. Le Renard argues for "Westerner" as an emergent racial category, instead of expatriate or white: "Even though Dubai's society is marked by British recent colonial history and white supremacy, Western-ness does not necessarily imply whiteness. Passport and nationality are central in a person's advantageous status as 'Westerner' on the job market. The boundaries of Western-ness are, however, unstable, blurred and shifting." Le Renard, "Hierarchical Intimacies," 3. Although in Dubai's broader business culture (and perhaps across the Gulf), "Westerner" does seem like a more expansive category for the elite racial formation that both Le Renard and I are discussing, I find it particularly important, given the context of American university settings, to also hold on to whiteness as an analytic for understanding the experiences of faculty and staff, and the way that they are presumed to embody a particular form of expertise required for Qatar's modernization.

22. Robyn Wiegman calls this the "hegemony of liberal whiteness." Wiegman, "Object Lessons," 145.

23. Syed Ali, *Gilded Cage*; Andrew Gardner, *City of Strangers*.

24. Walsh, "'Dad Says I'm Tied to a Shooting Star!'" and "'It Got Very Debauched, Very Dubai!',", explores how British expatriates, while enjoying national and racial privileges they might not at home, are also subject to financial insecurities, long working hours, and a wide range of concerns directly connected to their status as temporary guest workers in the Gulf.

25. Le Renard, "Hierarchical Intimacies."

26. Ali, *Gilded Cage*.

27. The 2013 Texas A&M contract with Qatar Foundation explicitly states that "TAMU shall be responsible for selecting, employing and supervising academic and administrative staff; establishing and implementing student admissions policies; and delivering a curriculum and degree program all according to educational, employment, nondiscrimination, and quality standards observed at the main campus of TAMU" (page 2 of 39). Nick Anderson, "Texas University Gets $76 Million Each Year to Operate in Qatar, Contract Says,"

Washington Post, March 8, 2016: https://www.washingtonpost.com/news/grade-point/wp/2016/03/08/texas-university-gets-76-million-each-year-to-operate-in-qatar-contract-says/?utm_term=.03f5dda1580c#contract (accessed December 3, 2017).

28. For a discussion on the technologies of kafala partnership and co-ethnic exploitation, see Neha Vora, "Unofficial Citizens," and *Impossible Citizens*, chap. 3.

29. See also Piya Chatterjee and Sunaina Maira, *Imperial University*.

30. The exit permit has now been moved to an online process that takes about twenty-four hours.

31. Koch, "We Entrepreneurial Academics."

32. Natalie Koch's interviewees highlighted the hypocrisy within these criticisms, how friends who made judgmental comments would also want to come through all the time and stay for free and be shown around as tourists in the Gulf. Koch, "We Entrepreneurial Academics."

33. Gay couples were employed in Education City but were not able to be openly married in Qatar. Some schools maintained antidiscrimination policies that included sexuality, while other schools, like Texas A&M, were bound by the homophobic policies of their home state.

34. Kirin Narayan calls these subjects "halfie" anthropologists. Narayan, "How Native Is a 'Native' Anthropologist?"

Conclusion

1. Carol Vogel, "Art, from Conception to Birth in Qatar," *New York Times*, October 7, 2013: http://www.nytimes.com/2013/10/08/arts/design/damien-hirsts-anatomical-sculptures-have-their-debut.html.

2. Marjorie Kelly, "Richard Serra, Damien Hirst, and Public Art in Qatar."

3. Talal Asad, *Anthropology and the Colonial Encounter*.

4. Since 2014, Qatar Foundation has restructured the relationship between the branch campuses and HBKU. HBKU is now listed as a separate national graduate research university distinct from the international branch campuses in Education City, which are considered partner institutions. Meanwhile, the campus life portions of HBKU are still promoted as Education City–wide initiatives. Qatar Foundation also opened the Qatar National Library within Education City in 2017, which it has branded as one of several heritage centers within the campus.

5. Kevin Mitchell, "Design for the Future," 44.

6. Mitchell, "Design for the Future"; Gokce Gunel, "Infinity of Water"; Natalie Koch, "Building Glass Refrigerators."

7. Tanya Kane, "Transplanting Education," 123.

8. Kristian Coates Ulrichsen, *Qatar*.

9. QNRF is similar to the National Science Foundation (NSF) in the United States.

10. Ameena Ahmadi, "City for Education," 53.

11. Of course, as I discussed in Chapter 5, for me these moments were mostly inconvenient in ways they could not be for my colleagues, who were faced with greater real or perceived job insecurity, or at least lesser quality of life at work (those who were not practicing Muslims, or felt that their liberal lifestyles were under threat, that is).

12. Roderick Ferguson, *Reorder of Things*, Introduction.

13. Georgetown is a Jesuit institution, so this might explain the Christmas tree, although Christmas trees are common in expatriate hotels and shopping malls in Doha.

14. See also Piya Chatterjee and Sunaina Maira, *Imperial University*.

15. Natalie Koch, "Orientalizing Authoritarianism."

16. No Dakota Access Pipeline was a movement to prevent drilling on sacred Native American land that could also pose a contamination threat to their waterways.

Bibliography

Abelmann, Nancy. *The Intimate University: Korean American Students and the Problems of Segregation*. Durham, NC: Duke University Press, 2009.

Abu-Lughod, Lila. *Do Muslim Women Need Saving?* Cambridge, MA: Harvard University Press, 2013.

Adams, David Wallace. *Education for Extinction: American Indians and the Boarding School Experience, 1875–1928*. Lawrence: University Press of Kansas, 1995.

Adely, Fida J. *Gendered Paradoxes: Educating Jordanian Women in Nation, Faith, and Progress*. Chicago, IL: University of Chicago Press, 2012.

Agnew, John. "The Territorial Trap: The Geographical Assumptions of International Relations Theory." *Review of International Political Economy* 1, no. 1 (1994): 53–80.

Ahmad, Attiya. "Beyond Labor: Foreign Residents in the Gulf States." In *Migrant Labor in the Gulf*, edited by Mehran Kamrava and Zahra Babar, 21–40. Doha: Center for International and Regional Studies, Georgetown School of Foreign Service Qatar, 2011.

———. *Everyday Conversions: Islam, Domestic Work, and South Asian Migrant Women in Kuwait*. Durham, NC: Duke University Press, 2017.

Ahmadi, Ameena. "A City for Education." In *UAE and the Gulf: Architecture and Urbanism*, special issue, *Architectural Design* 85, no. 1 (2015): 46–53.

Ahmed, Leila. *Women and Gender in Islam: Historical Roots of a Modern Debate*. New Haven, CT: Yale University Press, 1992.

Ahmed, Sara. *On Being Included*. Durham, NC: Duke University Press, 2012.

Aksan, Virginia. "How Do We 'Know' the Middle East?" *Review of Middle East Studies* 44, no. 1 (2010): 3–12.

Ali, Syed. *Dubai: Gilded Cage*. New Haven, CT: Yale University Press, 2010.

Alsudairi, Mohammed, and Rogaia Mustafa Abusharaf. "Migration in Pre-Oil Qatar: A Sketch." *Studies in Ethnicity and Nationalism* 15, no. 3 (2015): 511–21.

Altbach, Philip G. "Globalisation and the University: Myths and Realities in an Unequal World." *Tertiary Education and Management* 10, no. 1 (2004): 3–25.

Althusser, Louis. "Ideology and Ideological State Apparatuses." In *The Anthropology of the State*, edited by Aradhana Sharma and Akhil Gupta, 86–111. Malden, MA: Blackwell Publishing, 2006.

Anderson, Benedict. *Imagined Communities*. London: Verso, 1991.

Anderson, Betty. *The American University of Beirut: Arab Nationalism & Liberal Education*. Austin: University of Texas Press, 2011.

Anderson, Nick. "Northwestern Professor Raises Questions About Its Branch in Qatar." *Washington Post*, December 17, 2015. https://www .washingtonpost.com/news/grade-point/wp/2015/12/17/northwestern -professor-raises-questions-about-its-branch-in-qatar/?utm_term=.6e575 322c3a3.

Al-Ansari, Buthaina Hassan. *Qatari Women Before/After Oil & Gas*. Doha, Qatar: Strike, 2012.

Apple, Michael W. "Between Neoliberalism and Neoconservatism: Conservatism in a Global Context." In *Globalization and Education: Critical Perspectives*, edited by Nicholas C. Burbules and Carlos Alberto Torres, 57–77. London: Routledge, 2013.

Asad, Talal, ed. *Anthropology and the Colonial Encounter*. Ithaca, NY: Ithaca Press, 1973.

———. *Genealogies of Religion*. Baltimore, MD: Johns Hopkins University Press, 1993.

Asmi, Rehenuma. "Storytelling in Qatar: Language Ideologies, Schooling and Islam." PhD diss., Columbia University, 2012.

———. "Cultural Translation: The Problem with Policy Borrowing in RAND Qatar's 'Education for a New Era'." Unpublished paper, 2014.

Badran, Margot. *Feminism in Islam: Secular and Religious Convergence*. London: Oneworld, 2009.

Barrow, Clyde W. *Universities and the Capitalist State*. Madison: University of Wisconsin Press, 1990.

Bascara, Victor. "New Empire, Same Old University? Education in the American Tropics after 1898." In *The Imperial University: Academic Repression and Scholarly Dissent*, edited by Piya Chatterjee and Sunaina Maira, 53–77. Minneapolis: University of Minnesota Press, 2014.

Bayat, Asef. "Transforming the Arab World: The Arab Human Development Report and the Politics of Change." *Development and Change* 36, no. 6 (2005): 1225–37.

———. *Life as Politics: How Ordinary People Change the Middle East*. Palo Alto, CA: Stanford University Press, 2013.

Benhabib, Seyla. "Why I Oppose Yale in Singapore." *Yale Daily News*, May 18, 2011. https://yaledailynews.com/blog/2011/05/18/benhabib -why-i-oppose-yale-in-singapore.

Bollag, Burton. "America's Hot New Export: Higher Education." *Chronicle of Higher Education* 52, no. 24 (2006): A44–47.

Bristol-Rhys, Jane. *Emirati Women: Generations of Change.* New York: Columbia University Press, 2010.

Brodkin, Karen, Sandra Morgan, and Janis Hutchinson. "Anthropology as White Public Space?" *American Anthropologist* 113, no. 4 (2011): 545–56.

Brubaker, Rogers. *Ethnicity Without Groups.* Cambridge, MA: Harvard University Press, 2004.

Chalcraft, John. "Monarchy, Migration and Hegemony in the Arabian Peninsula." Research Paper No. 12 prepared for the Kuwait Programme on Development, Governance and Globalization in the Gulf States, LSE Middle East Centre, London, October 2010.

Chatterjee, Piya, and Sunaina Maira, eds. *The Imperial University.* Minneapolis: University of Minnesota Press, 2014.

Coles, Anne, and Katie Walsh. "From 'Trucial State' to 'Postcolonial' City? The Imaginative Geographies of British Expatriates in Dubai." *Journal of Ethnic and Migration Studies* 36, no. 8 (2010): 1317–33.

Cooke, Miriam. *Tribal Modern: Branding New Nations in the Arab Gulf.* Berkeley: University of California Press, 2014.

Crist, John T. "Innovation in a Small State: Qatar and the IBC Cluster Model of Higher Education." *The Muslim World* 105, no. 1 (2015): 93–115.

Crystal, Jill. *Oil and Politics in the Gulf: Rulers and Merchants in Kuwait and Qatar.* Cambridge: Cambridge University Press, 1995.

Davidson, Christopher. *Dubai: The Vulnerability of Success.* Oxford: Oxford University Press, 2009.

Dedinsky, Mary L. "Journalism and Scholarship: How One Learns in Qatar." In *Higher Education Investment in the Arab Gulf States: Strategies for Excellence and Diversity,* edited by Dale F. Eickelman and Rogaia Mustafa Abusharaf, 72–91. Berlin: Gerlach Press, 2017.

Deeb, Lara, and Jessica Winegar. *Anthropology's Politics: Disciplining the Middle East.* Stanford, CA: Stanford University Press, 2016.

Erskine-Loftus, Pamela, Victoria Penziner Hightower, and Mariam Ibrahim al-Mulla, eds. *Representing the Nation: Heritage, Museums, National Narratives and Identity in the Arab Gulf States.* London: Routledge, 2014.

Exell, Karen. "Locating Qatar on the World Stage: Museums, Foreign Expertise and the Construction of Qatar's Contemporary Identity." In Erskine-Loftus, Hightower, and al-Mulla, *Representing the Nation,* 27–42.

Exell, Karen, and Trinidad Rico, eds. *Cultural Heritage in the Arabian Peninsula: Debates, Discourses and Practices.* Surrey, England: Ashgate, 2014.

Faier, Lieba, and Lisa Rofel. "Ethnographies of Encounter." *Annual Review of Anthropology* 43 (2014): 363–77.

Ferguson, Roderick A. *The Reorder of Things: The University and Its Pedagogies of Minority Difference.* Minneapolis: University of Minnesota Press, 2012.

Findlow, Sally. "Women, Higher Education and Social Transformation in the Arab Gulf." In *Aspects of Education in the Middle East and North Africa*, edited by Colin Brock and Lila Zia Levers, 57–77. Oxford: Symposium Books, 2007.

Fromhertz, Allen J. *Qatar: A Modern History.* Washington, DC: Georgetown University Press, 2012.

Gardner, Andrew. *City of Strangers: Gulf Migration and the Indian Community in Bahrain.* Ithaca, NY: Cornell University Press, 2010.

———. "Gatekeepers, Imagineers, and the Development of Qatar's Knowledge-Based Economy." Paper presented at the Knowledge-Based Economy in the Gulf conference, American University of Kuwait, Salmiya, Kuwait, March 13, 2015.

Gonzalez, Alessandra. *Islamic Feminism in Kuwait: The Politics and Paradoxes.* New York: Palgrave Macmillan, 2013.

Gray, Kevin, Hassan Bashir, and Stephen Keck, eds. *Western Higher Education in Asia and the Middle East: Politics, Economics, and Pedagogy.* Lanham, MD: Lexington Books, 2017.

Gunel, Gokce. "The Infinity of Water: Climate Change Adaptation in the Arabian Peninsula." *Public Culture* 28, no. 2 (2016): 291–315.

Gusterson, Hugh. "Homework: Toward a Critical Ethnography of the University." *American Ethnologist* 44, no. 3 (2017): 435–50.

Gutierrez y Muhs, Gabriella, Yolanda Flores Neimann, Carmen G. Gonzalez, and Angela P. Harris, eds. *Presumed Incompetent: The Intersections of Race and Class for Women in Academia.* Logan: Utah State University Press, 2012.

Hall, Kathleen. "Science, Globalization, and Educational Governance: The Political Rationalities of the New Managerialism." *Indiana Journal of Global Legal Studies* 12, no. 1 (2005): 153–83.

Haraway, Donna. "Situated Knowledges: The Science Question in Feminism and the Privilege of Partial Perspective." *Feminist Studies* 14, no. 3 (1988): 575–99.

Jones, Calvert W. "Seeing Like an Autocrat: Liberal Social Engineering in an Illiberal State." *Perspectives on Politics* 13, no. 1 (2015): 24–41.

Kaminer, Ariel. "N.Y.U.'s Global Leader Is Tested by Faculty at Home." *New York Times*, March 9, 2013. http://www.nytimes.com/2013/03/10/nyregion/john-sexton-is-tested-by-nyu-faculty.html.

Kamrava, Mehran. "A Response to MESA President Virginia Aksan's Keynote Address." *Review of Middle East Studies* 44, no. 1 (2010): 132.

———. *Qatar: Small State, Big Politics*. Ithaca, NY: Cornell University Press, 2013.

Kane, Tanya. "Transplanting Education: A Case Study of the Production of 'American-Style' Doctors in a Non-American Setting." PhD diss., University of Edinburgh, 2011.

———. "Education in a Globalized World: Education City and the Recalibration of Qatari Citizens." In *Deconstructing Global Citizenship: Political, Cultural, and Ethical Perspectives*, edited by Hassan Bashir and Phillip W. Gray, 271–84. Lanham, MD: Lexington Books, 2015.

Kanna, Ahmed. "'A Group of Like-Minded Lads in Heaven': Everydayness and the Production of Dubai Space." *Journal of Urban Affairs* 36, no. 2 (2014): 605–20.

Karmani, Sohail. "English, 'Terror,' and Islam." *Applied Linguistics* 26, no. 2 (2005): 262–67.

Katodrytis, George, and Kevin Mitchell. "The Gulf Urbanization." In *UAE and the Gulf: Architecture and Urbanism*, special issue, *Architectural Design* 85, no. 1 (2015): 8–19.

Kelly, Marjorie. "Issues in the Development of a Gulf Studies Program at the American University of Kuwait: An Ethnography." *Review of Middle East Studies* 14, no. 2 (2010): 152–65.

———. "Richard Serra, Damien Hirst, and Public Art in Qatar." *Public Art Dialogue* 6, no. 2 (2016): 229–40.

Koch, Natalie. "'Building Glass Refrigerators in the Desert': Discourses of Urban Sustainability and Nation-Building in Qatar." *Urban Geography* 35, no. 8 (2014). doi:10.1080/02723638.2014.952538.

———. "Is Nationalism Just for Nationals? Civic Nationalism for Noncitizens and Celebrating National Day in Qatar and the UAE." *Political Geography* 54 (Sept. 2016): 43–53.

———. "We Entrepreneurial Academics: Creating Spatial Hierarchies and Interpreting Diasporic Academics' Motives to Work in Qatar and the UAE." *Territory, Politics, Governance* 4, no. 4 (2016): 438–52.

———. "Orientalizing Authoritarianism: Narrating US Exceptionalism in Popular Reactions to the Trump Election and Presidency." *Political Geography*. Published online February 28, 2017. doi:10.1016/j.polgeo.2017.03.001.

Al-Kuwari, Ali Khalifa. *The People Want Reform . . . In Qatar, Too*. Beirut, 2012.

Le Renard, Amelie. *A Society of Young Women: Opportunities of Place, Power, and Reform in Saudi Arabia*. Stanford, CA: Stanford University Press, 2014.

———. "Hierarchical Intimacies. Producing 'Westerners' as a Hegemonic Group in Dubai." *Gender, Place, Culture* (under review).

Levitt, Peggy, and Sally Merry. "Vernacularization on the Ground: Local Uses of Global Women's Rights in Peru, China, India and the United States." *Global Networks* 9, no. 4 (2009): 441–61.

Li, Guofang, Gulbahar Beckett, and Shirley Geok-Lin Lim, eds. *"Strangers" of the Academy: Asian Women Scholars in Higher Education.* Sterling, VA: Stylus Publishing, 2006.

Lim, Eng-Ben. "Performing the Global University." *Social Text* 27, no. 4 (2009): 25–44.

Limbert, Mandana. "Caste, Ethnicity, and the Politics of Arabness in Southern Arabia." *Comparative Studies of South Asia, Africa and the Middle East* 34, no. 3 (2014): 590–98.

Lindsey, Ursula. "Qatar Sets Its Own Terms for US Universities." *Chronicle of Higher Education*, November 18, 2013. https://www.chronicle.com /article/Qatar-Welcomes-American/143087.

Litzinger, Ralph. "Going Global." *Duke Magazine*, October 1, 2010. http://dukemagazine.duke.edu/article/going-global.

Lockman, Zachary. *Field Notes: The Making of Middle East Studies in the United States.* Stanford, CA: Stanford University Press, 2016.

Longva, Ahn Nga. *Walls Built on Sand: Migration, Exclusion, and Society in Kuwait.* Boulder, CO: Westview Press, 1999.

Lori, Noora. "National Security and the Management of Migrant Labor: A Case Study of the United Arab Emirates." *Asian and Pacific Migration Journal* 20, nos. 3–4 (2011): 315–37.

———. "Temporary Workers or Permanent Migrants? The Kafala System and Contestations over Residency in the Arab Gulf States." Policy paper prepared for the Center for Migrations and Citizenship, November 2012.

Lowe, Lisa. *The Intimacies of Four Continents.* Durham, NC: Duke University Press, 2015.

Lyons, Jonathan. *The House of Wisdom: How the Arabs Transformed Western Civilization.* New York: Bloomsbury Press, 2009.

Mahmood, Saba. "Secularism, Sovereignty, and Religious Difference: A Global Genealogy?" *Environment and Planning D: Society and Space* 35, no. 2 (2017): 197–209.

Mahmud, Lilith. "We Have Never Been Liberal: Occidentalist Myths and the Impending Fascist Apocalypse." *Hot Spots* (blog of *Cultural Anthropology*), October 27, 2016. https://culanth.org/fieldsights/981-we -have-never-been-liberal-occidentalist-myths-and-the-impending-fascist -apocalypse.

Massad, Joseph A. *Islam in Liberalism.* Chicago, IL: University of Chicago Press, 2015.

Menoret, Pascal. "The Imperial Liberal University: The Making of an Enclave in Abu Dhabi." Paper presented at New Directions in Arabian Peninsula Studies, Yale University, April 30, 2016.

Miller-Bernal, Leslie, and Susan L. Poulson, eds. *Going Co-Ed: Women's Experiences in Formerly Men's Colleges and Universities, 1950–2000.* Nashville, TN: Vanderbilt University Press, 2004.

Mir-Hosseini, Ziba. "Gender Rights and Islamic Legal Tradition: An Exploration." In Sonbol, *Gulf Women*, 343–66.

Al-Misnad, Sheikha. *The Development of Modern Education in the Gulf.* London: Ithaca Press, 1985.

Mitchell, Jocelyn. "Beyond Allocation: The Politics of Legitimacy in Qatar." PhD diss., Georgetown University, 2013.

Mitchell, Kevin. "Design for the Future: Educational Institutions in the Gulf." In *UAE and the Gulf: Architecture and Urbanism*, special issue, *Architectural Design* 85, no. 1 (2015): 38–45.

Mitchell, Timothy. *Carbon Democracy: Political Power in the Age of Oil.* London: Verso, 2011.

Morey, Ann I. "Globalization and the Emergence of For-Profit Higher Education." *Higher Education* 48, no. 1 (2004): 131–50.

Nagy, Sharon. "The Search for Miss Philippines Bahrain: Possibilities for Representation in Expatriate Communities." *City & Society* 20, no. 1 (2008): 79–104.

Al-Nakib, Farah. *Kuwait Transformed: A History of Oil and Urban Life.* Stanford, CA: Stanford University Press, 2016.

Narayan, Kirin. "How Native Is a 'Native' Anthropologist?" *American Anthropologist* 95, no. 3 (1993): 671–86.

Navarro, Tami. "But Some of Us Are Broke: Race, Gender, and the Neoliberalization of the Academy." *American Anthropologist* 119, no. 3 (2017): 506–17.

Navarro, Tami, Bianca Williams, and Attiya Ahmad. "Sitting at the Kitchen Table: Fieldnotes from Women of Color in Anthropology." *Cultural Anthropology* 28, no. 3 (2013): 443–63.

Newfield, Christopher. *Unmaking the Public University.* Cambridge, MA: Harvard University Press, 2008.

Olds, Kris, and Nigel Thrift. "Cultures on the Brink: Reengineering the Soul of Capitalism—On a Global Scale." In *Global Assemblages: Technology, Politics and Ethics as Anthropological Problems*, edited by Aihwa Ong and Stephen Collier, 270–90. Oxford: Blackwell, 2005.

Ong, Aihwa. *Flexible Citizenship: The Cultural Logics of Transnationality.* Durham, NC: Duke University Press, 1999.

———. *Neoliberalism as Exception.* Durham, NC: Duke University Press, 2006.

Onley, James. "Gulf Arab Headdress Before Oil: A Study in Cultural Diversity and Hybridity." Paper presented at the MESA conference, San Francisco, November 23, 2004.

Poovey, Mary. "The Twenty-First-Century University and the Market: What Price Economic Viability?" *Differences: A Journal of Feminist Cultural Studies* 12, no. 1 (2001): 1–16.

Pratt, Mary Louise. "Arts of the Contact Zone." *Profession* 91 (1991): 33–40.

———. *Imperial Eyes: Travel Writing and Transculturation*. London: Routledge, 1992.

Qatar National Vision 2030. Qatar Ministry of Development Planning and Statistics. http://www.mdps.gov.qa/en/qnv1/pages/default.aspx.

Rajakumar, Mohanalakshmi. "Assessing the Rhetoric of Sheikha Moza: Mistress of Ethos." In *Global Women Leaders: Studies in Feminist Political Rhetoric*, edited by Michelle Lockhart and Kathleen Mollick, 127–43. Lanham, MD: Lexington Books, 2014.

———. "My American Academia: At Home and Abroad." In *Experiences of Immigrant Professors: Challenges, Cross-Cultural Differences, and Lessons for Success*, edited by Charles Hutchinson, 223–33. London: Routledge, 2015.

Rajakumar, Mohanalakshmi, Mariam Bengali, Rushma Shahzad, and Tanya Kane. "Education, Marriage, and Professionalization: The Modern Qatari Women's Dilemma." *Gender* 9, no. 1 (2017): 82–98.

Readings, Bill. *The University in Ruins*. Cambridge, MA: Harvard University Press, 1996.

Rensimer, Lee. "'Going Global' Without Going Anywhere: Practices and Performances of British Higher Education in the United Arab Emirates." Paper presented at Symposium on the Global University, American University of Sharjah, March 9, 2015.

Ridge, Natasha. *Education and the Reverse Gender Divide in the Gulf States*. New York: Teachers College Press, 2014.

Roberts, Jon H., and James Turner. *The Sacred and the Secular University*. Princeton, NJ: Princeton University Press, 2000.

Roitman, Janet. *Anti-Crisis*. Durham, NC: Duke University Press, 2014.

Rosaldo, Renato. "Cultural Citizenship and Educational Democracy." *Cultural Anthropology* 9, no. 3 (1994): 402–11.

Ross, Andrew. "Human Rights, Academic Freedom, and Offshore Academics." *Academe* (Jan.–Feb. 2011). https://www.aaup.org/article /human-rights-academic-freedom-and-offshore-academics# .WlFM8ktG0xc.

El-Saadi, Hoda. "Women and Economy: Pre-Oil Gulf States." In Sonbol, *Gulf Women*, 147–66.

Salaita, Steven. *Uncivil Rites: Palestine and the Limits of Academic Freedom*. Chicago, IL: Haymarket Books, 2015.

Salih, Ruba. "Shifting Meanings of 'Home': Consumptions and Identity in Moroccan Women's Transnational Practices Between Italy and Morocco." In *New Approaches to Migration? Transnational Communities and the Transformation of Home*, edited by N. al-Ali and K. Koser, 51–67. London: Routledge, 2002.

Al-Sayegh, Fatma. "Women of the Gulf During the First Half of the Twentieth Century: A Comparative Study of American Missionary Archives and Local Memory." In Sonbol, *Gulf Women*, 241–76.

Schrecker, Ellen W. *No Ivory Tower: McCarthyism and the Universities*. Oxford: Oxford University Press, 1986.

Scott, Joan. *The Politics of the Veil*. Princeton, NJ: Princeton University Press, 2007.

Sheikh, Sa'diyya. *Sufi Narratives of Intimacy: Ibn 'Arabi, Gender, and Sexuality*. Chapel Hill: University of North Carolina Press, 2012.

Smith, Benjamin. *Market Orientalism: Cultural Economy and the Arab Gulf States*. Syracuse, NY: Syracuse University Press, 2015.

Sonbol, Amira el-Azhary, ed. *Gulf Women*. Doha: Bloomsbury Qatar Foundation Publishing, 2012.

Soudy, Nada. "Home and Belonging: A Comparative Study of 1.5 and Second-Generation Egyptian 'Expatriates' in Qatar and 'Immigrants' in the U.S." *Journal of Ethnic and Migration Studies*. Published online November 1, 2016. doi: 10.1080/1369183X.2016.1241136.

Taylor, Charles. "The Politics of Recognition." In *Multiculturalism and "The Politics of Recognition,"* 25–73. Princeton, NJ: Princeton University Press, 1992.

Tetrault, Mary Ann. "Identity and Transplant-University Education in the Gulf: The American University of Kuwait." *Journal of Arabian Studies* 1, no. 1 (2011): 81–98.

Torab, Azam. *Performing Islam: Gender and Ritual in Iran*. Leiden: Brill, 2007.

Ulrichsen, Kristian Coates. *Qatar and the Arab Spring*. New York: Oxford University Press, 2014.

Vitalis, Robert. *America's Kingdom*. Palo Alto, CA: Stanford University Press, 2006.

Vogel, Carol. "Art, from Conception to Birth in Qatar." *New York Times*, October 7, 2013.

Vora, Neha. "Unofficial Citizens: Indian Entrepreneurs and the State-Effect in Dubai, UAE." *International Labor and Working-Class History* 79, no. 1 (2011): 122–39.

———. "Free Speech and Civil Discourse: Producing Cosmopolitans and Locals in UAE English-Language Blogs." *Journal of the Royal Institute of Anthropology* 18, no. 4 (2012): 787–807.

———. *Impossible Citizens: Dubai's Indian Diaspora*. Durham, NC: Duke University Press, 2013.

———. "Between Global Citizenship and Qatarization: Negotiating Qatar's New Knowledge Economy Within American Branch Campuses." *Ethnic & Racial Studies* 37, no. 12 (2014): 2243–60.

———. "Expat/Expert Camps: Redefining Labor within Gulf Migration." In *Transit States: Labour, Migration & Citizenship in the Gulf*, edited by Omar Al-Shehabi, Adam Hanieh, and Abdulhadi Khalaf, 170–197. Pluto Press, 2014.

———. "Is the University Universal? Mobile (Re)Constitutions of American Academia in the Gulf Arab States." *Anthropology & Education Quarterly* 46, no. 1 (2015): 19–36.

Vora, Neha, and Natalie Koch. "Everyday Inclusions: Rethinking Ethnocracy, *Kafala*, and Belonging in the GCC." *Studies in Ethnicity and Nationalism* 15, no. 3 (2015): 540–52.

Wadud, Amina. *Inside the Gender Jihad: Women's Reform in Islam*. London: Oneworld, 2006.

Wakefield, Sarina. "Heritage, Cosmopolitanism and Identity in Abu Dhabi." In Exell and Rico, *Cultural Heritage in the Arabian Peninsula*, 99–116.

Walsh, Katie. "'Dad Says I'm Tied to a Shooting Star!' Grounding (Research on) British Expatriate Belonging." *Area* 38, no. 3 (2006): 268–78.

———. "'It Got Very Debauched, Very Dubai!' Heterosexual Intimacy Amongst Single British Expatriates." *Social & Cultural Geography* 8, no. 4 (2007): 507–33.

———. "Negotiating Migrant Status in the Emerging Global City: Britons in Dubai." *Encounters* (2010): 235–55.

Wasserman, Gary. *The Doha Experiment: Arab Kingdom, Catholic College, Jewish Teacher*. New York: Skyhorse Publishing, 2017.

Wiegman, Robyn. *Object Lessons*. Durham, NC: Duke University Press, 2012.

Wildavsky, Ben. *The Great Brain Race: How Global Universities Are Reshaping the World*. Princeton, NJ: Princeton University Press, 2010.

Wilder, Craig Steven. *Ebony & Ivy: Race, Slavery, and the Troubled History of America's Universities*. New York: Bloomsbury Press, 2013.

Wilhelm, Ian. "Duke Faculty Question the University's Global Ambitions." *Chronicle of Higher Education*, October 26, 2011. https://www.chronicle.com/article/Duke-Faculty-Question-the/129536.

Wippel, Steffen, Katrin Bromber, Christian Steiner, and Birgit Kraweitz, eds. *Under Construction: Logics of Urbanism in the Gulf Region*. Surrey, England: Ashgate, 2014.

Zahlan, Rosemarie Said. *The Creation of Qatar*. London: Croon Helm, 1979.

Zhan, Mei. *Other-Worldly: Making Chinese Medicine Through Transnational Frames*. Durham, NC: Duke University Press, 2009.

Index

Note: Page numbers in *italics* refer to illustrations.